Exploring Data

Exploring Data was prepared under the auspices of the American Statistical Association—National Council of Teachers of Mathematics Joint Committee on the Curriculum in Statistics and Probability.

This book is part of the Quantitative Literacy Project, which was funded in part by the National Science Foundation.

Exploring Data

James M. Landwehr
AT&T Bell Laboratories
Murray Hill, New Jersey

Ann E. Watkins
Los Angeles Pierce College
Woodland Hills, California

DALE SEYMOUR PUBLICATIONS

Cover Design: John Edeen
Technical Art: Pat Rogondino

This publication was prepared as part of the American Statistical
Association Project—Quantitative Literacy—with partial support of the
National Science Foundation Grant No. DPE-8317656. Any opinions,
findings, conclusions, or recommendations expressed in this publication
are those of the authors and do not necessarily represent the views of
the National Science Foundation.

ISBN 0-86651-321-3
Order Number DS01617

DALE
SEYMOUR
PUBLICATIONS
P.O. BOX 10888
PALO ALTO, CA 94303

cdefghij-MA-98432109

CONTENTS

PREFACE

Exploring Data is an introduction to statistics. In addition to learning the most up-to-date statistical techniques, you will have an opportunity to practice techniques in other areas of mathematics.

Familiar statistical topics, such as tables of data, the mean (average), and scatter plots, are included in this book. Less familiar topics, such as the median, stem-and-leaf plots, box plots, and smoothing, are also included. All of these techniques are part of a new emphasis in statistics called *data analysis.* Data analysis de-emphasizes the use of algebraic formulas for analyzing data. Instead, data analysis stresses the importance of organizing and displaying data so that it reveals its patterns and surprises. The techniques of data analysis are easy to use and are frequently graphical.

John W. Tukey, an influential statistician who recently retired from Princeton University and AT&T Bell Laboratories, was the leader in this new approach to statistics. He first published these techniques in the 1960s and 1970s. Nowhere else in your study of mathematics will you learn methods developed so recently.

The techniques in this material encourage you to ask questions about data. This is an important part of data analysis. By using these methods you will be able to interpret data that are interesting and important to you.

———————

The authors gratefully acknowledge the inspiration and leadership of Jim Swift in the preparation of materials on data analysis for secondary students.

I. LINE PLOTS

The 1984 Winter Olympics were held in Sarajevo, Yugoslavia. The table below lists the total number of gold, silver, and bronze medals won, by country.

Country	Total Medals	Country	Total Medals
Austria	1	Italy	2
Canada	4	Japan	1
Czechoslovakia	6	Liechtenstein	2
Finland	13	Norway	9
France	3	Sweden	8
Germany, East	24	Switzerland	5
Germany, West	4	USSR	25
Great Britain	1	United States	8
		Yugoslavia	1

Source: *The World Almanac and Book of Facts*, 1985 edition.

Let's make a *line plot* of these data. First, make a horizontal line.

Then, put a scale of numbers on this line using a ruler. Since the smallest number of medals is 1 and the largest is 25, the scale might run from 0 to 25 as shown below.

The first country, Austria, won one medal. To represent Austria, put an X above the line at the number 1.

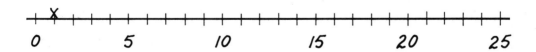

Continuing this way with the other countries, we can complete the line plot as shown below.

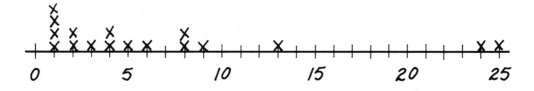

1

From a line plot, features of the data become apparent that were not as apparent from the list. These features include:

- *Outliers* — data values that are substantially larger or smaller than the other values

- *Clusters* — isolated groups of points

- *Gaps* — large spaces between points

It is also easy to spot the largest and smallest values from a line plot. If you see a cluster, try to decide if its members have anything special in common. For example, in the previous line plot the two largest values form a cluster. They are the USSR and East Germany — both eastern European countries. These two values are quite a bit larger than the rest, so we could also consider these points to be outliers.

Often, we would like to know the location of a particular point of interest. For these data, we might want to know how well the United States did compared to the other countries.

Discussion Questions

1. How many countries won only one medal?

2. How many countries won ten or more medals?

3. Do the countries seem to fall into clusters on the line plot?

4. Describe how the United States compares with the other countries.

5. In this book, you will often be asked to "describe what you learned from looking at the plot." Try to do this now with the plot of medal winners, then read the following sample.

Seventeen countries won medals in the 1984 Winter Olympics. Two countries, the USSR with 25 and East Germany with 24, won many more medals than the next country, Finland, with 13. The remaining countries were all clustered, with from 1 to 9 medals each. The United States won 8 medals, more than 11 countries but not many in comparison to the leaders. One noticeable feature about these 17 countries is that, with the exception of the United States, Canada, and Japan, they are all in Europe.

The list does not say how many countries did not win any medals. This might be interesting to find out.

Writing descriptions is probably new to you. When you look at the plot, jot down any observations you make and any questions that occur to you. Look specifically for outliers, clusters, and the other features we mentioned. Then organize and write your paragraphs as if you were composing them for your English teacher. The ability to organize, summarize, and communicate numerical information is a necessary skill in many occupations and is similar to your work with science projects and science laboratory reports.

Application 1

Rock Albums

The following list of the top 10 record albums in the first five months of 1985 is based on *Billboard* magazine reports.

Artist	Title	Total Points
Bruce Springsteen	"Born in the U.S.A."	183
Madonna	"Like a Virgin"	149
Phil Collins	"No Jacket Required"	108
John Fogerty	"Centerfield"	97
Wham!	"Make It Big"	97
Soundtrack	"Beverly Hills Cop"	93
Tina Turner	"Private Dancer"	69
Prince	"Purple Rain"	59
Foreigner	"Agent Provocateur"	54
USA for Africa	"We Are the World"	49

Source: *Los Angeles Times*, May 25, 1985.

The total points were calculated by giving 10 points for each week an album was number 1 on the *Billboard* charts, 9 points for each week it was number 2, 8 points for each week it was number 3, and so forth.

1. If a record was number 1 for 3 weeks, number 2 for 5 weeks, and number 3 for 2 weeks, how many total points would it have?

2. How many points does a record earn by being number 5 for 1 week?

3. If a record was number 4 for 3 weeks and number 5 for 1 week, how many total points would it have?

4. Find two ways for a record to earn 25 points.

5. There were about 21 weeks in the first five months of 1985. Find a way for "Born in the U.S.A." to earn 183 points in these 21 weeks.

The following line plot was constructed from these data.

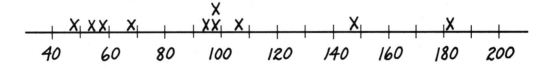

6. Which record(s) is an outlier?

7. Do the records seem to cluster into more than one group?

8. List the records in the lowest group.

9. List the records in the next lowest group.

10. Write a description of what you learned from studying this plot.

3

Causes of Death

The United States Public Health Service issues tables giving death rates by cause of death. These are broken down by age group, and the table below is for people 15-24 years of age. It gives death rates per 100,000 population for 16 leading causes of death. As an example, a death rate of 1.7 for leukemia means that out of 100,000 people in the United States aged 15-24, we can expect 1.7 of them will die annually from leukemia.

Cause of Death	Death Rate (per 100,000 people aged 15-24 per year)
heart diseases	2.9
leukemia	1.7
cancers of lymph and blood other than leukemia	1.0
other cancers	3.6
strokes	1.0
motor vehicle accidents	44.8
other accidents	16.9
chronic lung diseases	0.3
pneumonia and influenza	0.8
diabetes	0.3
liver diseases	0.3
suicide	12.3
homicide	15.6
kidney diseases	0.3
birth defects	1.4
blood poisoning	0.2

Source: National Center for Health Statistics, Monthly Vital Statistics Report, August 1983.

1. Of 100,000 people aged 15-24, how many would you expect to die annually from pneumonia and influenza?

2. Of 1,000,000 people aged 15-24, how many would you expect to die annually from pneumonia and influenza?

3. Suppose there are 200,000 people, and 3 die from a certain cause. What is the death rate per 100,000 people?

4. Of 250,000 people aged 15-24, about how many would you expect to die annually from motor vehicle accidents?

5. Construct a line plot of these data. To avoid crowding when plotting the X's, round each death rate to the nearest whole number.

6. Which cause of death is an outlier?

7. Which three causes of death are in the cluster below the outlier?

8. Which medical problem has the largest death rate?

9. Write a summary of the information communicated by the line plot. Include a list of any questions you have about the data. (For example, in which category are drug overdoses included?)

10. (For class discussion) Suppose you want to reduce the total death rate for 15-24 year olds, and you have $10 million to spend. How would you spend it? On medical research, medical treatment, or in some other way?

Line Plots — Summary

Line plots are a quick, simple way to organize data. They work best when there are fewer than 25 numbers. With many more, the plot starts to look crowded.

From a line plot it is easy to spot the largest and smallest values, outliers, clusters, and gaps in the data. It is also possible to find the relative position of particular points of interest. Sometimes you can notice outliers, clusters, and gaps from the table of data. However, the line plot is easy to make and has several advantages. It makes it easy to spot these features, it gives a graphical picture of the relative sizes of the numbers, and it helps you to make sure that you aren't missing any important information.

When making line plots, be sure to place the X's for values that are approximately the same on top of each other rather than crowding them in. It is also usual to number the scale in multiples of 1, 5, 10, 100, or some other round number.

Suggestions for Student Projects

Collect data on one of the ideas listed below or on your own topic. Make a line plot of the data and write a summary of the information displayed by the plot.

1. heights of students in your class

2. grades on your math tests this year

3. grades on the last test for the members of your class

4. ages of the mothers of students in your class

5. number of hours of television you watch each day for two weeks

6. number of miles each student drives in a week

7. number of students in your class born in each of the 12 months (On the number line, 1 would represent January, 2 would represent February, and so forth.)

II. STEM-AND-LEAF PLOTS

The table below gives the amounts of calories, fat, carbohydrates (sugar and starch), and sodium (salt) in each serving of various fast food items. Fat and carbohydrates are measured in grams; sodium in milligrams.

Item	Calories	Fat (gm)	Carbohydrates (gm)	Sodium (mg)
HAMBURGERS				
Burger King Whopper	660	41	49	1083
Jack-in-the-Box Jumbo Jack	538	28	44	1007
McDonald's Big Mac	591	33	46	963
Wendy's Old Fashioned	413	22	29	708
SANDWICHES				
Roy Rogers Roast Beef	356	12	34	610
Burger King Chopped-Beef Steak	445	13	50	966
Hardee's Roast Beef	351	17	32	765
Arby's Roast Beef	370	15	36	869
FISH				
Long John Silver's	483	27	27	1333
Arthur Treacher's Original	439	27	27	421
McDonald's Filet-O-Fish	383	18	38	613
Burger King Whaler	584	34	50	968
CHICKEN				
Kentucky-Fried Chicken Snack Box	405	21	16	728
Arthur Treacher's Original Chicken	409	23	25	580
SPECIALTY ENTREES				
Wendy's Chili	266	9	29	1190
Pizza Hut Pizza Supreme	506	15	64	1281
Jack-in-the-Box Taco	429	26	34	926

Source: *Consumer Reports*, September 1979.

Suppose you decide to order a McDonald's Big Mac. It contains 33 grams of fat. How does this compare to the other items? By looking at the table, about all we can see is that it does not have the most fat nor the least. So that we can get a better picture of the grams of fat per serving, let's make a stem-and-leaf plot.

First, find the smallest value and the largest value.

The smallest value is 9 for Wendy's Chili and the largest is 41 for the Burger King Whopper.

The smallest value, 9, has a 0 in the ten's place and the largest value, 41, has a 4 in the ten's place. Therefore, we choose the *stems* to be the digits from 0 to 4.

7

Second, write these stems vertically with a line to their right.

```
0 |
1 |
2 |
3 |
4 |
```

Third, separate each value into a stem and a leaf and put the leaves on the plot to the right of the stem.

For example, the first value in the list is 41, for a Burger King Whopper. Its stem is 4 and its leaf is 1. It is placed on the plot as follows:

```
0 |
1 |
2 |
3 |
4 | 1
```

The second value in the list is 28. Its stem is 2 and its leaf is 8. Now the plot looks as shown below.

```
0 |
1 |
2 | 8
3 |
4 | 1
```

Continuing in this way gives the following plot:

```
0 | 9
1 | 2 3 7 5 8 5
2 | 8 2 7 7 1 3 6
3 | 3 4
4 | 1
```

Next, on a new plot arrange the leaves so they are ordered from smallest value to largest. (This final step is often omitted.)

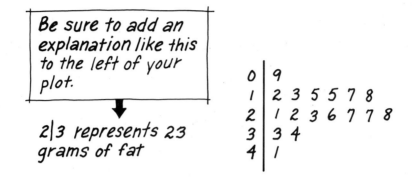

Be sure to add an explanation like this to the left of your plot.

2|3 *represents* 23 *grams of fat*

```
0 | 9
1 | 2 3 5 5 7 8
2 | 1 2 3 6 7 7 8
3 | 3 4
4 | 1
```

The plot shows that most of the food items have grams of fat in the 10's and 20's and that there are a few large values. The McDonald's Big Mac with 33 grams has one of the larger amounts of fat.

If we rotate the stem-and-leaf plot 90° counterclockwise, we get a plot that resembles a bar graph or histogram.

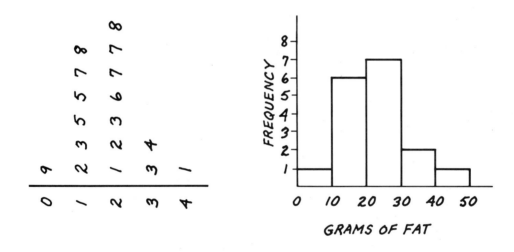

The stem-and-leaf plot is often better than the bar graph or histogram because it is easier to construct and all the original data values are displayed.

It is sometimes worthwhile to label specific items. For example, we might want to label the smallest value, the largest value, and a value of special interest such as McDonald's Big Mac. This is shown below.

```
0 | 9 ←───────────── WENDY'S CHILI
1 | 2 3 5 5 7 8
2 | 1 2 3 6 7 7 8
3 | 3 4 ←─────────── McDONALD'S BIG MAC
4 | 1 ←──────────── BURGER KING WHOPPER
```

Also, it is sometimes interesting to replace the leaves in the stem-and-leaf plot by symbols identifying the items. For example, replace each of the four hamburger leaves with an *H*, each of the four sandwich leaves with an *S*, each of the four fish leaves with an *F*, each of the two chicken leaves with a *C*, and each of the three special entree leaves with an *O* (for other). Replacing the leaves by symbols gives the following:

```
0 | O
1 | S S S O S F
2 | C H C O F F H
3 | H F
4 | H
```

When writing a description of a stem-and-leaf plot, look for the same features that you looked for with a line plot:

- largest and smallest values

- outliers

- clusters

- gaps

- the relative position of any item important to you

Our description of what we learned about fat in the fast food items from the stem-and-leaf plots follows:

There are no outliers separated far from the rest nor any large internal gaps among these values. Of these fast foods, the type that is generally highest in fat is the hamburger, which has three of the highest four values. One hamburger is lower in fat than the others and lies in about the middle of all these values; it is Wendy's Old Fashioned. Some possible reasons for its lower value are: it might be smaller than the others, it might be made from meat with a lower fat content, or it might be cooked differently.

From the data, the type of food that is second highest in fat is fish; the values are only slightly smaller than those for hamburgers. Again, one fish value, McDonald's Filet-O-Fish, is smaller than the other fish values. Although we generally think of fish as having a lot less fat than beef, perhaps these fish items are all fried and therefore high in fat.

The type of food lowest in fat is the roast beef sandwich, and chicken falls near the middle in these data. It is surprising that both the lowest and highest items are beef, but perhaps the sandwich is lowest because it is not fried. The other specialty items are spread throughout the data, but they include the single lowest item, Wendy's Chili. Is it just a coincidence that the hamburger that was lowest in fat was also from Wendy's?

When analyzing data throughout this book, you will need to examine the plots and to think about other information you may have from outside mathematics that can help to interpret the results. Sometimes, this process will lead to questions and possibilities about the problem that cannot be answered just from the data.

The stem-and-leaf plot shows the shape of the set of data more clearly than a line plot. The "shape" of a set of data is called its *distribution*. For example, some common types of distribution follow:

```
3 | 4                         2 | 5 5 8
4 | 6 9 9                     3 | 2 3 4 4 5 9
5 | 2 4 4 5 5 9               4 | 6 7 7
6 | 1 1 7                     5 | 4
7 | 8                         6 | 1 1 3 8
                              7 | 0 1 3 4 4 5 6 8 8
                              8 | 2 3 5 5
```

     MOUND-SHAPED   U-SHAPED

```
3 | 4                         3 | 2 2 3 8
4 | 7 8                       4 | 1 5 7
5 | 2 2 3                     5 | 0 4 4 9
6 | 1 1 2 4 4 5 7 8           6 | 1 1 5 7
7 | 0 1 2 2 2 3 6 8 8 9 9     7 | 3 6 8 8 9
```

     J-SHAPED   RECTANGULAR-SHAPED

The mound-shaped distribution, sometimes called bell-shaped, is a shape that occurs often. The data values are fairly symmetrical, with lows balancing the highs. If the data follow a U-shaped distribution, it may be because there are really two underlying groups, each of which is mound-shaped, corresponding to the two peaks. Thus, when a U-shaped plot is observed, it is a good idea to see if there is any reason to treat the observations as two separate groups.

The J-shaped plot or the backward J-shaped plot does not occur as often as the first two types. Typically, it occurs because it is impossible to have observations above (or below) a particular limit. In the example above, this limit might be 80. In some problems, there is a lower limit of 0. If you observe a J-shaped plot, try to determine if there is a limit, what it is, and why it is there. For a rectangular-shaped distribution, sometimes called flat or uniform, there are often both lower and upper limits with the data values spread evenly between them. For the previous example, the limits might be 30 and 80. As with the J-shaped plot, you should try to understand if there are limits to the possible values of the data, and what the limits might mean.

11

Discussion Questions

1. Make a stem-and-leaf plot of the grams of carbohydrates in the fast food items. Label the smallest value, the largest value, and McDonald's Big Mac.

2. Make another stem-and-leaf plot of the grams of carbohydrates, but replace the leaves by the symbols:
   H for hamburger
   S for sandwich
   F for fish
   C for chicken
   O for other

3. Write a description of the information displayed in the stem-and-leaf plot of the grams of carbohydrates. Mention any interesting patterns. How does this plot compare to the one for fat?

4. All of the fast food information was given on a per item basis. However, the sizes of the items are different. Do you think this should be taken into account? How might you do this? Should price also be considered?

5. In judging fast food items, which is most important to you: calories, fat, carbohydrates, or sodium?

6. Give an example of data that are distributed a) U-shaped. b) mound-shaped. c) J-shaped. d) rectangular-shaped.

Application 3

Ages of U.S. Presidents at Their Death

The table below lists the presidents of the United States and the ages at which they died.

Washington	67	Filmore	74	Roosevelt	60
Adams	90	Pierce	64	Taft	72
Jefferson	83	Buchanan	77	Wilson	67
Madison	85	Lincoln	56	Harding	57
Monroe	73	Johnson	66	Coolidge	60
Adams	80	Grant	63	Hoover	90
Jackson	78	Hayes	70	Roosevelt	63
Van Buren	79	Garfield	49	Truman	88
Harrison	68	Arthur	57	Eisenhower	78
Tyler	71	Cleveland	71	Kennedy	46
Polk	53	Harrison	67	Johnson	64
Taylor	65	McKinley	58		

1. Make a stem-and-leaf plot of the ages using these stems.

```
4 |
5 |
6 |
7 |
8 |
9 |
```

2. How many presidents died in their forties or fifties?

3. Who lived to be the oldest?

4. Label the four presidents who were assassinated.

5. What is the shape of this distribution?

6. Write a one-paragraph description of the information shown in the stem-and-leaf plot, including information about the presidents who were assassinated.

Application 4

Thunderstorms

The table below lists 81 U.S. cities with the number of days per year with thunderstorms.

Area	Number of Days	Area	Number of Days	Area	Number of Days
Akron, OH	39	Detroit, MI	33	Oklahoma City, OK	51
Albany, NY	28	El Paso, TX	36	Omaha, NE	51
Albuquerque, NM	43	Fargo, ND	30	Orlando, FL	85
Anchorage, AK	1	Fresno, CA	5	Philadelphia, PA	42
Atlanta, GA	50	Grand Rapids, MI	37	Phoenix, AZ	20
Austin, TX	40	Great Falls, MT	27	Pittsburgh, PA	35
Bakersfield, CA	3	Hartford, CT	28	Portland, ME	20
Baltimore, MD	24	Honolulu, HI	7	Portland, OR	7
Baton Rouge, LA	80	Houston, TX	59	Providence, RI	21
Beaumont, TX	63	Indianapolis, IN	47	Raleigh, NC	45
Biloxi, MS	80	Kansas City, MO	50	Richmond, VA	37
Birmingham, AL	65	Las Vegas, NV	13	Rochester, NY	29
Boise, ID	15	Little Rock, AR	56	Sacramento, CA	5
Boston, MA	19	Louisville, KY	52	Salt Lake City, UT	41
Buffalo, NY	30	Los Angeles, CA	6	San Antonio, TX	35
Burlington, VT	27	Manchester, NH	24	San Diego, CA	3
Charleston, SC	58	Memphis, TN	50	San Francisco, CA	2
Charleston, WV	45	Miami, FL	71	Seattle, WA	6
Chicago, IL	36	Milwaukee, WI	37	Shreveport, LA	58
Cincinnati, OH	52	Minneapolis, MN	36	Sioux Falls, SD	47
Cleveland, OH	38	Mobile, AL	86	St. Louis, MO	43
Columbia, SC	52	Nashville, TN	52	Tampa, FL	91
Columbus, OH	36	Nassau-Suffolk, NY	18	Tucson, AZ	28
Corpus Christi, TX	32	Newark, NJ	25	Tulsa, OK	53
Dallas, TX	41	New Orleans, LA	73	Washington, DC	28
Denver, CO	38	New York, NY	18	Wichita, KS	53
Des Moines, IA	55	Norfolk, VA	36	Wilmington, DE	30

Source: United States Weather Bureau.

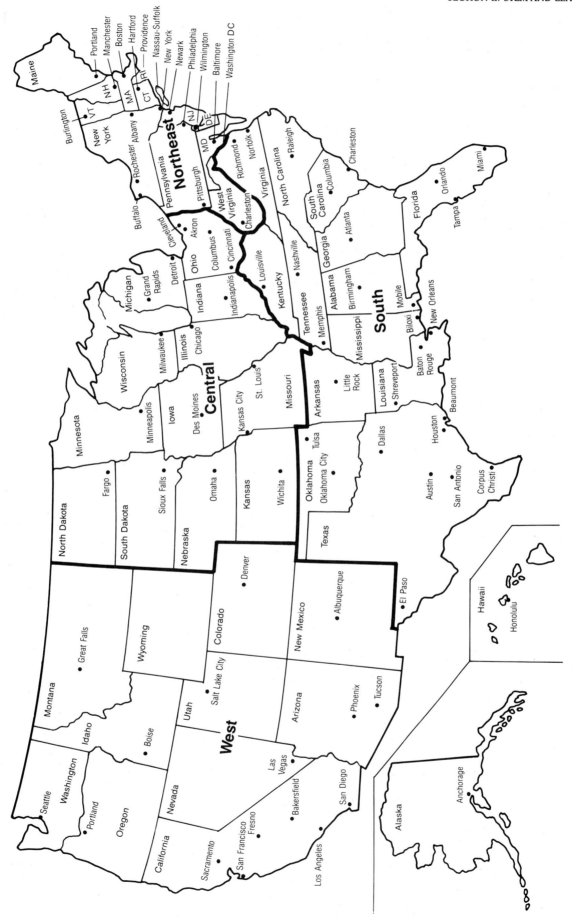

A stem-and-leaf plot of the number of days of thunderstorms is shown below. Notice that the stem for numbers less than 10 is 0.

```
0 | 1 2 3 3 5 5 6 6 7 7

1 | 3 5 8 8 9

2 | 0 0 1 4 4 5 7 7 8 8 8 8 9

3 | 0 0 0 2 3 5 5 6 6 6 6 7 7 7 8 8 9

4 | 0 1 1 2 3 3 5 5 7 7

5 | 0 0 0 1 1 2 2 2 2 3 3 5 6 8 8 9

6 | 3 5

7 | 1 3

8 | 0 0 5 6

9 | 1
```

6|3 REPRESENTS
63 THUNDERSTORMS
PER YEAR

1. How does your city, or the city nearest you, compare to the other cities?

2. Which five cities have the largest number of days with thunderstorms? What do these five cities have in common?

3. The map on page 15 shows the United States divided into four regions: west, south, central, and northeast. Make a stem-and-leaf plot, replacing each city with the label for its location:

   W for WEST
   S for SOUTH
   C for CENTRAL
   N for NORTHEAST

4. Write a summary of what you can see in this stem-and-leaf plot.

Application 5

Soft Drinks

The table below shows the number of *gallons* of soft drinks sold per person in 1977 for each state.

State	Gallons per Person	State	Gallons per Person
Alabama (AL)	36.8	Nebraska (NE)	32.9
Alaska (AK)	29.5	Nevada (NV)	34.5
Arizona (AZ)	29.1	New Hampshire (NH)	28.4
Arkansas (AR)	33.3	New Jersey (NJ)	28.7
California (CA)	32.2	New Mexico (NM)	28.7
Colorado (CO)	30.0	New York (NY)	31.7
Connecticut (CT)	31.3	North Carolina (NC)	39.9
Delaware (DE)	32.5	North Dakota (ND)	23.2
Florida (FL)	39.7	Ohio (OH)	34.1
Georgia (GA)	39.4	Oklahoma (OK)	31.0
Hawaii (HI)	31.3	Oregon (OR)	23.8
Idaho (ID)	20.7	Pennsylvania (PA)	26.5
Illinois (IL)	33.2	Rhode Island (RI)	28.5
Indiana (IN)	28.8	South Carolina (SC)	39.1
Iowa (IA)	29.0	South Dakota (SD)	25.5
Kansas (KS)	35.9	Tennessee (TN)	36.4
Kentucky (KY)	35.3	Texas (TX)	35.9
Louisiana (LA)	36.7	Utah (UT)	28.0
Maine (ME)	29.2	Vermont (VT)	26.6
Maryland (MD)	34.9	Virginia (VA)	38.3
Massachusetts (MA)	31.6	Washington (WA)	25.1
Michigan (MI)	33.4	Washington, D.C. (DC)	36.0
Minnesota (MN)	33.0	West Virginia (WV)	34.2
Mississippi (MS)	38.2	Wisconsin (WI)	28.8
Missouri (MO)	36.4	Wyoming (WY)	20.6
Montana (MT)	23.3		

Source: *Beverage World*, March 1978.

(After each state is its two-letter postal abbreviation. In some applications we will use these for identifying the states, so you may need to refer back to this list to check any that are unfamiliar.)

1. How many ounces are in a gallon?

2. In Alabama, 36.8 gallons were sold per person. How many ounces were sold per person? How many 12-ounce cans would 36.8 gallons fill?

3. For the number of gallons per person in your state, find the equivalent number of 12-ounce cans of soft drinks.

4. These data are different from previous sets of data since the numbers contain decimals. The values go from 20.6 to 39.9, so we choose the stems to be 20, 21, 22, ..., 39. Copy and complete this stem-and-leaf plot of the gallons per person. The plot has been started with the values for Alabama and Alaska.

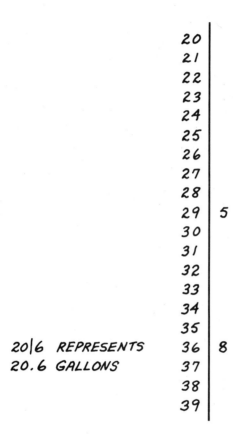

20|6 REPRESENTS
20.6 GALLONS

```
20
21
22
23
24
25
26
27
28
29 | 5
30
31
32
33
34
35
36 | 8
37
38
39
```

5. Label your state.

6. Label the states that have the lowest soft drink consumption.

7. Label the states that have the highest soft drink consumption.

8. Which region of the country consumes the most soft drinks per person? What is your explanation for this?

9. (For class discussion) How could these data have been collected?

Back-to-Back Stem-and-Leaf Plots and Spreading Out Stem-and-Leaf Plots

Sometimes we want to compare two sets of data. For example, look at the following tables that contain the home run leaders for the National League and American League from 1921 to 1985.

Year	National League	HR	American League	HR
	Home Run Leaders			
1921	George Kelly, New York	23	Babe Ruth, New York	59
1922	Rogers Hornsby, St. Louis	42	Ken Williams, St. Louis	39
1923	Cy Williams, Philadelphia	41	Babe Ruth, New York	41
1924	Jacques Foumier, Brooklyn	27	Babe Ruth, New York	46
1925	Rogers Hornsby, St. Louis	39	Bob Meusel, New York	33
1926	Hack Wilson, Chicago	21	Babe Ruth, New York	47
1927	Hack Wilson, Chicago Cy Williams, Philadelphia	30	Babe Ruth, New York	60
1928	Hack Wilson, Chicago Jim Bottomley, St. Louis	31	Babe Ruth, New York	54
1929	Charles Klein, Philadelphia	43	Babe Ruth, New York	46
1930	Hack Wilson, Chicago	56	Babe Ruth, New York	49
1931	Charles Klein, Philadelphia	31	Babe Ruth, New York Lou Gehrig, New York	46
1932	Charles Klein, Philadelphia Mel Ott, New York	38	Jimmy Foxx, Philadelphia	58
1933	Charles Klein, Philadelphia	28	Jimmy Foxx, Philadelphia	48
1934	Rip Collins, St. Louis Mel Ott, New York	35	Lou Gehrig, New York	49
1935	Walter Berger, Boston	34	Jimmy Foxx, Philadelphia Hank Greenberg, Detroit	36
1936	Mel Ott, New York	33	Lou Gehrig, New York	49
1937	Mel Ott, New York Joe Medwick, St. Louis	31	Joe DiMaggio, New York	46
1938	Mel Ott, New York	36	Hank Greenberg, Detroit	58
1939	John Mize, St. Louis	28	Jimmy Foxx, Boston	35
1940	John Mize, St. Louis	43	Hank Greenberg, Detroit	41
1941	Dolph Camilli, Brooklyn	34	Ted Williams, Boston	37
1942	Mel Ott, New York	30	Ted Williams, Boston	36
1943	Bill Nicholson, Chicago	29	Rudy York, Detroit	34
1944	Bill Nicholson, Chicago	33	Nick Etten, New York	22
1945	Tommy Holmes, Boston	28	Vern Stephens, St. Louis	24
1946	Ralph Kiner, Pittsburgh	23	Hank Greenberg, Detroit	44
1947	Ralph Kiner, Pittsburgh John Mize, New York	51	Ted Williams, Boston	32
1948	Ralph Kiner, Pittsburgh John Mize, New York	40	Joe DiMaggio, New York	39
1949	Ralph Kiner, Pittsburgh	54	Ted Williams, Boston	43
1950	Ralph Kiner, Pittsburgh	47	Al Rosen, Cleveland	37
1951	Ralph Kiner, Pittsburgh	42	Gus Zernial, Chicago-Philadelphia	33
1952	Ralph Kiner, Pittsburgh Hank Sauer, Chicago	37	Larry Doby, Cleveland	32

Source: *The World Almanac and Book of Facts*, 1985 edition.

Home Run Leaders

Year	National League	HR	American League	HR
1953	Ed Mathews, Milwaukee	47	Al Rosen, Cleveland	43
1954	Ted Kluszewski, Cincinnati	49	Larry Doby, Cleveland	32
1955	Willie Mays, New York	51	Mickey Mantle, New York	37
1956	Duke Snider, Brooklyn	43	Mickey Mantle, New York	52
1957	Hank Aaron, Milwaukee	44	Roy Sievers, Washington	42
1958	Ernie Banks, Chicago	47	Mickey Mantle, New York	42
1959	Ed Mathews, Milwaukee	46	Rocky Colavito, Cleveland	42
			Harmon Killebrew, Washington	
1960	Ernie Banks, Chicago	41	Mickey Mantle, New York	40
1961	Orlando Cepeda, San Francisco	46	Roger Maris, New York	61
1962	Willie Mays, San Francisco	49	Harmon Killebrew, Minnesota	48
1963	Hank Aaron, Milwaukee	44	Harmon Killebrew, Minnesota	45
	Willie McCovey, San Francisco			
1964	Willie Mays, San Francisco	47	Harmon Killebrew, Minnesota	49
1965	Willie Mays, San Francisco	52	Tony Conigliaro, Boston	32
1966	Hank Aaron, Atlanta	44	Frank Robinson, Baltimore	49
1967	Hank Aaron, Atlanta	39	Carl Yastrzemski, Boston	44
			Harmon Killebrew, Minnesota	
1968	Willie McCovey, San Francisco	36	Frank Howard, Washington	44
1969	Willie McCovey, San Francisco	45	Harmon Killebrew, Minnesota	49
1970	Johnny Bench, Cincinnati	45	Frank Howard, Washington	44
1971	Willie Stargell, Pittsburgh	48	Bill Melton, Chicago	33
1972	Johnny Bench, Cincinnati	40	Dick Allen, Chicago	37
1973	Willie Stargell, Pittsburgh	44	Reggie Jackson, Oakland	32
1974	Mike Schmidt, Philadelphia	36	Dick Allen, Chicago	32
1975	Mike Schmidt, Philadelphia	38	George Scott, Milwaukee	36
			Reggie Jackson, Oakland	
1976	Mike Schmidt, Philadelphia	38	Graig Nettles, New York	32
1977	George Foster, Cincinnati	52	Jim Rice, Boston	39
1978	George Foster, Cincinnati	40	Jim Rice, Boston	46
1979	Dave Kingman, Chicago	48	Gorman Thomas, Milwaukee	45
1980	Mike Schmidt, Philadelphia	48	Reggie Jackson, New York	41
			Ben Oglivie, Milwaukee	
1981	Mike Schmidt, Philadelphia	31	Bobby Grich, California	22
			Tony Armas, Oakland	
			Dwight Evans, Boston	
			Eddie Murray, Baltimore	
1982	Dave Kingman, New York	37	Gorman Thomas, Milwaukee	39
			Reggie Jackson, California	
1983	Mike Schmidt, Philadelphia	40	Jim Rice, Boston	39
1984	Mike Schmidt, Philadelphia	36	Tony Armas, Boston	43
	Dale Murphy, Atlanta			
1985	Dale Murphy, Atlanta	37	Darrell Evans, Detroit	40

Source: *The World Almanac and Book of Facts,* 1985 edition.

In which league does the leader tend to hit more home runs? To find out, we make the following back-to-back stem-and-leaf plot of these data. Notice that the stems are in the center of the plot.

NATIONAL LEAGUE		AMERICAN LEAGUE
9 8 8 8 7 3 3 1	2	2 2 4
9 9 8 8 8 7 7 7 6 6 6 6 5 4 4 3 3 1 1 1 1 0 0	3	2 2 2 2 2 2 2 3 3 3 4 5 6 6 6 7 7 7 7 9 9 9 9
9 9 8 8 8 7 7 7 7 6 6 5 5 4 4 4 4 3 3 3 2 2 1 1 0 0 0 0	4	0 0 1 1 1 2 2 2 3 3 3 4 4 4 4 5 5 6 6 6 6 7 8 8 9 9 9 9 9 9
6 4 2 2 1 1	5	2 4 8 8 9
	6	0 1

|2|4 REPRESENTS 24 HOME RUNS

There are too many leaves per stem, so we will spread out the stem-and-leaf plot using the stems that follow.

NATIONAL LEAGUE		AMERICAN LEAGUE
	2	
	·	
	3	
	·	
	4	
	·	
	5	
	·	
	6	

We will put the leaves 0, 1, 2, 3, and 4 on the first line for each stem and the leaves 5, 6, 7, 8, and 9 on the second line. The reorganized plot is shown as follows:

NATIONAL LEAGUE		AMERICAN LEAGUE
3 3 1	2	2 2 4
9 8 8 8 7	·	
4 4 3 3 1 1 1 1 0 0	3	2 2 2 2 2 2 3 3 3 4
9 9 8 8 8 7 7 7 6 6 6 5	·	5 6 6 6 7 7 7 7 9 9 9 9
4 4 4 4 3 3 3 2 2 1 1 0 0 0 0	4	0 0 1 1 1 2 2 2 3 3 3 4 4 4 4
9 9 8 8 8 7 7 7 7 6 6 5 5	·	5 5 6 6 6 6 7 8 8 9 9 9 9 9 9
4 2 2 1 1	5	2 4
6	·	8 8 9
	6	0 1

|2|4 REPRESENTS 24 HOME RUNS

Discussion Questions

1. Does the American League champion or the National League champion tend to hit the most home runs?

2. Which three years were unusually low in home runs hit in the American League? What happened in these three years?

3. Make a new back-to-back stem-and-leaf plot using the stems that follow. The home runs for the National League have been done for you. To construct this plot, you don't have to go back to the original list of data. Instead, take the values from one of the stem-and-leaf plots already constructed.

   For each stem, put the leaves:

   - 0 and 1 on the first line
   - 2 and 3 on the second line
   - 4 and 5 on the third line
   - 6 and 7 on the fourth line
   - 8 and 9 on the last line

```
        NATIONAL LEAGUE                    AMERICAN LEAGUE
_____
                            1 | 2 |
                          3 3 | · |
                              | · |
                            7 | · |
                        9 8 8 | · |
              / / / / 0 0 | 3 |
                          3 3 | · |
                        5 4 4 | · |
              7 7 7 6 6 6 | · |
                      9 9 8 8 | · |
                / / 0 0 0 | 4 |
                  3 3 3 2 2 | · |
              5 5 4 4 4 4 | · |
              7 7 7 7 6 6 | · |
                  9 9 8 8 8 | · |
                        / / | 5 |
                          2 2 | · |
                            4 | · |
                            6 | · |
                              | · |
  9|3| REPRESENTS              |   |
  39  HOME RUNS              | 6 |
```

4. Which of the three back-to-back stem-and-leaf plots for the home run data do you think displays the data best? Why?

From a back-to-back plot like this, we can see that there tends to be a slightly larger number of home runs in the American League. We reach this conclusion because the values at the high end, in the upper 50's and 60's, come more often from the American League. Also, the values at the low end, in the 20's, come more often from the National League. For the stems in the 30's and the 40's, the numbers of leaves for the two leagues are about equal. The lower 50's has more values in the National League, but the American League makes up for this by having more values in the upper 50's and 60's.

Back-to-back stem-and-leaf plots are useful for comparing two sets of data. Before making comparisons, however, check to see first that both sets have about the same total number of values. Also, make sure that the plot is drawn accurately with each leaf taking up the same amount of space. These checks are important because we make the comparisons mainly through comparing the numbers of leaves on both sides. If one side has more data values or each leaf takes more space on one side than on the other, it can be hard to make accurate comparisons. To get the sizes correct, it helps to construct the plot on graph paper.

To decide if one data set generally has larger values than the other, compare the number of leaves on the two sides for both the largest and smallest stems. Also, note if there are outliers or gaps in the data that are not the same on both sides, and whether or not the two sides have about the same shape.

Application 6

Traffic Deaths

The table below lists the 50 states and the District of Columbia with the number of deaths in 1983 per 100 million vehicle miles driven.

Motor Vehicle Traffic Deaths by State per 100 Million Vehicle Miles

State	Rate	State	Rate
Alabama	3.2	Montana	4.0
Alaska	3.9	Nebraska	2.1
Arizona	2.6	Nevada	3.8
Arkansas	3.2	New Hampshire	2.6
California	2.6	New Jersey	1.7
Colorado	2.6	New Mexico	4.3
Connecticut	2.1	New York	2.5
Delaware	2.3	North Carolina	2.8
District of Columbia	1.8	North Dakota	2.1
Florida	3.3	Ohio	2.1
Georgia	3.1	Oklahoma	2.7
Hawaii	2.2	Oregon	2.7
Idaho	3.2	Pennsylvania	2.4
Illinois	2.3	Rhode Island	1.6
Indiana	2.5	South Carolina	3.4
Iowa	2.5	South Dakota	2.6
Kansas	2.2	Tennessee	2.9
Kentucky	3.0	Texas	3.0
Louisiana	4.3	Utah	2.5
Maine	2.8	Vermont	2.3
Maryland	2.1	Virginia	2.1
Massachusetts	1.7	Washington	2.2
Michigan	2.1	West Virginia	4.4
Minnesota	1.8	Wisconsin	2.2
Mississippi	4.1	Wyoming	3.2
Missouri	2.5		

Source: National Safety Council.

1. If a state had 685 traffic deaths for 20,000,000,000 vehicle miles, what rate would be listed in the table above?

2. Alabama had a total of 940 auto deaths in 1983. How many miles were driven in Alabama that year?

3. How do the states east of the Mississippi River compare with the states west of it? To decide, construct a back-to-back stem-and-leaf plot with the stems spread out. You may want to use the map on page 15. Leave the values for Minnesota and Louisiana off the plot as the river goes through both states.

4. Which states east of the Mississippi River might be considered outliers?

5. Which state west of the Mississippi River has the highest traffic death rate? Would you call it an outlier?

6. Do states in the east or the west generally have larger traffic death rates?

7. Summarize what you learned from this back-to-back stem-and-leaf plot.

8. What factors do you think might help to explain the difference between the east and the west?

9. (For class discussion) How could these data have been collected?

Stem-and-Leaf Plots Where the Data Should be Truncated

The following table lists the buildings in San Francisco that are over 360 feet tall.

Building	Height in Feet
Transamerica Pyramid	853
Bank of America	778
101 California Street	600
5 Fremont Center	600
Embarcadero Center, Number 4	570
Security Pacific Bank	569
One Market Plaza, Spear Street	565
Wells Fargo Building	561
Standard Oil	551
One Sansome-Citicorp	550
Shaklee Building	537
Aetna Life	529
First & Market Building	529
Metropolitan Life	524
Crocker National Bank	500
Hilton Hotel	493
Pacific Gas & Electric	492
Union Bank	487
Pacific Insurance	476
Bechtel Building	475
333 Market Building	474
Hartford Building	465
Mutual Benefit Life	438
Russ Building	435
Pacific Telephone Building	435
Pacific Gateway	416
Embarcadero Center, Number 3	412
Embarcadero Center, Number 2	412
595 Market Building	410
101 Montgomery Street	405
California State Automobile Association	399
Alcoa Building	398
St. Francis Hotel	395
Shell Building	386
Del Monte	378
Pacific 3-Apparel Mart	376
Meridien Hotel	374

Source: *The World Almanac and Book of Facts*, 1985 edition.

The shortest building, the Meridien Hotel, is 374 feet tall. The tallest, the Transamerica Pyramid, is 853 feet tall. Start the stem-and-leaf plot as follows:

```
3
.
4
.
5
.
6
.
7
.
8
.
```

To place the 778-feet tall Bank of America Building on the plot, truncate (cut off) the last digit. This leaves 77, which goes on the plot as follows:

```
3
.
4
.
5
.
6
.
7
. 7
8
.
```

The finished plot follows.

```
3
. 7 7 7 8 9 9 9
4 0 1 1 1 1 3 3 3
. 6 7 7 7 8 9 9
5 0 2 2 2 3
. 5 5 6 6 6 7
6 0 0
.
7
. 7
8
. 5
```

3|7 REPRESENTS
370 - 379 FEET

Discussion Questions

1. What heights can 8|5 represent?

2. The heights of all but two buildings stop abruptly at 600 feet. Can you think of a possible explanation for this?

3. The following table lists Los Angeles buildings taller than 360 feet.

Building	Height in Feet
First Interstate Bank	858
Crocker Center, North	750
Security Pacific National Bank	735
Atlantic Richfield Plaza (2 buildings)	699
Wells Fargo Bank	625
Crocker-Citizen Plaza	620
Century Plaza Towers (2 buildings)	571
Union Bank Square	516
City Hall	454
Equitable Life Building	454
Transamerica Center	452
Mutual Benefit Life Insurance Building	435
Broadway Plaza	414
1900 Avenue of Stars	398
1 Wilshire Building	395
The Evian	390
Bonaventure Hotel	367
400 South Hope Street	365
Beaudry Center	365
California Federal Savings & Loan Building	363
Century City Office Building	363

Source: *The World Almanac and Book of Facts*, 1985 edition.

Complete this back-to-back stem-and-leaf plot for the two cities.

```
     LOS ANGELES                SAN FRANCISCO
  _____|_____
                       |  3  |
                       |  •  |
                       |  4  |
                       |  •  |
                       |  5  |
                       |  •  |
                       |  6  |
                       |  •  |
                       |  7  |
                       |  •  |
                       |  8  |
```

Notice that San Francisco has 37 tall buildings, while Los Angeles has only 21. We don't need a stem-and-leaf plot to tell us that San Francisco has more tall buildings than Los Angeles. This plot can, however, help us answer the question of which city's buildings are relatively taller, apart from the total numbers of tall buildings. Unlike the last section, we cannot just look at the number of leaves, since San Francisco has more values and thus will generally have more leaves for each stem. Instead, we need to compare the two *shapes*, making a mental adjustment for the fact that San Francisco has about twice as many data values. Follow this procedure to answer the following question.

4. Considering only buildings over 360 feet tall, does Los Angeles or San Francisco tend to have relatively taller buildings?

5. In the previous stem-and-leaf plots, both the San Francisco and Los Angeles heights were truncated. Instead of truncating, we will now *round* each height to the nearest ten. Then we will see if the back-to-back stem-and-leaf plot gives the same impression as before. The San Francisco side of the plot below was made by rounding. Copy the plot and complete the Los Angeles side using rounding. The symbol 3|7 now represents 365-374 feet.

LOS ANGELES		SAN FRANCISCO
	3	
	.	7 8 8 9
	4	0 0 0 1 1 1 1 2 4 4 4
	.	7 7 8 8 9 9 9
	5	0 2 3 3 4
	.	5 5 6 7 7 7
	6	0 0
	.	
	7	
	.	8
	8	
	.	5

3|7 REPRESENTS
365 - 374 FEET

6. Is it faster to round or to truncate?

7. Does the back-to-back stem-and-leaf plot with rounded numbers give the same general impression as the one with truncated numbers? Are there any differences in what you learn from the two plots?

8. Do you think truncating is an appropriate procedure, or should the data be rounded?

30

If you are like many students, you may feel that there is something wrong about truncating. It seems less accurate than rounding, and therefore worse. But is using 3|7 to represent 365-374 feet really more accurate for our purposes than using 3|7 to represent 370-379 feet?

Another point to consider is that the data we have may already be either rounded or truncated, and we don't know which. Are all the building heights exact multiples of one foot, with no inches or fractions of inches, as listed in the tables?

Finally, it is easy to make a mistake when rounding. In order to truncate, all we do is use a straightedge to cover the columns of digits not needed. To decide if truncating is appropriate for a specific problem, ask yourself if it is likely to make any difference in the interpretations you reach.

Children's Books

The following table lists the children's books published in the U.S. since 1895 that have sold one million or more copies.

Green Eggs and Ham, by Dr. Seuss. 1960	5,940,776
One Fish, Two Fish, Red Fish, Blue Fish, by Dr. Seuss. 1960	5,842,024
Hop on Pop, by Dr. Seuss. 1963	5,814,101
Dr. Seuss' ABC, by Dr. Seuss. 1963	5,648,193
The Cat in the Hat, by Dr. Seuss. 1957	5,394,741
The Wonderful Wizard of Oz, by L. Frank Baum. 1900	(estimate) 5,000,000
Charlotte's Web, by E. B. White. 1952	4,670,516
The Cat in the Hat Comes Back, by Dr. Seuss. 1958	3,431,917
The Little Prince, by Antoine de Saint-Exupery. 1943	2,811,478
The Little House on the Prairie, by Laura Ingalls Wilder. 1953 edition	2,732,666
The Little House in the Big Woods, by Laura Ingalls Wilder. 1953 edition	2,527,203
My First Atlas. 1959	2,431,000
Love and the Facts of Life, by Evelyn Duvall and Sylvanus Duvall. 1950	2,360,000
Egermeier's Bible Story Book, by Elsie E. Egermeier. 1923	2,326,577
Go Ask Alice, Anonymous. 1971	2,245,605
Benji, by Leonore Fleischer. 1974	2,235,694
The Little Engine That Could, by Watty Piper. 1926	2,166,000
Stuart Little, by E. B. White. 1945	2,129,591
Freckles, by Gene Stratton Potter. 1904	2,089,523
The Girl of the Limberlost, by Gene Stratton Porter. 1909	2,053,892
Sounder, by William Armstrong. 1969	1,815,401
Harry, the Dirty Dog, by Gene Zion. 1956	1,690,339
Seventeen, by Booth Tarkington. 1916	(estimate) 1,682,891
Where the Wild Things Are, by Maurice Sendak. 1963	1,632,020
Laddie, by Gene Stratton Porter. 1913	1,586,529
The Big Book of Mother Goose. 1950	1,500,000
The Golden Dictionary, by Ellen Wales Walpole. 1944	1,450,000
A Friend is Someone Who Likes You, by Joan Walsh Anglund. 1958	1,423,432
Rebecca of Sunnybrook Farm, by Kate Douglas Wiggin. 1904	1,357,714
Love Is a Special Way of Feeling, by Joan Walsh Anglund. 1960	1,308,293
The Real Mother Goose. 1915	1,296,140
The Pigman, by Paul Zindel. 1968	1,265,876
Better Homes and Gardens Story Book. 1951	1,220,728
Trouble after School, by Jerrold Beim. 1957	1,145,570
Better Homes and Gardens Junior Cook Book. 1955	1,100,182
Pollyanna, by Eleanor H. Porter. 1913	1,059,000
Le Petit Prince, by Antoine de Saint-Exupery. 1943	1,018,373
Mary Poppins, by Pamela L. Travers. 1934	1,005,203
Winnie-the Pooh, by A. A. Milne. 1926	1,005,000
Pollyanna Grows Up, by Eleanor H. Porter. 1915	1,000,000
Little Black Sambo, by Helen Bannerman. 1899	(estimate) 1,000,000

Source: A. P. Hackett and J. H. Burke, *Eighty Years of Best Sellers.*

1. Make a stem-and-leaf plot of these data using these stems. *Green Eggs and Ham* has been placed on the plot to get you started. Truncate all digits except those in the millions and hundred-thousands places.

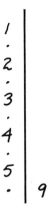

```
1
 .
2
 .
3
 .
4
 .
5
 . | 9
```

1|0 REPRESENTS 1,000,000 THROUGH 1,099,999 BOOKS SOLD

2. Underline all digits representing books by Dr. Seuss.

3. Circle the digits representing the books you have read. Do these circles tend to be at the top or the bottom of the diagram? Why?

4. If another line were added to the top of the plot for books that sold 500,000-999,999 copies, how long do you think it would be? Why?

5. Write a summary of the information displayed in the plot.

Stem-and-Leaf Plots — Summary

Stem-and-leaf plots are a new way to quickly organize and display data. Unlike line plots, they are best used when there are more than 25 pieces of data. Statisticians use stem-and-leaf plots as a substitute for the less informative histograms and bar graphs.

Variations of stem-and-leaf plots that you should know how to construct are as follows:

- back-to-back
- truncated and rounded
- spread out

From a stem-and-leaf plot it is easy to identify the largest and smallest values, outliers, clusters, gaps, the relative position of any important value, and the shape of the distribution.

Suggestions for Student Projects

1. Collect data on a topic that interests you, make a stem-and-leaf plot, and then write a summary of the information displayed in the plot. Use one of the topics listed below or think of your own.

    a. Compare the ages in months of the boys and the girls in your class.

    b. Compare the heights of the boys and the girls in your class.

    c. Compare the heights of the buildings in two cities near you.

    d. Compare the gas mileage of foreign and domestic cars. (This information can be found in many almanacs.)

    e. Compare the scores of two different classes taking the same math test.

    The next two projects involve comparing line plots with stem-and-leaf plots.

2. Devise a way to use symbols in a line plot to replace the individual data values, as we did for the stem-and-leaf plots in the fast foods and thunderstorm examples. Then, construct a line plot for one of these examples, using your method. Do the line and stem-and-leaf plots show any different information? Which is easier to interpret? Which do you prefer?

3. Devise a way of modifying a line plot to get a back-to-back line plot. Then, redo Application 6, or the building heights example, using your back-to-back line plot. Which is easier to construct, the back-to-back line plot or the stem-and-leaf plot? Do they show any different information? Which shows the information more clearly? Which do you prefer? Can you think of situations in which you might prefer the other plot?

4. In order to compare truncating and rounding, take any of the data in this section and make a back-to-back stem-and-leaf plot of the truncated against the rounded values. Do you see any difference, and if so what is it? Could you have predicted this?

5. In the fast foods example at the beginning of this section, we showed the type of food in the stem-and-leaf plot by replacing the leaves by letters. A way to show both the specific numerical values and labels is to keep the numerical leaf in the plot, and follow it by a label in parentheses. For instance, the next-to-bottom row in the fast foods example would be 3|3(H), 4(F). By keeping the number in the plot, we retain as much detailed numerical information as is generally needed. This idea is especially useful for displaying data where there is one number for each of the 50 states. The two-letter postal abbreviation can be used to identify each state. Find some interesting data where there is one value for each state. A good example would be each state's current population as found in an almanac. Make the plot just described, and write a summary of the information displayed.

III. MEDIAN, MEAN, QUARTILES, AND OUTLIERS

Median and Mean

You have probably learned how to compute the average of a set of numbers. For example, if Sally gets scores of 80, 96, 84, 95, and 90 on five math tests, then her average is:

$$\frac{80 + 96 + 84 + 95 + 90}{5}$$

$$= \frac{445}{5}$$

$$= 89.$$

Whenever we compute an average this way, we will call it the *mean*. Thus, the mean of Sally's test scores is 89. We need a new word for the average because there are other kinds of averages. Another type of average is the *median*. To find the median of Sally's test scores, first put them in order from smallest to largest.

$$80 \quad 84 \quad \boxed{90} \quad 95 \quad 96$$

The middle score, 90, is the median. Half of Sally's five test scores are lower than or equal to the median and half are higher than or equal to the median.

What do you do if there is an even number of scores? If Sally takes a sixth test and gets a 25, her scores are now:

$$25 \quad 80 \quad \boxed{84 \quad 90} \quad 95 \quad 96.$$

There are two scores in the middle, 84 and 90. The median is halfway between these two scores:

$$\frac{84 + 90}{2}$$

$$= \frac{174}{2}$$

$$= 87.$$

Half of her six test scores are lower than 87 and half are higher.

Discussion Questions

1. Compute the mean of Sally's six test scores. (Round to the nearest tenth.)

2. On the basis of this grading scale what grade would Sally receive if the mean of the six tests is used to determine her grade?

   A 90-100   B 80-89   C 70-79   D 60-69   E 0-59

3. What grade would she receive if the median of the six tests is used to determine her grade?

4. Does one extreme score cause a greater change in the median or in the mean?

5. Do you need to know all of the data values in order to find the median? For example, suppose that Sally has taken 6 tests and you only know 5 of her scores. Can you calculate the median?

6. Give a reason for choosing the median to summarize Sally's test scores.

7. Give a reason for choosing the mean to summarize Sally's test scores.

8. Which do you think is better to use, the mean or median?

9. Why do you think the median is generally used when discussing ages, average house prices, or average incomes, as in the following newspaper and magazine examples?

   a. "When only first-time marriages were considered, the agency [National Center for Health Statistics] placed the median age for brides at 21.8 years in 1980, up from 20.3 years in 1963. The median age for bridegrooms was 23.6 years, up from 22.5 years in 1963." *(Los Angeles Times 2/17/84)*

   b. According to the Census Bureau, "the counties with the highest median value of owner-occupied dwellings are: Pitkin, CO - $200,000; Marin, CA - $151,000; Honolulu, HI - $130,400; San Mateo, CA - $124,400; Maui, HI - $113,600." *(USA Today 3/8/84)*

   c. According to the Census Bureau, "the median time spent on homework for students in American elementary and high schools was 5.4 hours a week...the sharpest difference was between types of schools, with students in private high schools doing 14.2 hours of homework weekly, as against 6.5 hours by their public school counterparts." *(The New York Times 11/29/84)*

   d. "The following drawing shows typical allowances (rounded to the nearest 25¢) for 8-to-13-year-olds, as reported by the 811 students in our survey who received allowances. The allowances of the 8-to-11-year-olds are all pretty much the same. They range from $2.00 to $2.75. But for the 12-year-olds, there's a jump of $1, and an even bigger jump for kids one year older.

      The figures don't mean that all the three hundred thirty-eight 11-year-olds in our survey who receive an allowance are pocketing $2.75 every week. That $2.75 is the *median* allowance for that age. Median means right in the middle. Half the 11-year-olds are getting more than $2.75, and half are getting less. In fact, one-third report a weekly allowance of under $2, and about the same amount get more than $4 a week.

169 get less	$2.75	169 get more

      The amount of your allowance seems to depend a lot on your age. But where you live and whether you are a boy or a girl do *not* seem to affect how much you get per week. Students all across the country, in cities and small towns, said they received pretty much the same amount. Boys and girls also reported similar allowances." (*Penny Power* 2/3/83)

10. In the following newspaper story, what do you think is the meaning of the word "average"? Give your reasons.

"[In a study of jury awards in civil trials, they] found that while the average award against corporate defendants was more than $120,000, the average against individuals was $18,500. The average against government defendants was $38,000, but it was $97,000 in cases that involved hospitals and other nonprofit entities.

'To some degree, the average awards against corporations and hospitals were so great because of a few extraordinarily large awards,' the report explained." (*Newark Star-Ledger* 8/20/85)

11. The following information seems to be incorrect.

"According to the latest enrollment analysis by age-categories, half of the [Los Angeles Community College] district's 128,000 students are over the age of 24. The average student is 29." (*Los Angeles Times* 9/20/81)

"In the region we are traveling west of Whitney, precipitation drops off and the average snow depth on April 1 for the southern Sierra is a modest 5 to 6 feet. And two winters out of three, the snow pack is below average." Ezra Bowen, *The High Sierra* (New York: Time-Life Books, 1972), p. 142.

   a. Give an example of four students with a mean age of 29 and median age of 24.

   b. Give an example of the snow depth for three winters that makes the quote from *The High Sierra* true.

Both the median and the mean summarize the data by giving a measure of the center of the data values. *For the kinds of data in this book*, the median generally gives a more reasonable summary since it is not affected by a few extreme values. When there are no outliers, there will generally not be much difference between the median and mean, and which we choose won't matter. Using a calculator, the mean is easy to compute. To find the median, however, the data must be ordered from smallest to largest. This can be tedious, but an easy method is to construct a stem-and-leaf plot.

Neither the median nor the mean can tell us as much about the data as a plot showing all the values, such as a line plot or a stem-and-leaf plot.

Application 8

How Many Moons?

A visitor from the star Alpha Centauri has selected you to provide her with information about our solar system. She is filling out a form and asks how many moons are "average" for a planet in our solar system.

Study the table below.

Planet	Number of Moons
Mercury	0
Venus	0
Earth	1
Mars	2
Jupiter	16
Saturn	23
Uranus	15*
Neptune	2
Pluto	1

Source: The World Book, 1984.
*The published figure is 5 moons, but in January 1986, Voyager 2 discovered 10 additional moons around Uranus.

1. Compute the mean number of moons.

2. Compute the median number of moons.

3. Which three planets are the most different in number of moons compared to the others? Do you know any explanation for this?

4. Do you think the visitor from Alpha Centauri would get a more accurate impression about the typical number of moons from the median or the mean? Is either summary number adequate? Give your reasons.

Next, the visitor asks about the length of a typical day in our solar system. Study the following table.

Planet	Approximate Length of a Day in Earth Hours
Mercury	1416
Venus	5832
Earth	24
Mars	24.5
Jupiter	10
Saturn	11
Uranus	22
Neptune	16
Pluto	153

5. Compute the mean length of a day in our solar system in hours.

6. How many Earth days is this?

7. Find the median length of a day in our solar system.

8. Do you think it is better to give your visitor the mean length of a day or the median length of a day? Why? Are you happy about giving your visitor one single number? Why or why not?

Application 9

The Pop Meter

Six of the pop music reviewers for the *Los Angeles Times* and a teenage actress and singer, Molly Ringwald, rated five new albums as follows:

Albums	Dennis Hunt	Lori E. Pike	Richard Cromelin	Connie Johnson	Chris Willman	Patrick Goldstein	Molly Ringwald
"Little Creatures" Talking Heads	75	84	85	75	88	91	95
"Who's Zoomin' Who?" Aretha Franklin	86	82	70	83	62	79	98
"Youthquake" Dead or Alive	78	72	50	30	12	36	70
"Boy in the Box" Corey Hart	60	60	20	49	25	51	75
"Invasion of Your Privacy" Ratt	65	20	20	25	27	66	90

The ratings system: 90-100, excellent; 70-89, good; 50-69, fair; 30-49, weak; 0-29, melt down.

Source: *Los Angeles Times*, September 1, 1985.

1. Compute the mean rating for each album.
2. Compute the median rating for each album.
3. a) For which album are the mean and median farthest apart?

   b) Which reviewer caused this?

   c) Is the mean or the median more representative of this album's overall rating?

4. a) If you judge by the mean rating, which reviewer is the hardest grader?

   b) If you judge by the median rating, which reviewer is the hardest grader?

   c) Which reviewer tends to be the most different from the others?

Range, Quartiles, and Interquartile Range

The number of grams of carbohydrates (starch and sugar) in a 1-ounce serving of thirteen breakfast cereals is shown below.

Cereal	Carbohydrates	Cereal	Carbohydrates
Life	19	Grape Nuts	23
Super Sugar Crisp	26	Special K	21
Rice Krispies	25	Raisin Bran	28
Product 19	24	Wheaties	23
Total	23	Puffed Rice	13
Sugar Corn Pops	26	Sugar Smacks	25
		Cheerios	20

To find the *range*, subtract the smallest number from the largest. The range for the carbohydrates is:

$$28 - 13 = 15 \text{ grams.}$$

We will also learn how to find the *lower quartile* and the *upper quartile*. If the numbers are arranged in order from smallest to largest, the lower quartile, the median, and the upper quartile divide them into four groups of roughly the same size.

X X X X X X X X X X X X X X X X X X X X X X X X X

LOWER EXTREME	LOWER QUARTILE	MEDIAN	UPPER QUARTILE	UPPER EXTREME

To find the quartiles of the previous numbers, first arrange the numbers in order:

13   19   20   21   23   23   23   24   25   25   26   26   28

Second, find the median and draw a vertical line through it.

13   19   20   21   23   23   2|3   24   25   25   26   26   28

The median is 23. Six numbers are below this 23 and six are above it.

Third, consider only the data values to the left of the line.

13   19   20 | 21   23   23

The median of these six numbers is between 20 and 21. This is the lower quartile. Thus, the lower quartile is 20.5. We have drawn a vertical line at the median of these values in the same way as before.

Finally, consider only the data values to the right of the line and find their median. This is the upper quartile. The upper quartile is 25.5.

$$24 \quad 25 \quad 25 \mid 26 \quad 26 \quad 28$$

We have divided the numbers into four groups:

$$13 \quad 19 \quad 20 \mid 21 \quad 23 \quad 23 \quad 23 \quad 24 \quad 25 \quad 25 \mid 26 \quad 26 \quad 28$$

Notice that there are three numbers in each group.

The *interquartile range* is the difference between the upper quartile and the lower quartile. The interquartile range of the given numbers is:

$$25.5 - 20.5 = 5.$$

The *lower extreme* is the smallest value in the data. In this case, it is 13. Similarly, the *upper extreme* is the largest number in the data. In this case, it is 28.

The fastest way to order the numbers from smallest to largest is to make a stem-and-leaf plot of the data, with the leaves ordered. Then, count in from the top and bottom to mark the median and quartiles. As an example, suppose we did not have Cheerios in the list of cereals and we wanted the median and quartiles of the remaining 12 cereals. The median will then be between the sixth and seventh values. We draw the first line there and consider only the data values below and above this line, as before, to get the quartiles.

```
1 | 3
• | 9
2 | 1 | 3  3  3 | 4
• | 5  5 | 6  6 | 8
```

The vertical lines here are dotted. The median is 23.5, the lower quartile is 22, and the upper quartile is 25.5.

Discussion Questions

1. In these data, the median is the mean of the quartiles. Will the median always be the mean of the quartiles?

2. Is the interquartile range half of the range?

3. Cross the 13 grams from Puffed Rice off the list and find the new median and quartiles.

4. By how much did these values change?

5. Recompute the range and interquartile range.

6. By how much did these values change?

7. Find two different sets of seven numbers with:

> lower extreme - 3
> lower quartile - 5
> median - 10
> upper quartile - 12
> upper extreme - 13

8. The median is always between the two quartiles. Do you think the *mean* is always between the two quartiles?

9. Find a set of seven numbers where the mean is above the upper quartile.

10. Find a set of seven numbers where the mean is below the lower quartile.

Application 10

Motocross Bike Ratings

The list below contains the ratings by *Penny Power* magazine of 22 motocross bikes.

Rating	Brand	Model	Price
Very Good	Raleigh	R-10 TUFF BMF	$190
Very Good	Raleigh	R-10 MK III	$150
Very Good	Schwinn	B43 Scrambler	$196
Very Good	Mongoose	BMX Wirewheel	$190
Very Good	Mongoose	BMX Freemag	$215
Good	Vista	GTX99	$125
Good	J.C.Penney	Eagle V	$190
Fair	Ross	142-25 THX	$165
Fair	Ross	Slinger	$125
Fair	Sears	Free Spirit BMX FS500	$150
Fair	Schwinn	B511 Thrasher	$143
Fair	Sears	BMX FS100	$100
Fair	Murray	X-20 Team Murray	$141
Fair	AMF	Hawk 4 BMX	$139
Fair	Huffy	Pro Thunder BMX	$160
Fair	Columbia	Pro Am 2236	$160
Poor	Murray	Team Murray BMX	$130
Poor	J.C.Penney	Dirt Tracker II	$110
Poor	Wards	BMX 34 Open Road	$80
Poor	AMF	Avenger Motocross	$100
Poor	Columbia	Formula 16 BMX	$110
Poor	Huffy	Thunder BMX	$100

Source: *Penny Power*, February 3, 1983.

1. What is the most expensive bike?

2. What is the least expensive bike?

3. Find the median price of the bikes rated:

   a. very good

   b. good

   c. fair

   d. poor

4. In general, do bikes with a higher price have a higher rating?

5. What is the range of the bike prices?

6. Find the lower quartile for all bikes.

7. Find the upper quartile.

8. What is the interquartile range of the bike prices?

9. Which of the bikes rated "very good" is priced below the upper quartile? Is this bike a good buy?

10. Which of the bikes rated "poor" is priced above the lower quartile? Is this bike a good buy?

Outliers

The following table lists all 15 records that reached number 1 for the first time in 1959, and the total number of weeks that each record held the number 1 spot.

Weeks	Record Title	Artist
3	"Smoke Gets in Your Eyes"	Platters
4	"Stagger Lee"	Lloyd Price
5	"Venus"	Frankie Avalon
4	"Come Softly to Me"	Fleetwoods
1	"The Happy Organ"	Dave 'Baby' Cortez
2	"Kansas City"	Wilbert Harrison
6	"The Battle of New Orleans"	Johnny Horton
4	"Lonely Boy"	Paul Anka
2	"A Big Hunk o' Love"	Elvis Presley
4	"The Three Bells"	Browns
2	"Sleep Walk"	Santo & Johnny
9	"Mack the Knife"	Bobby Darin
1	"Mr. Blue"	Fleetwoods
2	"Heartaches by the Number"	Guy Mitchell
1	"Why"	Frankie Avalon

Source: *The Billboard Book of Top 40 Hits*, 1985.

We have already used the word *outlier* several times to indicate values that are widely separated from the rest of the data. Would you say that any record in the list above is an outlier? If we think we have spotted an outlier, it is worth some special thought about why it is different from the rest. Trying to make sense out of the outliers can be an important part of interpreting data.

It is not reasonable, however, to automatically call the upper and lower extremes outliers. Any data set has extremes, and we don't want to put extra energy into trying to interpret them unless they are separated from the rest of the data. We could decide if an observation is an outlier by looking at a plot and making a decision, as we have done so far. However, it is helpful to have a rule to aid in making the decision, especially when there are a moderate to large number of observations (say 25 or more).

Thus, we say that an *outlier* is any number more than 1.5 interquartile ranges above the upper quartile, or more than 1.5 interquartile ranges below the lower quartile. A line plot of the hit record data, with the median (M) and quartiles (LQ and UQ) labeled, follows.

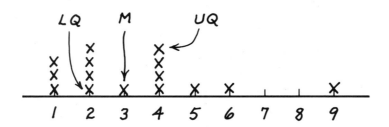

The interquartile range (IQR) is $4 - 2 = 2$, so $1.5 \times IQR = 3$. Thus, the upper cut-off is $4 + 3 = 7$. Since the data value 9 ("Mack the Knife") is greater than 7, we call it an outlier. For the lower end, the cut-off is $2 - 3 = -1$. Since no data value can be less than -1, there are no outliers at the lower end. An interpretation we can draw is that "Mack the Knife" was not only the most popular record in 1959, but that it really stands out as substantially more popular than the other 14 top hits. Before doing this calculation, did you feel that "Mack the Knife" was an outlier?

The rule just described is quick, easy, and straightforward to use. Multiplying the IQR by 1.5 rather than 1.0 or 2.0 generally produces results that are what we would like, if we were to decide which values should be labeled outliers. You might experiment using multipliers such as 1.0, 1.5, and 2.0 to decide which you prefer.

Ice Cream Cone Prices

In September 1985, the prices of a single-scoop ice cream cone at 17 Los Angeles stores are given in the table below.

Store (brand)	Price
Andi's (homemade)	$ .90
Baskin-Robbins	.75
Carvel	.95
Cecelia's (Dreyers)	.90
Cinema Sweet (homemade)	1.20
Clancy Muldoon	.95
Creamery (homemade)	1.05
Farrell's	.70
Foster's Freeze	.53
Haagen-Dazs	1.10
Humphrey Yogart	.95
Leatherby's (homemade)	.91
Magic Sundae (Buds)	.96
Robb's (homemade)	.95
Swensons	1.00
Thrifty Drug	.25
Will-Wright's (own recipe)	1.15

1. Make a stem-and-leaf plot of the prices.

2. Are there any gaps in the prices? Where?

3. Find the median price of an ice cream cone using the stem-and-leaf plot.

4. Find the mean price of an ice cream cone.

5. Thrifty Drug's cone is much cheaper than the others. If it is taken off the list, do you think the median or the mean will increase the most?

6. Cross Thrifty Drug's price off the list before determining the following:

   a. Find the median price of the remaining cones.

   b. Find the mean price of the remaining cones.

   c. Which increased more, the median or the mean?

7. Find the range in prices. (Include Thrifty Drug from exercise 7 through 13).

8. Find the lower quartile of the prices.

9. Find the upper quartile of the prices.

10. Is there a larger difference between the median and the lower quartile or between the median and the upper quartile?

11. Find the interquartile range.

12. Use the 1.5 × IQR rule to find any outliers.

13. How is the outlier different from the others? Can you think of any possible explanations for this?

Median, Mean, Quartiles, and Outliers — Summary

Both the median and the mean are single numbers that summarize the location of the data. Neither alone can tell the whole story about the data, but sometimes we do want a single, concise, summary value. Generally, the median is more valuable than the mean, especially if there is any possibility of having even a few unusually large or small values in the data.

The lower quartile, median, and upper quartile divide the data into four parts with approximately the same number of observations in each part. The interquartile range (IQR), the third quartile minus the first quartile, is a measure of how spread out the data are. If a number is more than 1.5 times the interquartile range above the upper quartile or below the lower quartile, we call it an outlier. If the data are grouped fairly tightly, there will be no outliers. When we do find an outlier, we should study it closely. It is worthwhile to try to find reasons for it, as they can be an important part of the overall interpretation of the data.

Suggestions for Student Projects

1. Choose 5 or 6 current popular records. Your teacher should select 5 or 6 reviewers from students in your class. These reviewers will fill in ratings as in Application 9, and the entire class will analyze the results.

2. Find examples of the use of the words "mean," "median," or "average" in a local newspaper. If you find "average," can you tell if they used the median, the mean, or some other method? If you find "mean" or "median," discuss whether or not the appropriate method was used.

3. The following data give the Number 1 hit records in each of 10 years. The class will work in groups. Each group takes the data from one year, makes a line plot, and identifies outliers using several different rules (for example, multipliers of 1.0, 1.5, and 2.0, or other appropriate multipliers). Then, each group decides which rule it likes the best for its data. Finally, discuss the results among the whole class. What is your choice?

1960

Weeks	Record Title	Artist
2	El Paso	Marty Robbins
3	Running Bear	Johnny Preston
2	Teen Angel	Mark Dinning
9	Theme from 'A Summer Place'	Percy Faith
4	Stuck on You	Elvis Presley
5	Cathy's Clown	Everly Brothers
2	Everybody's Somebody's Fool	Connie Francis
1	Alley-Oop	Hollywood Argyles
3	I'm Sorry	Brenda Lee
1	Itsy Bitsy Teeny Weeny Yellow Polkadot Bikini	Brian Hyland
5	It's Now or Never	Elvis Presley
1	The Twist	Chubby Checker
2	My Heart Has a Mind of Its Own	Connie Francis
1	Mr. Custer	Larry Verne
3	Save the Last Dance for Me	Drifters
1	I Want to Be Wanted	Brenda Lee
1	Georgia on My Mind	Ray Charles
1	Stay	Maurice Williams & The Zodiacs
6	Are You Lonesome Tonight?	Elvis Presley

Source: *The Billboard Book of Top 40 Hits*, 1985.

1962

Weeks	Record Title	Artist
2	The Twist	Chubby Checker
3	Peppermint Twist	Joey Dee & The Starliters
3	Duke of Earl	Gene Chandler
3	Hey! Baby	Bruce Channel
1	Don't Break the Heart That Loves You	Connie Francis
2	Johnny Angel	Shelley Fabares
2	Good Luck Charm	Elvis Presley
3	Soldier Boy	Shirelles
1	Stranger on the Shore	Mr. Acker Bilk
5	I Can't Stop Loving You	Ray Charles
1	The Stripper	David Rose
4	Roses Are Red	Bobby Vinton
2	Breaking Up Is Hard to Do	Neil Sedaka
1	The Loco-Motion	Little Eva
2	Sheila	Tommy Roe
5	Sherry	4 Seasons
2	Monster Mash	Boris Pickett & The Crypt Kickers
2	He's A Rebel	Crystals
5	Big Girls Don't Cry	4 Seasons
3	Telstar	Tornadoes

Source: *The Billboard Book of Top 40 Hits*, 1985.

1964

Weeks	Record Title	Artist
4	There! I've Said It Again	Bobby Vinton
7	I Want to Hold Your Hand	Beatles
2	She Loves You	Beatles
5	Can't Buy Me Love	Beatles
1	Hello, Dolly!	Louis Armstrong
2	My Guy	Mary Wells
1	Love Me Do	Beatles
3	Chapel of Love	Dixie Cups
1	A World Without Love	Peter & Gordon
2	I Get Around	Beach Boys
2	Rag Doll	4 Seasons
2	A Hard Day's Night	Beatles
1	Everybody Loves Somebody	Dean Martin
2	Where Did Our Love Go?	Supremes
3	The House of the Rising Sun	Animals
3	Oh, Pretty Woman	Roy Orbison
2	Do Wah Diddy Diddy	Manfred Mann
4	Baby Love	Supremes
1	Leader of the Pack	Shangri-Las
1	Ringo	Lorne Greene
1	Mr. Lonely	Bobby Vinton
2	Come See About Me	Supremes
3	I Feel Fine	Beatles

Source: *The Billboard Book of Top 40 Hits*, 1985.

1966

Weeks	Record Title	Artist
2	The Sounds of Silence	Simon & Garfunkle
3	We Can Work It Out	Beatles
2	My Love	Petula Clark
1	Lightnin' Strikes	Lou Christie
1	These Boots Are Made for Walkin'	Nancy Sinatra
5	The Ballad of the Green Berets	Sgt. Barry Sadler
3	(You're My) Soul and Inspiration	Righteous Brothers
1	Good Lovin'	Young Rascals
3	Monday, Monday	Mamas & Papas
2	When a Man Loves a Woman	Percy Sledge
2	Paint It Black	Rolling Stones
2	Paperback Writer	Beatles
1	Strangers in the Night	Frank Sinatra
2	Hanky Panky	Tommy James & The Shondells
2	Wild Thing	Troggs
3	Summer in the City	Lovin' Spoonful
1	Sunshine Superman	Donovan
2	You Can't Hurry Love	Supremes
3	Cherish	Association
2	Reach Out I'll Be There	Four Tops
1	96 Tears	? & The Mysterians
1	Last Train to Clarksville	Monkees
1	Poor Side of Town	Johnny Rivers
2	You Keep Me Hangin' On	Supremes
3	Winchester Cathedral	New Vaudeville Band
1	Good Vibrations	Beach Boys
7	I'm a Believer	Monkees

Source: *The Billboard Book of Top 40 Hits*, 1985.

1968

Weeks	Record Title	Artist
2	Judy in Disguise (With Glasses)	John Fred & His Playboy Band
1	Green Tambourine	Lemon Pipers
5	Love Is Blue	Paul Mauriat
4	(Sittin' on) The Dock of the Bay	Otis Redding
5	Honey	Bobby Goldsboro
2	Tighten Up	Archie Bell & The Drells
3	Mrs. Robinson	Simon & Garfunkel
4	This Guy's in Love with You	Herb Alpert
2	Grazing in the Grass	Hugh Masekela
2	Hello, I Love You	Doors
5	People Got to Be Free	Rascals
1	Harper Valley P.T.A.	Jeannie C. Riley
9	Hey Jude	Beatles
2	Love Child	Diana Ross & The Supremes
7	I Heard It Through the Grapevine	Marvin Gaye

Source: *The Billboard Book of Top 40 Hits*, 1985.

1980

Weeks	Record Title	Artist
1	Please Don't Go	KC & The Sunshine Band
4	Rock with You	Michael Jackson
1	Do That to Me One More Time	Captain & Tenille
4	Crazy Little Thing Called Love	Queen
4	Another Brick in the Wall (Part II)	Pink Floyd
6	Call Me	Blondie
4	Funkytown	Lipps, Inc.
3	Coming Up (Live at Glasgow)	Paul McCartney & Wings
2	It's Still Rock and Roll to Me	Billy Joel
4	Magic	Olivia Newton-John
1	Sailing	Christopher Cross
4	Upside Down	Diana Ross
3	Another One Bites the Dust	Queen
3	Woman In Love	Barbra Streisand
6	Lady	Kenny Rogers
5	(Just Like) Starting Over	John Lennon

Source: *The Billboard Book of Top 40 Hits*, 1985.

1981

Weeks	Record Title	Artist
1	The Tide Is High	Blondie
2	Celebration	Kool & The Gang
2	9 to 5	Dolly Parton
2	I Love a Rainy Night	Eddie Rabbitt
1	Keep on Loving You	REO Speedwagon
2	Rapture	Blondie
3	Kiss on My List	Daryl Hall & John Oates
2	Morning Train (Nine to Five)	Sheena Easton
9	Bette Davis Eyes	Kim Carnes
1	Stars on 45 Medley	Stars on 45
1	The One That You Love	Air Supply
2	Jessie's Girl	Rick Springfield
9	Endless Love	Diana Ross & Lionel Richie
3	Arthur's Theme (Best That You Can Do)	Christopher Cross
2	Private Eyes	Daryl Hall & John Oates
10	Physical	Olivia Newton-John

Source: *The Billboard Book of Top 40 Hits*, 1985.

1982

Weeks	Record Title	Artist
1	I Can't Go for That (No Can Do)	Daryl Hall & John Oates
6	Centerfold	J. Geils Band
7	I Love Rock 'n Roll	Joan Jett & The Blackhearts
1	Chariots of Fire	Vangelis
7	Ebony and Ivory	Paul McCartney/Stevie Wonder
3	Don't You Want Me	Human League
6	Eye of the Tiger	Survivor
2	Abracadabra	Steve Miller Band
2	Hard to Say I'm Sorry	Chicago
4	Jack & Diane	John Cougar
1	Who Can It Be Now?	Men at Work
3	Up Where We Belong	Joe Cocker & Jennifer Warnes
2	Truly	Lionel Richie
1	Mickey	Toni Basil
4	Maneater	Daryl Hall & Joan Oates

Source: *The Billboard Book of Top 40 Hits*, 1985.

1983

Weeks	Record Title	Artist
4	Down Under	Men at Work
1	Africa	Toto
2	Baby, Come to Me	Patti Austin & James Ingram
7	Billie Jean	Michael Jackson
1	Come On Eileen	Dexys Midnight Runners
3	Beat It	Michael Jackson
1	Let's Dance	David Bowie
6	Flashdance...What a Feeling	Irene Cara
8	Every Breath You Take	Police
1	Sweet Dreams (Are Made of This)	Eurythmics
2	Maniac	Michael Sembello
1	Tell Her About It	Billy Joel
4	Total Eclipse of the Heart	Bonnie Tyler
2	Islands in the Stream	Kenny Rogers with Dolly Parton
4	All Night Long (All Night)	Lionel Richie
6	Say Say Say	Paul McCartney & Michael Jackson

Source: *The Billboard Book of Top 40 Hits*, 1985.

1984

Weeks	Record Title	Artist
2	Owner of a Lonely Heart	Yes
3	Karma Chameleon	Culture Club
5	Jump	Van Halen
3	Footloose	Kenny Loggins
3	Against All Odds (Take a Look at Me Now)	Phil Collins
2	Hello	Lionel Richie
2	Let's Hear It for the Boy	Deniece Williams
2	Time After Time	Cyndi Lauper
2	The Reflex	Duran Duran
5	When Doves Cry	Prince
3	Ghostbusters	Ray Parker, Jr.
3	What's Love Got to Do with It?	Tina Turner
1	Missing You	John Waite
2	Let's Go Crazy	Prince
3	I Just Called to Say I Love You	Stevie Wonder
2	Caribbean Queen (No More Love on the Run)	Billy Ocean
3	Wake Me Up Before You Go-Go	WHAM!
2	Out of Touch	Daryl Hall & John Oates
6	Like a Virgin	Madonna

Source: *The Billboard Book of Top 40 Hits*, 1985.

IV. BOX PLOTS

In the last section, we learned how to find the extremes, the quartiles and the median. These five numbers tell us a great deal about a set of data. In this section, we will describe a way of using them to make a plot.

The following tables give the ratings for national prime-time television for the week of April 29 through May 5, 1985, as compiled by the A. C. Nielsen Co. The 25.5 rating for *The Cosby Show* means that out of every 100 houses with televisions, 25.5 were watching *The Cosby Show* at the time it was on. Each ratings point represents 849,000 TV households.

TELEVISION RATINGS

	Program	Network	Rating
1.	The Cosby Show	NBC	25.5
2.	Family Ties	NBC	21.9
3.	Dallas	CBS	21.4
4.	Cheers	NBC	19.7
5.	Newhart	CBS	18.4
6.	Falcon Crest	CBS	18.3
7.	"Alfred Hitchcock Presents"	NBC	18.0
8.	60 Minutes	CBS	17.9
9.	Knots Landing	CBS	17.8
10.	A-Team	NBC	17.6
11.	Murder, She Wrote	CBS	17.6
12.	Night Court	NBC	17.6
13.	Highway to Heaven	NBC	17.0
14.	Facts of Life	NBC	16.8
15.	"Missing, Have You Seen This Person?"	NBC	16.5
16.	Kate & Allie	CBS	16.3
17.	Sara	NBC	16.3
18.	Who's the Boss?	ABC	15.9
19.	Trapper John, M.D.	CBS	15.7
20.	Love Boat	ABC	15.5
21.	Scarecrow & Mrs. King	CBS	15.4
22.	"Miss Hollywood '85"	ABC	15.4
23.	"Lace II," Part I	ABC	15.3
24.	Miami Vice	NBC	15.2
25.	Simon & Simon	CBS	15.2
26.	Riptide	NBC	15.2
27.	Cagney & Lacey	CBS	15.0
28.	"Adam"	NBC	14.9
29.	Crazy Like a Fox	CBS	14.6
30.	MacGruder and Loud	ABC	14.3
31.	20/20	ABC	14.3
32.	"Life's Embarrassing Moments"	ABC	14.2
33.	Hill Street Blues	NBC	14.0

Source: A.C. Nielsen Company.

TELEVISION RATINGS

	Program	Network	Rating
34.	St. Elsewhere	NBC	13.9
35.	Three's a Crowd	ABC	13.8
36.	Hail to the Chief	ABC	13.7
37.	"Joanna"	ABC	13.0
38.	Airwolf	CBS	12.7
39.	Remington Steele	NBC	12.6
40.	"Loving Couples"	CBS	12.4
41.	"Apocalypse Now"	ABC	12.4
42.	"Survival Anglia"	CBS	12.0
43.	Gimme a Break	NBC	12.0
44.	Knight Rider	NBC	11.8
45.	Hunter	NBC	11.6
46.	"Anything for a Laugh"	ABC	11.6
47.	T. J. Hooker	ABC	11.5
48.	Double Trouble	NBC	11.5
49.	Magnum, P. I.	CBS	11.4
50.	Diff'rent Strokes	NBC	10.7
51.	Benson	ABC	10.7
52.	"Ray Mancini Story"	CBS	10.6
53.	Mike Hammer	CBS	10.5
54.	Webster	ABC	10.4
55.	Under One Roof	NBC	10.4
56.	Half-Nelson	NBC	10.4
57.	Double Dare	CBS	9.6
58.	Best Times	NBC	9.5
59.	"Dr. No"	ABC	9.5
60.	Punky Brewster	NBC	9.0
61.	Ripley's Believe It or Not	ABC	8.5
62.	Cover Up	CBS	8.3
63.	Eye to Eye	ABC	8.3
64.	Street Hawk	ABC	7.9
65.	Silver Spoons	NBC	7.8
66.	Lucie Arnaz Show	CBS	7.5
67.	Jeffersons	CBS	7.1

Source: A.C. Nielsen Company.

The following instructions will teach you how to make a box plot of the ratings of the 67 programs:

Step 1   Find the median rating.

There are 67 ratings, thus the median will be the 34th show. The 34th show, *St. Elsewhere,* has a rating of 13.9.

Step 2   Find the median of the upper half.

There are 33 ratings above the median. The median of these ratings is at the 17th show. This show is *Sara* with a rating of 16.3. This number 16.3 is the upper quartile.

Step 3   Find the median of the lower half.

There are 33 ratings below the median. The median of these ratings is at the 51st show, which is *Benson* with a rating of 10.7. This number 10.7 is the lower quartile.

Step 4   Find the extremes.

The lowest rating is 7.1 and the highest is 25.5.

Step 5   Mark dots for the median, quartiles, and extremes below a number line.

Step 6   Draw a box between the two quartiles. Mark the median with a line across the box. Draw two "whiskers" from the quartiles to the extremes.

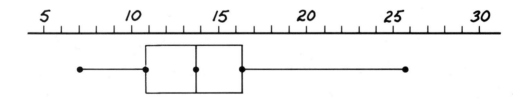

Discussion Questions

About what percent of the ratings are:

1. Below the median?

2. Below the lower quartile?

3. Above the lower quartile?

4. In the box?

5. In each whisker?

6. Is one whisker longer than the other? What does this mean?

7. Why isn't the median in the center of the box?

8. On May 8, 1985, CBS announced that it was cancelling *The Jeffersons*, *Cover Up*, *The Lucie Arnaz Show*, and *Double Dare*. The future of *Mike Hammer* was in doubt. Why do you think CBS is cancelling these shows? Are there any other programs CBS should consider cancelling?

9. Which shows do you think ABC cancelled?

The executives of the networks are interested in how the three compare in ratings. We learned that a back-to-back stem-and-leaf plot is good for such comparisons. Unfortunately, it has only two sides and there are three networks. Box plots are effective for comparing two or more sets of data. For example, let's plot the ratings for CBS, NBC, and ABC on separate box plots.

CBS has 22 shows listed. Their ratings are:

21.4	18.4	18.3	17.9	17.8	17.6	16.3	15.7
15.4	15.2	15.0	14.6	12.7	12.4	12.0	11.4
10.6	10.5	9.6	8.3	7.5	7.1		

The median is halfway between the 11th and 12th ratings, which are 15.0 and 14.6. Thus, the median is:

$$\frac{15.0 + 14.6}{2} = \frac{29.6}{2} = 14.8 .$$

The lower quartile is 10.6 and the upper quartile is 17.6. The extremes are 7.1 and 21.4.

The box plots for CBS, NBC, and ABC are shown below.

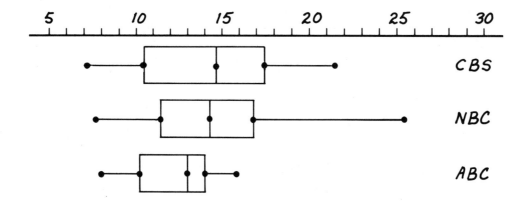

Discussion Questions

1. Use the box plot to estimate the median, quartiles, and extremes for NBC.

2. Use the box plot to estimate the median, quartiles, and extremes for ABC.

3. Study the box plots to decide which network has the largest interquartile range.

4. If you say that the winning network is the one with the highest-rated show, which network is the winner? Which is second? Which is third?

5. If you say that the winning network is the one with the largest upper quartile, which network is the winner? Which is second? Which is third?

6. If you say that the winning network is the one with the largest median, which network is the winner? Which is second? Which is third?

7. Use the box plot to estimate if there are any outliers for NBC. (Hint: The length of the box is one interquartile range!)

8. Are any shows outliers for CBS or ABC?

9. Why are box plots a better way to compare the relative positions of the three networks than line plots or stem-and-leaf plots?

10. Write a description of the relative standings of the three networks. Then (don't peek) read the following example.

The median ratings of the three networks are very close — each around 14. The lower quartiles and lower extremes are also very close — around 11 and 7, respectively. This means that if you look at just the shows in the bottom half for each network, the three networks do about the same in the ratings. However, when looking at the top half of the ratings, NBC and CBS do much better than ABC. The ratings for ABC are all packed tightly between 13.0 and 15.9. In contrast, about 25% of the ratings for both CBS and NBC are larger than 17. It is clear that ABC is the losing network, but whether NBC or CBS is the winner is not so clear.

Even if ABC had cancelled the bottom quarter of their shows and replaced them all by shows that received a higher rating than their current top show — for example between 17 and 22 — they would still be a bit behind NBC and CBS in terms of the top shows. (As an exercise, redraw the boxplot for ABC to reflect this hypothetical situation.)

Application 12

Prices of Corn Poppers

The box plot below shows the dollar prices of twenty popcorn poppers as listed in *Consumer Reports Buying Guide*, 1981.

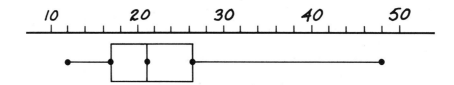

Source: *Consumer Reports Buying Guide*, 1981.

1. Approximately how much did the most expensive popcorn popper cost?

2. Approximately how much did the least expensive popcorn popper cost?

3. What was the median price for a popcorn popper?

4. What percentage of the poppers cost more than $26.50 (the upper quartile)?

5. What percentage of the poppers cost more than $17.00 (the lower quartile)?

6. If you had $21.00, how many of the twenty poppers could you afford?

7. If you had $26.50, how many of the twenty poppers could you afford?

8. Are any of the prices outliers? How can you tell?

9. Write a short description of the price of popcorn poppers.

Application 13

Roller Skating Clubs

The following table gives the number of roller skating clubs by state for 45 states.

State	Number	State	Number
Alabama	11	Nebraska	8
Arizona	6	Nevada	1
Arkansas	5	New Hampshire	1
California	102	New Jersey	24
Colorado	11	New Mexico	1
Connecticut	7	New York	18
Delaware	2	North Carolina	15
Florida	39	Ohio	47
Georgia	8	Oklahoma	5
Hawaii	1	Oregon	13
Illinois	35	Pennsylvania	41
Indiana	21	Rhode Island	5
Iowa	7	South Carolina	2
Kansas	7	Tennessee	10
Kentucky	6	Texas	40
Louisiana	10	Utah	2
Maine	1	Vermont	1
Maryland	15	Virginia	33
Massachusetts	13	Washington	22
Michigan	29	West Virginia	4
Minnesota	4	Wisconsin	8
Mississippi	3	Wyoming	2
Missouri	22		

Source: Roller Skating Rink Operators Association.

1. Why do you think the data include only 45 and not 50 states? What values might the 5 remaining states have? Which states are missing?

2. Make a box plot of the 45 values. (Hint: The numbers must be put in order before you find the median and the quartiles. A quick way to do this is to use a stem-and-leaf plot.)

3. Show that California is an outlier.

4. Look at the upper whisker. Why is it so long? If you were to omit California from the list, how would the box plot change?

5. There is an alternate way to construct the box plot when there is an outlier, such as California. Copy your box plot, but stop the upper whisker at Ohio's 47. Then, put an asterisk at California's 102. Thus, there is a gap in the plot, corresponding to the gap between the largest and second-largest values.

6. Which of these plots do you think gives a more accurate picture of these data? Why?

7. Write a description of the information given in the box plot you constructed for question 5.

Application 14

Sugar in Cereals

Percentage of Sugar in Cereals

Product	% Sugar	Product	% Sugar
Sugar Smacks (K)	56.0	Kellogg Raisin Bran (A)	29.0
Apple Jacks (K)	54.6	C. W. Post, Raisin, (A)	29.0
Froot Loops (K)	48.0	C. W. Post (A)	28.7
General Foods Raisin Bran (A)	48.0	Frosted Mini Wheats (K)	26.0
Sugar Corn Pops (K)	46.0	Country Crisp (K)	22.0
Super Sugar Crisp (K)	46.0	Life, cinnamon (K)	21.0
Crazy Cow, chocolate (K)	45.6	100% Bran (A)	21.0
Corny Snaps (K)	45.5	All Bran (A)	19.0
Frosted Rice Krinkles (K)	44.0	Fortified Oat Flakes (A)	18.5
Frankenberry (K)	43.7	Life (A)	16.0
Cookie Crisp, vanilla (K)	43.5	Team (A)	14.1
Cap'n Crunch, crunch berries (K)	43.3	40% Bran (A)	13.0
Cocoa Krispies (K)	43.0	Grape Nuts Flakes (A)	13.3
Cocoa Pebbles (K)	42.6	Buckwheat (A)	12.2
Fruity Pebbles (K)	42.5	Product 19 (A)	9.9
Lucky Charms (K)	42.2	Concentrate (A)	9.3
Cookie Crisp, chocolate (K)	41.0	Total (A)	8.3
Sugar Frosted Flakes of Corn (K)	41.0	Wheaties (A)	8.2
Quisp (K)	40.7	Rice Krispies (K)	7.8
Crazy Cow, strawberry (K)	40.1	Grape Nuts (A)	7.0
Cookie Crisp, oatmeal (K)	40.1	Special K (A)	5.4
Cap'n Crunch (K)	40.0	Corn Flakes (A)	5.3
Count Chocula (K)	39.5	Post Toasties (A)	5.0
Alpha Bits (K)	38.0	Kix (K)	4.8
Honey Comb (K)	37.2	Rice Chex (A)	4.4
Frosted Rice (K)	37.0	Corn Chex (A)	4.0
Trix (K)	35.9	Wheat Chex (A)	3.5
Cocoa Puffs (K)	33.3	Cheerios (K)	3.0
Cap'n Crunch, peanut butter (K)	32.2	Shredded Wheat (A)	0.6
Golden Grahams (A)	30.0	Puffed Wheat (A)	0.5
Cracklin' Bran (A)	29.0	Puffed Rice (A)	0.1

Source: United States Department of Agriculture, 1979.

1. What do you think the table means when it says that "the percentage of sugar" in Sugar Smacks is 56.0?

We divided the list into "kid" and "adult" cereals as indicated by a (K) or an (A) following each name. (You may disagree and change some of these.)

The following box plots show the amount of sugar in "kid" and "adult" cereals.

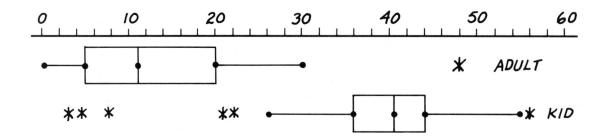

2. For the "kid" cereals, estimate:
   a. the lower extreme
   b. the upper extreme
   c. the median
   d. the lower quartile
   e. the upper quartile

3. For the "adult" cereals, estimate
   a. the lower extreme
   b. the upper extreme
   c. the median
   d. the lower quartile
   e. the upper quartile

4. Write a paragraph comparing the percentage of sugar in "kid" and "adult" cereals.

Application 15

Automobile Safety

The Highway Loss Data Institute rated 181 models of 1982-84 cars based on the number of insurance claims filed for personal injury coverage. The cars are rated in relative terms; 100 represents the average for all cars. Lower numbers mean a better safety record. A rating of 122, for example, means 22% worse than average.

Station Wagons and Passenger Vans

Small Cars	Injury Rating	Midsize Cars	Injury Rating	Large Cars	Injury Rating
Volkswagen Vanagon	73	Volvo 240	56	Olds. Custom Cruiser	54
Mercury Lynx	83	American Eagle 30	69	Buick Electra	59
Toyota Tercel 4WD	91	Ford LTD	76	Dodge Caravan	63
Ford Escort	95	Oldsmobile Firenza	80	Plymouth Voyager	67
Subaru DL/GL 4WD	98	Chevrolet Celebrity	83	Chevrolet Caprice	69
Subaru DL/GL	100	Dodge Aries	91	Mercury Grand Marquis	69
Nissan Sentra	108	Plymouth Reliant	93	Ford Crown Victoria	70
		Pontiac 2000	94		
		Chevrolet Cavalier	94		
		Chrysler LeBaron	95		
		Nissan Maxima	100		

Source: Highway Loss Data Institute.

Sports and Specialty Models

Small Cars	Injury Rating	Midsize Cars	Injury Rating	Large Cars	Injury Rating
Mercedes 380SL Coupe	57	Lincoln Continental	72	Mercedes 300SD/380SE	60
Chevrolet Corvette	63	BMW 528e/533i	74	Jaguar X16	63
Porsche 944 Coupe	71	Audi 5000 4D	79	Mercedes-Benz 300D	64
Nissan 300ZX	100	BMW 318i/325e	81	Oldsmobile Toronado	65
VW Rabbit Convertible	102	Chrys. LeBaron Conv.	87	Cadillac De Ville 4D	67
Mazda RX-7	104	Ford Mustang Convertible	98	Cadillac Eldorado	71
Pontiac Fiero	119	Toyota Celica Supra	102	Lincoln Town Car	72
Ford EXP	124	Pontiac Firebird	107	Buick Riviera	73
		Mercury Capri	114	Cadillac Brougham 4D	75
		Chevrolet Camaro	116	Cadillac Seville	76
		Ford Mustang	127	Cadillac De Ville 2D	81

Source: Highway Loss Data Institute.

Four-Door Models

Small Cars	Injury Ratings	Midsize Cars	Injury Ratings	Large Cars	Injury Ratings
Saab 900	71	Chrysler E Class	75	Oldsmobile Delta 88	59
Honda Accord	89	Oldsmobile Cutlass	76	Buick LeSabre	62
Volkswagen Rabbit	92	Buick Regal	79	Oldsmobile Ninety Eight	62
Volkswagen Jetta	97	Pontiac Bonneville	80	Mercury Grand Marquis	65
Mazda 626	100	Mercury Topaz	81	Buick Electra	66
Nissan Stanza	107	Pontiac 6000	85	Chevrolet Caprice	68
Dodge Omni	114	Mercury Marquis	86	Ford LTD Crown Victoria	68
Renault Alliance	114	Dodge 600	86	Chrys. 5th Ave.	69
Ford Escort	117	Oldsmobile Ciera	86	Dodge Diplomat	72
Plymouth Horizon	118	Chrysler New Yorker	87	Chevrolet Impala	79
Mercury Lynx	120	Buick Century	87	Plymouth Grand Fury	101
Toyota Corolla	122	Chrysler LeBaron	88		
Subaru DL/GL Sedan	125	Volvo 240	89		
Toyota Tercel	127	Ford LTD	89		
Mazda GLC	130	Peugeot 505	91		
Pontiac 1000	139	Toyota Camry	91		
Isuzu T-Car/I-Mark	140	Toyota Cressida	92		
Chevrolet Chevette	143	Buick Skylark	92		
Dodge Colt	144	Cadillac Cimarron	93		
Nissan Sentra	145	Chevrolet Celebrity	94		
Mitsubishi Tredia	155	Chevrolet Citation	94		
Plymouth Colt	156	Audi 4000	96		
		Oldsmobile Omega	98		
		Ford Tempo	100		
		Pontiac Phoenix	101		
		Pontiac 2000	109		
		Dodge Aries	111		
		Plymouth Reliant	112		
		Chevrolet Cavalier	112		
		Oldsmobile Firenza	113		
		Buick Skyhawk	113		
		Nissan Maxima	121		

Source: Highway Loss Data Institute.

Two-Door Models

Small Cars	Injury Ratings	Midsize Cars	Injury Ratings	Large Cars	Injury Ratings
Saab 900	70	Oldsmobile Cutlass	88	Ford Crown Victoria	65
Honda Accord	102	Buick Regal	90	Buick LeSabre	70
Nissan Stanza	105	Oldsmobile Ciera	91	Oldsmobile Delta 88	70
Volkswagen Rabbit	106	Pontiac Grand Prix	92	Oldsmobile Ninety Eight	71
Mazda 626	106	Oldsmobile Omega	92	Mercury Grand Marquis	76
Volkswagen Scirocco	108	Pontiac 6000	94	Chevrolet Caprice	77
Mazda GLC	110	Buick Skylark	94	Buick Electra	81
Honda Prelude	114	Chevrolet Monte Carlo	98		
Honda Civic	115	Chrysler LeBaron	99		
Subaru Hardtop	117	Ford Thunderbird	100		
Renault Fuego	118	Buick Century	100		
Toyota Celica	120	Volvo 240	104		
Dodge Daytona	122	Dodge 400/600	105		
Subaru Hatchback	125	Chevrolet Celebrity	107		
Plymouth Horizon	128	Dodge Aries	109		
Chrysler Laser	128	Mercury Cougar	109		
Toyota Tercel	129	Chevrolet Citation	111		
Ford Escort	130	Pontiac Phoenix	112		
Renault Encore	130	Pontiac 2000	118		
Dodge Charger	132	Ford Tempo	118		
Mercury Lynx	137	Plymouth Reliant	119		
Nissan Sentra	137	Buick Skylark	123		
Renault Alliance	138	Oldsmobile Firenza	123		
Toyota Starlet	148	Chevrolet Cavalier	126		
Plymouth Colt	148				
Dodge Colt	149				
Mitsubishi Cordia	151				
Chevrolet Chevette	154				
Pontiac 1000	155				
Nissan Pulsar	158				

Source: Highway Loss Data Institute.

1. Which of the four groups of cars is the safest?

2. Which is the most dangerous group?

3. The box plot for all of the small cars and for midsize cars is shown below. (All four types of models were combined.) Make the box plot for large cars. Show any outliers as in Application 13, question 5.

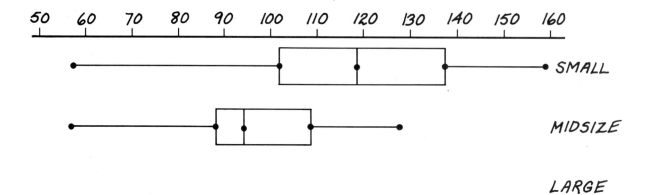

4. Which would you say are closer in safety, small and midsize cars, or midsize and large cars? Why?

5. Write a paragraph giving an overall summary of the plots.

6. (Optional) Make box plots for American small cars and for Japanese small cars, or two other categories that interest you, and write a summary of the plots.

7. (For class discussion) Do you think that these injury ratings reflect just the inherent safety of these cars? Might they also relate to other factors such as different characteristics of the drivers, different mileages, or different types of driving that the cars receive? What other ways can you think of for comparing the safety of different automobiles?

Application 16

High School Eligibility

Data from the *Los Angeles Times* appear in the following table.

| High School | % Ineligible in Selected Activities | | | | | |
	Band	Drama	Yearbook	Baseball	Boys Track	Girls Track
Banning	27	19	0	9	38	24
Bell	37	19	—	0	22	13
Belmont	—	3	7	19	14	7
Birmingham	52	31	—	—	24	—
Canoga Park	30	19	20	17	25	33
Carson	—	0	—	13	21	—
Chatsworth	25	19	33	9	20	31
Cleveland	11	—	7	16	15	—
Crenshaw	68	36	—	20	19	17
Dorsey	8	28	—	15	31	31
Eagle Rock	0	—	0	—	—	—
El Camino Real	7	15	13	3	16	15
Fairfax	35	23	—	21	51	30
Francis Poly	4	28	—	0	22	31
Franklin	48	33	21	17	29	44
Fremont	—	43	—	32	32	38
Gardena	34	—	17	19	20	20
Garfield	21	—	—	7	16	23
Granada Hills	14	29	—	15	21	28
Grant	—	3	—	17	26	—
Hamilton	36	27	0	24	12	0
Hollywood	3	3	8	—	—	—
Huntington Park	40	33	44	15	22	—
Jefferson	61	58	—	8	62	—

High School	% Ineligible in Selected Activities					
	Band	Drama	Yearbook	Baseball	Boys Track	Girls Track
Jordan	49	70	50	38	32	—
Kennedy	20	14	18	0	18	20
Lincoln	32	28	71	6	17	13
Locke	30	—	67	45	30	57
Los Angeles	27	100	39	43	37	17
Manual Arts	45	35	38	21	18	25
Marshall	14	19	—	16	31	15
Monroe	23	30	6	3	21	24
Narbonne	21	35	0	—	—	—
North Hollywood	18	50	—	—	—	—
Palisades	4	14	—	14	30	30
Reseda	24	53	0	—	—	—
Roosevelt	—	39	—	12	12	35
San Fernando	19	64	24	24	44	33
San Pedro	11	10	—	8	18	0
South Gate	38	8	5	19	15	28
Sylmar	10	32	—	0	21	13
Taft	—	11	0	10	27	27
University	20	30	43	16	14	9
Van Nuys	22	21	0	17	30	7
Venice	11	21	—	5	16	13
Verdugo Hills	8	35	10	14	39	39
Washington	29	31	25	16	18	14
Westchester	19	11	0	17	3	0
Wilson	—	—	—	—	—	—

Source: *Los Angeles Times*, May 17, 1983.

Following a policy established by the Los Angeles Board of Education, students must maintain a C average and have no failing grades in order to participate in extracurricular activities. The table shows how the policy is affecting activities at high schools. Numbers represent the percentage of students in the activity who were declared ineligible. For example, 25% of band members at Chatsworth and 38% of the athletes in girls' track at Fremont were declared ineligible and could no longer participate.

1. The newspaper does not say why the table contains blanks. How do you know that a blank does not mean that no students were ineligible? What do you think a blank means? For the rest of this activity , ignore the blanks.

2. The class should be divided into six groups. One group should construct a box plot of the percentage of students declared ineligible in band; one group should construct the plot for drama; another for yearbook, and so on. Use an asterisk for any outliers, as in Application 13, question 5.

3. Make a number line on the blackboard or overhead projector. A representative from each group should draw its box plot under this number line.

4. Do band members or baseball players tend to have higher rates of ineligibility?

5. Why is there no lower whisker on the yearbook box plot?

6. Write a paragraph or two summarizing what you see in the six box plots.

The Use of Box Plots

It is becoming more and more common to use a box plot to tell people their results on a test. For example, students sometimes take tests to see how interested they are in various occupations. The results from one such test are reproduced below.

BASIC INTEREST SCALES

NATURE	33	V-LOW	
ADVENTURE	55	MOD-H	
MILITARY ACTIVITIES	41	V-LOW	
MECHANICAL ACTIVITIES	40	AVER.	
SCIENCE	36	LOW	
MATHEMATICS	59	HIGH	
MEDICAL SCIENCE	34	LOW	
MEDICAL SERVICE	43	MOD-L	
MUSIC/DRAMATICS	29	V-LOW	
ART	32	V-LOW	
WRITING	26	V-LOW	
TEACHING	28	V-LOW	
SOCIAL SERVICE	43	MOD-L	
ATHLETICS	52	AVER.	
DOMESTIC ARTS	41	LOW	
RELIGIOUS ACTIVITIES	48	AVER.	
PUBLIC SPEAKING	37	MOD-L	
LAW/POLITICS	33	LOW	
MERCHANDISING	45	AVER.	
SALES	46	AVER.	
BUSINESS MANAGEMENT	40	MOD-L	
OFFICE PRACTICES	55	AVER.	

Let's examine the "Nature" result more carefully. There are two box plots for "Nature." The top one is for girls and the bottom one is for boys. The top box plot shows that the median interest score in nature for girls is about 51. (The scale is above "Mechanical Activities.") The score of the girl who took the test is marked on each scale by a ★. Thus, her interest in nature is very low compared to other girls who have taken the test previously.

Discussion Questions

1. For which subject(s) is this girl's interest score in the top 25% of all girls?

2. For which subjects is this girl's interest lowest?

3. Which subjects are girls much more interested in than are boys?

4. Which subjects are boys much more interested in than are girls?

5. Write a letter to this girl recommending possible career choices.

Box Plots — Summary

You may have found it difficult to see the advantages of using box plots. Some students are disturbed by the fact that most of the data disappears and only five summary numbers (the median, quartiles, and extremes) remain. It is true that we can no longer spot clusters and gaps, nor can we identify the shape of the distribution as clearly as with line plots or stem-and-leaf plots. However, we are able to focus on the relative positions of different sets of data and thereby compare them more easily.

Box plots are especially useful when the set of data contains hundreds or even thousands of numbers. A line plot or stem-and-leaf plot would be unwieldy with thousands of numbers on it!

To compare two (or more) sets of data using box plots, first look at the boxes to get an idea whether or not they are located in about the same place. Also, study their lengths, to determine whether or not the variabilities in the data sets are about the same. Then, you can focus on details. Check whether or not one data set has median, upper and lower quartiles, and extremes that are all larger than the corresponding values in the second data set. If it does, then the data in the first set tend to be larger than those in the second no matter which criterion we use for comparing them. If it does not, then there is more uncertainty about which data set is larger. In either case, the plot has helped us learn some details about the similarities and differences between the two data sets. Also, check to see if the pattern of outliers is the same in both data sets.

Notice that even if two (or more) sets of data have unequal numbers of values, this does not cause problems for making comparisons with box plots. This was not true for stem-and-leaf plots.

Suggestions for Student Projects

1. Collect some data on a topic that interests you, construct box plots, and interpret them. Topics that other students have used include:

   - number of hours students work per week

   - number of hours of TV watched per week by different types of students

   - allowances of girls and of boys in your class

   - scores of all the students in a school that take a certain test, separated so you can compare the different classes

2. One variation of box plots involves changing the width in proportion to the number of data values represented. For example, if a box representing 100 values is 1 cm wide, then a box representing 50 values would be 0.5 cm wide and a box representing 200 values would be 2 cm wide. Make box plots under the same number line for the small two-door models, midsize two-door models and large two-door models from Application 15. Make the width of the box proportional to the number of cars represented. Discuss the merit of this variation.

V. REVIEW OF ONE-VARIABLE TECHNIQUES

Which Method to Use?

This section is different from the previous four. Each of the previous four introduced some statistical method that can help to interpret data. Then, the method was used on several examples. Often more than one of these methods *could* be used to display and to help interpret a particular set of data. This section helps you to choose an appropriate method by giving some comparisons among them.

Before using any statistical method it is a good idea to ask yourself a few basic questions about the data. How were the numbers obtained? Are the values plausible? What would you like to learn from the data? Are there any specific questions that you know need answers? The purpose of statistical methods is to help us learn something useful or interesting from the data, so it is a good idea to keep questions such as these in mind throughout the analysis.

Suppose we have the starting weekly wage for 23 different jobs. We could display the values using a line plot (Section I), a stem-and-leaf plot (Section II), or a box plot (Section IV). We could calculate statistics such as the median, mean, range, and interquartile range (Section III). Which of these methods should we use, or, at least, which should we use first? There is no single, correct answer. However, there are some guidelines that can help you to make an appropriate choice of methods.

A reasonable general strategy is to use the simpler methods first. Then, if the interpretations of the data are very clear, there is no need to go on to more complicated displays and methods.

One Group and One Variable

Consider the above example of the starting wage for several jobs. In this example there is one *variable*, the wage. We can treat the various jobs as forming one *group* of jobs. Thus, we have measurements for *one group on one variable*. This is the simplest type of problem for which statistical methods and displays are needed. Most of the examples in Sections I, II, and III are this type of problem.

The line plot, the stem-and-leaf plot, and the box plot are three different displays that can be used for the one-group/one-variable situation. The following paragraphs describe their relative advantages and disadvantages.

> *Line Plot.* The line plot is easy to construct and interpret. It gives a clear graphical picture, and a few values can be labeled easily. Constructing a line plot is also a useful first step for calculating the median, extremes, and quartiles. These statements are all true providing the number of values is not too large — fewer than about 25. As the number of values becomes larger, the line plot can become unwieldy and more difficult to interpret. When a specific value is repeated several times or when there are many

75

nearby values, the line plot can also become jumbled. Another disadvantage is that it is hard to read the exact numerical values from the line plot. In conclusion, the line plot is a useful first display for the one-group/one-variable situation, providing there are about 25 or fewer values in the data.

Stem-and-Leaf Plot. The stem-and-leaf plot shares many advantages of the line plot. It is easy to construct and interpret, values can be labeled, and it is a useful first step for calculating the median, extremes, and quartiles. In addition, exact numerical values can be read from the stem-and-leaf plot and repeated values and nearby values in the data cause no special problems. Stem-and-leaf plots do not get as unwieldy as line plots when the number of data values becomes large. On the other hand, a disadvantage is that to construct the stem-and-leaf plot you may have to decide whether or not to truncate or round. Further disadvantages are the need to decide which values to use for the stems, and how to spread out the plot. Thus, it may take more thought to construct the stem-and-leaf plot than the line plot. The stem-and-leaf plot can display more values than the line plot without becoming too confusing in appearance. However, it also has a limit to the number of values that is *reasonable* to display. With more than about 100 values, you will most likely spread out the stem-and-leaf plot. Then it can be useful for up to about 250 values. Above 250 it will be too large and jumbled to interpret easily. In conclusion, for the one-group/one-variable situation with about 25 or fewer values, either the stem-and-leaf plot or the line plot is a reasonable first display. The choice is partly a matter of personal preference. With about 25 to 250 data values, the stem-and-leaf plot is the most useful first display.

Box Plot. The box plot is more complicated to construct, since you must calculate the median, extremes, and quartiles first. Generally, the simplest way to do this is to construct the stem-and-leaf plot first and then count in from the ends to get the quartiles and median. Unlike the stem-and-leaf plot, once the box plot is constructed, specific data values cannot be read from it (except for outliers and the median, quartiles, and extremes). The main advantage of the box plot is that it is not cluttered by showing all the data values. It highlights only a few *important* features of the data. Thus, the box plot makes it easier to focus attention on the median, extremes, and quartiles and comparisons among them. Another advantage of the box plot is that it does not become more complicated with more data values. It is useful with any number of values. A disadvantage of the box plot occurs when there are only a few data values — less than about 15. Then, the plotted values might change greatly if only one or a few of the observations were changed.

The box plot is a *summary display* since it shows only certain statistics, not all the data. In conclusion, the box plot is not as useful as the line or stem-and-leaf plots for showing details, but it enables us to focus more easily on the median, extremes, and quartiles. Since the line and stem-and-leaf plots are useful for computing the statistics needed to construct the box plot, it is generally reasonable to make one of these two plots first even if you will eventually construct and use the box plot.

Several Groups and One Variable

Think again about the starting weekly wage example mentioned at the beginning of this section. Instead of considering the 23 jobs as *one group* of jobs, we could divide them into those jobs that require a high school diploma and those that require a college diploma. The jobs are divided into *two groups*. We want to compare the various salaries in these two groups. This is an example of the *two-group/one-variable* problem. Many of the examples in Sections II and IV are this type. The following paragraphs describe the relative advantages and disadvantages of the line, stem-and-leaf, and box plots for this situation.

Line plots can be placed next to each other to compare two groups, although we did not give any examples of this type. However, this becomes confusing if the two groups overlap a lot or if there are more than a total of about 25 data values.

Back-to-back stem-and-leaf plots are more useful for comparing two groups. They are easy to construct. Comparisons can be made by judging the number of leaves for various stems. However, if the number of data values in the two groups is not roughly equal, the comparisons get more difficult. The details shown in the stem-and-leaf plots can become an obstacle. Furthermore, as the number of values becomes large these plots become unwieldy. In summary, for comparing two groups of about equal size with around 100 or fewer data values in each group, back-to-back stem-and-leaf plots are easy to construct and generally adequate.

Box plots below the same number line can also be used to compare two groups. This gives the easiest and most direct comparisons of the two minimums, the two lower quartiles, the two medians, the two upper quartiles, and the two maximums. Of course, this does not show any other details, but these quantities are usually sufficient for comparing two groups. Moreover, there are no special problems caused by having a large number of data values, or by having a different number of values in the two groups.

Often, we need to compare more than two groups. For example, the jobs could be broken down into those not requiring a high school diploma, those requiring a high school diploma, those requiring a college degree, and those requiring a graduate degree. This gives four groups. It is an example of a *many-group/one-variable* problem.

There is no way to construct a stem-and-leaf plot for this situation. Several line plots placed next to each other can be useful, if there are not many data values. Box plots are the best choice. The reasons are the same as those given for comparing two groups.

A more concise way to compare two groups than any of these is simply to calculate a single number, such as the mean or median, for each group. But this number hides all the other information in the data. It also loses the advantage of graphical displays. Thus, for purposes of exploring and interpreting data, any of the graphical displays will be more valuable than calculating just means or medians. If it is necessary to give a single number to summarize the data, and if there is a possibility of even a few outliers, then the median is usually more valuable than the mean.

As a general conclusion, line plots, stem-and-leaf plots, and box plots each have a useful role for exploring various kinds of data sets. Often, it is worthwhile to make more than one plot. There are no hard and fast rules about which plot should be used, but the previous comparisons can help you make good choices.

The following applications will help you compare the different methods.

Application 17

Letter Frequencies

The number of occurrences of each letter was counted in a very large amount of written material. The percentage that each letter occurred is given in the table below.

A	8.2	J	0.1	S	6.0
B	1.4	K	0.4	T	10.5
C	2.8	L	3.4	U	2.5
D	3.8	M	2.5	V	0.9
E	13.0	N	7.0	W	1.5
F	3.0	O	8.0	X	0.2
G	2.0	P	2.0	Y	2.0
H	5.3	Q	0.1	Z	0.07
I	6.5	R	6.8		

Source: National Council of Teachers of Mathematics.

1. What is the most-used letter?

2. What is the least-used letter?

3. How many *t*'s would you expect to find in a paragraph of 100 letters? In a paragraph of 500 letters?

4. As a group, vowels account for what percentage of letters used?

5. Make a line plot of the percentages.

6. Make a stem-and-leaf plot of the percentages.

7. Find the median percentage, the quartiles, and any outliers.

8. Make a box plot of the percentages.

9. Which two letters have the most unusual percentages? From which plot is it easiest to find this information?

10. Are most of the letters used rarely or used more frequently? From which plot is it easiest to find this information?

11. Make a back-to-back stem-and-leaf plot of vowels and consonants.

12. Why isn't it appropriate to make one box plot for vowels and another for consonants?

13. What conclusions can you make by looking at the stem-and-leaf plot you constructed for question 11?

Application 18

Salaries

The table below lists the median weekly salaries of workers employed full time. For example, the median salary for carpenters is $325 because half of the carpenters earn less than $325 and half earn more than $325.

Occupation	Median Weekly Earnings	Occupation	Median Weekly Earnings
Accountant	379	Machinist	356
Airplane Pilot	530	Mathematician	508
Architect	428	Newspaper Reporter	351
Auto Mechanic	285	Painter	271
Bank Teller	189	Pharmacist	463
Barber	327	Physician, Osteopath	501
Bookkeeper	227	Plumber	404
Carpenter	325	Police Officer	363
Cashier	168	Postal Clerk	400
Chemist	467	Printing Press Operator	320
Civil Engineer	505	Psychologist	394
College Teacher	444	Receptionist	200
Computer Programmer	422	Registered Nurse	332
Cooks and Chefs	171	Retail Sales Worker	178
Cosmetologist	179	School Counselor	396
Dental Assistant	183	Secondary Teacher	351
Dentist	352	Secretary	229
Drafter	343	Shoe Repairer	200
Electrician	419	Telephone Operator	240
Fire Fighter	362	Truck Driver (local)	314
Flight Attendant	365	Truck Driver (long distance)	517
Food Counter Worker	141	Typist	213
K-6 Teacher	322	Veterinarian	656
Lawyer	546	Waiter/Waitress	150
Librarian	320	Welder	334

Source: United States Bureau of Labor Statistics.

1. Which kind of worker earns the most?

2. Which kind of worker earns the least?

3. Which occupation listed would you most like to have someday?

4. Suppose you want to see how the salary of the occupation you chose compares to the other salaries. Which do you think is best for this use: a line plot, stem-and-leaf plot, or box plot?

5. Construct the plot you selected.

6. In one or two sentences, describe how the salary of the occupation you chose compares to the other salaries.

Application 19

Money Spent Per Student

The values in the table below are the amount of money spent on education per student in 1983-84 for each of the 50 states and Washington, D.C.

State	Expense	State	Expense
Alabama	$2,082	Montana	$3,691
Alaska	$6,378	Nebraska	$2,913
Arizona	$2,685	Nevada	$2,882
Arkansas	$2,214	New Hampshire	$2,765
California	$2,981	New Jersey	$4,677
Colorado	$3,188	New Mexico	$2,866
Connecticut	$4,055	New York	$4,821
Delaware	$3,848	North Carolina	$2,455
D.C.	$4,574	North Dakota	$2,952
Florida	$3,169	Ohio	$2,996
Georgia	$2,317	Oklahoma	$3,146
Hawaii	$3,395	Oregon	$3,771
Idaho	$2,174	Pennsylvania	$3,707
Illinois	$3,384	Rhode Island	$3,811
Indiana	$2,583	South Carolina	$2,271
Iowa	$3,251	South Dakota	$2,639
Kansas	$3,392	Tennessee	$2,141
Kentucky	$2,646	Texas	$2,960
Louisiana	$2,707	Utah	$2,047
Maine	$2,839	Vermont	$3,491
Maryland	$3,771	Virginia	$2,853
Massachusetts	$3,692	Washington	$3,129
Michigan	$3,315	West Virginia	$2,488
Minnesota	$3,322	Wisconsin	$3,677
Mississippi	$2,090	Wyoming	$4,488
Missouri	$2,814		

Source: National Education Association.

1. Using the value for your state, and an estimate of the number of students in your school, give a rough estimate of the total cost of running your school in 1983-84.

2. Suppose you want to know how your state compares to the others. Construct a plot to help you make this comparison, and label your state.

Then, write a paragraph describing the overall distribution of expenses, and the relative position of your state.

3. Pick 3 to 5 nearby states that are similar to yours. Label them on the plot. Write another sentence or two describing how the expenses in your state compare to those of your neighbors.

4. Using the map of the United States on page 15, classify each state as being in the Northeast, Central, South, or West. Then, construct a plot to show how the expenses per student compare in the four regions of the country. Write a paragraph summarizing the comparisons.

VI. SCATTER PLOTS

The table below gives the box score for the first game of the 1985 National Basketball Association Championship series.

Los Angeles Lakers 114, Boston Celtics 148

LOS ANGELES

	Min	FG-A	FT-A	R	A	P	T
Worthy	37	8-19	4-6	8	5	1	20
Rambis	22	4-6	0-0	9	0	2	8
Jabbar	22	6-11	0-0	3	1	3	12
Magic Johnson	34	8-14	3-4	1	12	2	19
Scott	30	5-14	0-0	2	0	2	10
Cooper	24	1-5	2-2	2	2	3	4
McAdoo	21	6-13	0-0	3	0	5	12
McGee	15	4-7	4-5	2	2	1	14
Spriggs	15	4-7	0-2	3	4	1	8
Kupchak	16	3-3	1-2	2	1	3	7
Lester	4	0-1	0-0	0	1	0	0
Totals	240	49-100	14-21	35	28	23	114

Shooting field goals, 49.0%, free throws, 66.7%

BOSTON

	Min	FG-A	FT-A	R	A	P	T
Bird	31	8-14	2-2	6	9	1	19
McHale	32	10-16	6-9	9	0	1	26
Parish	28	6-11	6-7	8	1	1	18
Dennis Johnson	33	6-14	1-1	3	10	1	13
Ainge	29	9-15	0-0	5	6	1	19
Buckner	16	3-5	0-0	4	6	4	6
Williams	14	3-5	0-0	0	5	2	6
Wedman	23	11-11	0-2	5	2	4	26
Maxwell	16	1-1	1-2	3	1	0	3
Kite	10	3-5	1-2	3	0	1	7
Carr	4	1-3	0-0	1	0	1	3
Clark	4	1-2	0-0	1	3	0	2
Totals	240	62-102	17-25	48	43	17	148

Shooting field goals, 60.8%, free throws, 68.0%

Key for table

Min	Minutes played
FG-A	Field goals made - field goals attempted
FT-A	Free throws made - free throws attempted
R	Rebounds
A	Assists
P	Personal fouls
T	Total points scored

Source: *Los Angeles Times*, May 28, 1985.

Discussion Questions

1. How many rebounds did Kevin McHale make?

2. Which player played the most minutes?

3. Which player had the most assists?

4. How many field goals did James Worthy make? How many did he attempt? What percentage did he make?

5. Five players are on the court at one time for each team. Determine how many minutes are in a game.

6. Which team made a larger percentage of free throws?

7. How is the T (total points scored) column computed? Verify that this number is correct for Magic Johnson and for Kevin McHale. (Caution: Some of the field goals for other players were three point shots.)

Do you think that the players who *attempt* the most field goals are generally the players that *make* the most field goals? Of course! We can see this from the box score. To further investigate this question, we will make a *scatter plot* showing field goals made (FG) and field goals attempted (FG-A). First, set up a plot with field goals attempted on the horizontal axis and field goals made on the vertical axis.

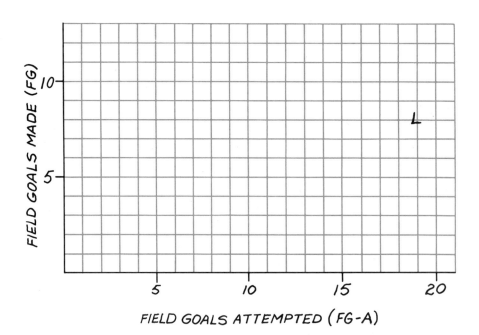

Worthy, the first player, attempted 19 field goals and made 8 of them. The L on the preceding plot represents Worthy. The L is above 19 and across from 8. We used an L to show that he is a Los Angeles player.

The completed scatter plot follows. Each B stands for a Boston player and each L for a Los Angeles player.

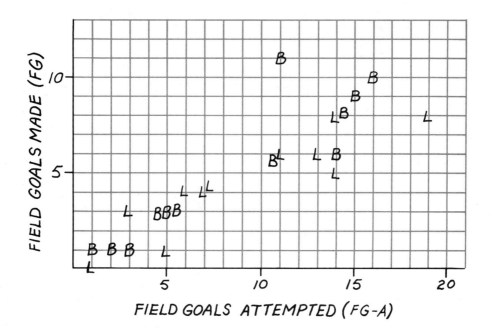

As we suspected, this plot shows that players who attempt more field goals generally make more field goals, and players who attempt few field goals make few field goals. Thus, there is a *positive* association between field goals attempted and field goals made.

However, we can see much more from this plot. First, a player who makes every basket will be represented by a point on the line through the points (0, 0), (1, 1), (2, 2), (3, 3), and so forth. Second, the players who are relatively far below this line were not shooting as well as the other players. Finally, we can observe the relative positions of the two teams in this plot.

Discussion Questions

1. Using the scatter plot, find the points that represent the three perfect shooters.

2. Why are all the points below a diagonal line running from lower left to upper right?

3. Is there a different pattern for Los Angeles and Boston players?

4. Which three Laker players were not shooting very well that game?

5. Suppose a player attempts 9 field goals. About how many would you expect him to make?

6. Write a brief description of the information conveyed by this scatter plot. Then read the following sample discussion. Did you notice any information not listed in this sample discussion?

In this plot, we were not surprised to see a positive association between the number of field goals attempted and the number of field goals made. There were three players, two from Boston and one from Los Angeles, who made all the field goals they attempted. One of these Boston players was truly outstanding as he made eleven out of eleven attempts. The Laker players who attempted a great number of field goals generally did not make as many of them as did the Celtics who attempted a great number of field goals. This could have been the deciding factor in the game.

The points seem to cluster into two groups. The cluster on the upper right generally contains players who played over 20 minutes and the one on the lower left contains players who played less than 20 minutes.

An assist is a pass that leads directly to a basket. A player is credited with a rebound when he recovers the ball following a missed shot. Do you think that players who get a lot of rebounds also make a lot of assists? It is difficult to answer this question just by looking at the box score.

To answer this question, we will make a scatter plot showing rebounds (R) and assists (A). This plot includes all players who made at least four rebounds or four assists.

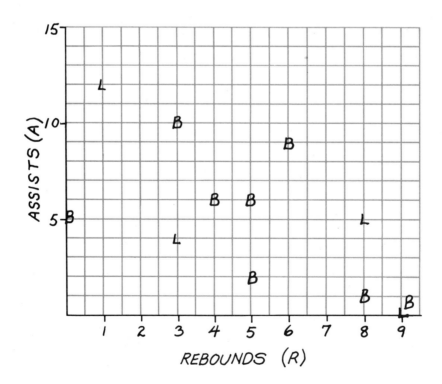

This plot shows that players who get *more* rebounds generally have *fewer* assists, and players who get *fewer* rebounds have *more* assists. Thus, there is a *negative* association between rebounds and assists.

Discussion Questions

1. Do the players who get the most rebounds also make the most assists?

2. Suppose a player had 7 rebounds. About how many assists would you expect this player to have?

3. Is there a different pattern for Boston players than for Los Angeles players?

4. Why do you suppose players who get a lot of rebounds do not make a lot of assists?

5. If you were the coach and you wanted a player to make more assists, would you instruct him to make fewer rebounds?

6. Why didn't we include players who would have been in the lower left-hand corner of this plot?

The following scatter plot shows total points and personal fouls for all players.

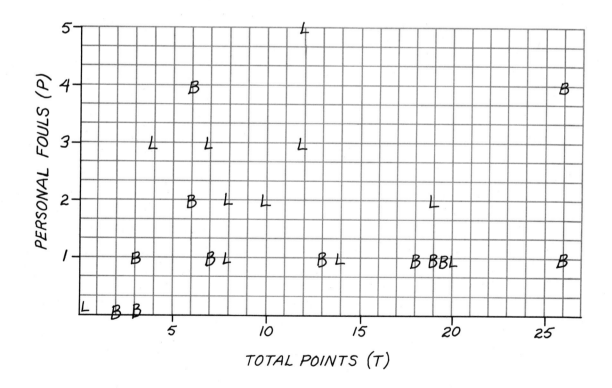

This plot shows *no association* between total points scored and the number of personal fouls committed.

In summary, the following scatter plots show *positive association*.

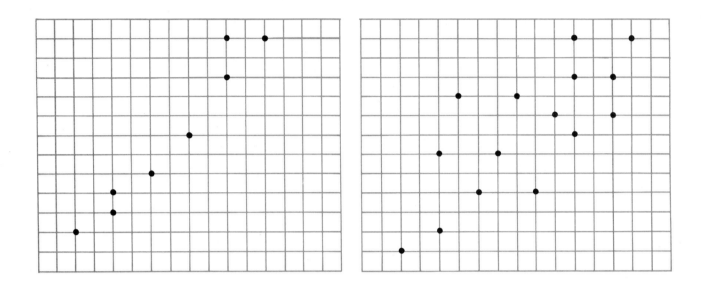

The following scatter plots show *negative association*.

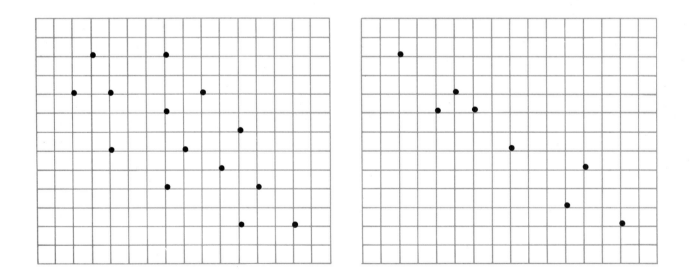

The following scatter plots show *no association*.

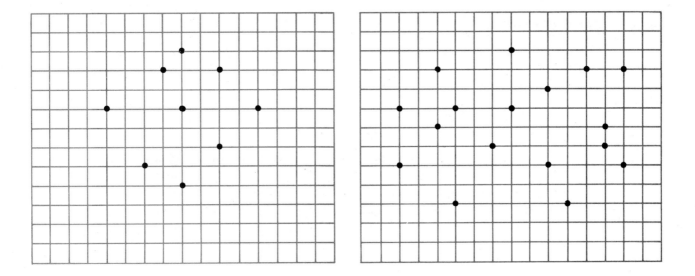

Sometimes one or two points can make it appear that there is a positive or negative association when there is really no association. If you can cover up one or two points and make it look as if there is no association, there probably really is none.

When describing the information displayed on a scatter plot, you can discuss

1. whether there is positive, negative, or no association;

2. whether there are any clusters of points and whether the points in the clusters have anything in common; and

3. whether any points do not follow the general pattern.

It's not always safe to conclude that one variable *causes* another to happen (or not happen) just because there is an association.

Box Office Hits

The table below shows production costs, promotion costs, and gross ticket sales for twelve of the most popular "dumb" movies. The box office grosses were obtained from studios and are estimates.

Dumbing for Dollars

	Year	Production Costs	Promotion Costs	Worldwide Ticket Sales
"Animal House"	1978	$2.9 million	$3 million	$150 million
"Meatballs"	1979	$1.4 million	$2 million	$70 million
"Caddyshack"	1980	$4.8 million	$4 million	$60 million
"Stripes"	1981	$10.5 million	$4.5 million	$85 million
"Spring Break"	1982	$4.5 million	$5 million	$24 million
"Porky's"	1982	$4.8 million	$9 million	$160 million
"Fast Times At Ridgemont High"	1982	$5 million	$4.9 million	$50 million
"Porky's II — The Next Day"	1983	$7 million	$7.5 million	$55 million
"Hot Dog — The Movie"	1984	$2 million	$4 million	$22 million
"Bachelor Party"	1984	$7 million	$7.5 million	$38 million
"Revenge of the Nerds"	1984	$7 million	$7.5 million	$42 million
"Police Academy"	1984	$4.5 million	$4 million	$150 million

Source: Peter H. Brown, "Dumbing for Dollars," *Los Angeles Times*, January 20, 1985.

The scatter plot for total costs (production costs + promotion costs) and worldwide ticket sales follows.

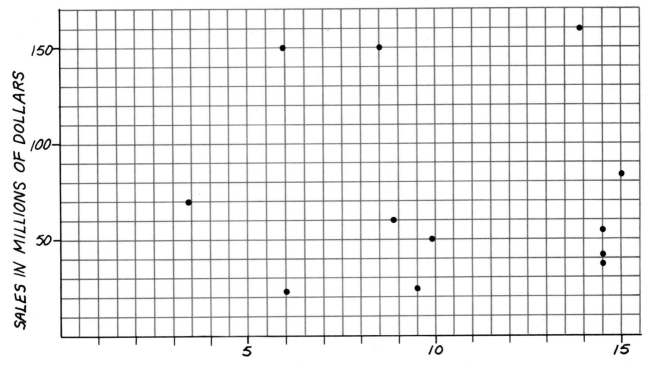

1. Is there positive association, negative association, or no association between total costs and worldwide ticket sales?

2. Which movie(s) would you say did the best when costs are compared to ticket sales?

3. Which movie(s) would you say did the worst when costs are compared to ticket sales?

4. Make a scatter plot of promotion costs against production costs. Put production costs on the horizontal axis and promotion costs on the vertical axis.

5. Is there a positive, negative, or no association between production costs and promotion costs?

6. If a studio spends $4 million on production costs, about how much money would you expect the studio to spend promoting the movie?

7. Which two movies stand out on the scatter plot you made in question 4?

8. Write a description of the information displayed by the two scatter plots.

Protein versus Fat

The following scatter plot shows the grams of fat against the grams of protein in individual servings of lunch and dinner items sold at various fast food restaurants.

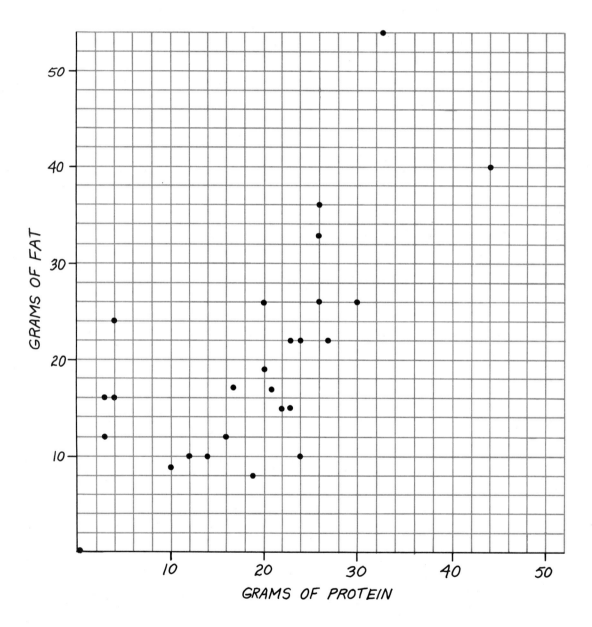

1. Suppose you want protein without much fat. Give the number of grams of protein and fat in the item that you would select.

2. What is the largest number of grams of protein in any item?

3. What is the number of grams of fat in the item in question 2?

4. Does the item in question 2 have an unusually large amount of fat considering how much protein it has?

5. What is the smallest number of grams of protein in any item?

6. How many grams of fat did the item in question 5 have?

7. Is there a positive, negative, or no association between grams of protein and grams of fat?

8. If a new item has 32 grams of protein, how many grams of fat would you expect it to have?

9. Do you see any clusters of points? Where?

The following table lists the items in the previous plot with their grams of protein and grams of fat.

	Protein grams	Fat grams
Big Mac — McDonald's	26	33
Cheeseburger — Hardee's	17	17
Double cheeseburger — Burger Chef	23	22
Cheeseburger w/Bacon Supreme — Jack-in-the-Box	33	54
Single — Wendy's	26	26
Double — Wendy's	44	40
Hamburger — McDonald's	12	10
Quarter Pounder — McDonald's	24	22
Whopper — Burger King	26	36
Roast beef — Arby's	22	15
Beef and cheese — Arby's	27	22
Roast beef — Hardee's	21	17
Big fish — Hardee's	20	26
Ham and cheese — Hardee's	23	15
Thick-crust cheese pizza — Pizza Hut	24	10
Super Supreme thin-crust pizza — Pizza Hut	30	26
Idiot's Delight pizza — Shakey's	14	10
Cheese pizza — Shakey's	16	12
Chicken McNuggets — McDonald's	20	19
Chili — Wendy's	19	8
French fries — McDonald's	3	12
Onion rings — Burger King	3	16
Chocolate shake — McDonald's	10	9
Apple turnover — Jack-in-the-Box	4	24
Chocolaty chip cookies — McDonald's	4	16
Carbonated beverages	0	0

Source: P. Hausman, *At-A-Glance Nutrition Counter*, 1984.

10. What is the item that you decided to order in question 1?

11. What kinds of items are in the cluster of question 9?

12. Do you see any single points in the scatter plot that could be outliers? That is, do you see points that don't follow the general relationship or that don't lie in a large cluster? If so, list the grams of protein and fat for those points. Which items are they? Can you give explanations for any of them?

13. With your fingers, cover up any points you identified for question 12 and the cluster from question 9, and look at the remaining points. Are they scattered fairly closely about a straight line?

14. Write a summary of the information displayed in the scatter plot.

Application 22

Walk-around Stereos

The following table lists 22 "walk-around stereos," each with its price and overall score. The overall score is based on "estimated overall quality as tape players, based on laboratory tests and judgments of features and convenience." A "perfect" walk-around stereo would have a score of 100. Consumers Union says that a difference of 7 points or less in overall score is not very significant.

Ratings of Walk-around Stereos		
Brand and Model	**Price**	**Overall Score**
AIWA HSP02	$120	73
AIWA HSJ02	180	65
JVC CQ1K	130	64
Sanyo MG100	120	64
Sony Walkman WM7	170	64
Sanyo Sportster MG16D	70	61
Toshiba KTVS1	170	60
JVC CQF2	150	59
Panasonic RQJ20X	150	59
Sharp WF9BR	140	59
Sony Walkman WM4	75	56
General Electric Stereo Escape II 35275A	90	55
KLH Solo S200	170	54
Sanyo Sportster MG36D	100	52
Koss Music Box A2	110	51
Toshiba KTS3	120	47
Panasonic RQJ75	50	46
Sears Cat. No. 21162	60	45
General Electric Great Escape 35273A	70	43
Sony Walkman WMR2	200	41
Sony Walkman WMF2	220	38
Realistic SCP4	70	37

Source: *Consumer Reports Buying Guide*, 1985.

1. Which walk-around stereo do you think is the best buy?
2. A scatter plot will give a better picture of the relative price and overall score of the walk-around stereos. Make a scatter plot with price on the horizontal axis. You can make the vertical axis as follows:

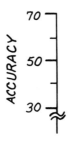

The ≈ lines indicate that part of the vertical axis is not shown, so that the plot is not too tall.

3. Which stereo appears to be the best buy according to the scatter plot?

4. Is there a positive, negative, or no association between price and overall score?

5. Given their overall scores, which walk-around stereos are too expensive?

Application 23

SAT Scores

The following plot shows the SAT math scores in each state in 1985 against the percentage of seniors in each state who took the test. Each state is identified by its postal code. For example, Mississippi is MS. The nationwide mean was 475.

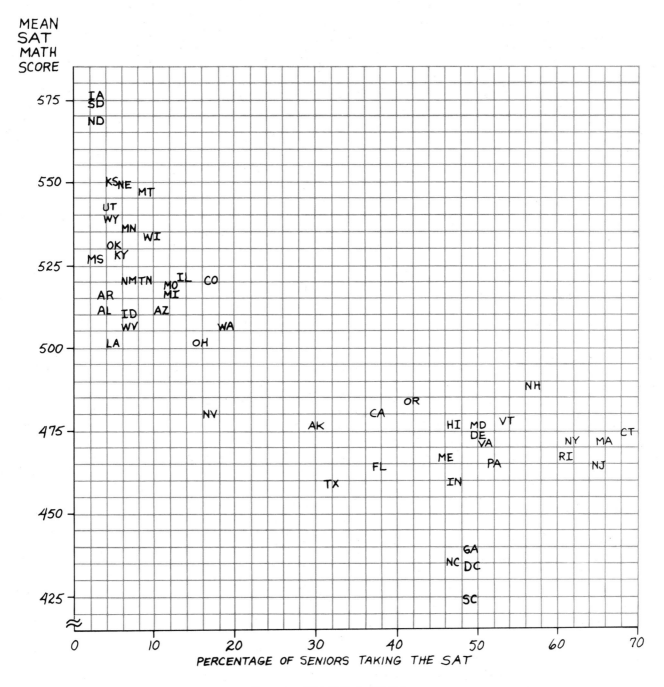

Source: The College Board.

1. In general, as a larger percentage of students take the test, what happens to the SAT math score?

2. Find the two clusters of states. Within the cluster on the left, is there a positive, negative, or no association between the percentage taking the test and the score?

3. Within the cluster on the right, is there a positive, negative, or no association?

4. Taking into account the percentage of students taking the test, which state(s) do you think have the best SAT math score? Which have the worst?

5. Using the facts you discovered in questions 1 through 4, write a summary of the information given in the scatter plot. Include an analysis of the position of your state.

Time Series Plots

Some scatter plots have year or some other time interval on the horizontal axis. Since there is only one value per year, we can connect the points in order to see the general trend. For example, the following *plot over time* shows how many 12-ounce soft drinks the average person in the U.S. drank each year from 1945 to 1984.

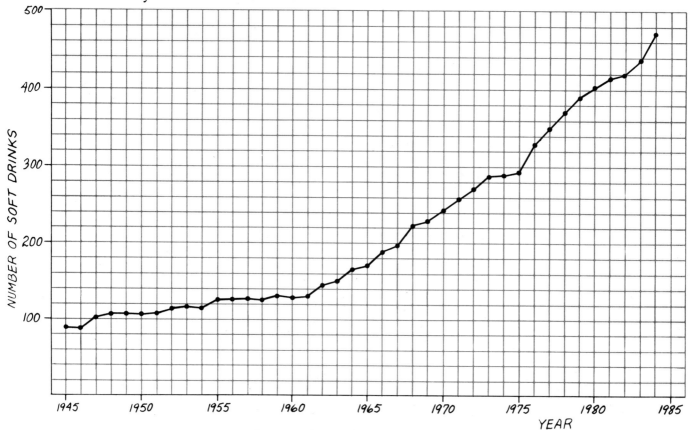

Source: National Soft Drink Association.

Discussion Questions

1. About how many soft drinks did the average person drink in 1950? In 1970?

2. About how many six-packs of soft drinks did the average person drink in 1980?

3. About how many soft drinks did the average person drink *per week* in 1950? In 1980?

4. If the trend continues, about how many 12-ounce soft drinks will the average person drink each year in 1990?

5. In what year did soft drink consumption start to "take off"? Can you think of any reason for this?

6. Who is the "average person"?

7. Write a summary of the trend in soft drink consumption shown by the plot. (Our summary of this plot follows.)

In the U.S. from 1945 until 1961, soft drink consumption rose gradually from about 90 twelve-ounce servings per year per person to about 130 twelve-ounce servings. In 1962, soft drink consumption started to rise rapidly until it was about 400 twelve-ounce servings in 1980. In other words, in these 18 years, soft drink consumption more than tripled in the United States.

What happened in 1962? Some ideas are as follows:

• Diet drinks might have been introduced.

• Soft drinks in aluminum cans might have become available.

• The economy might have improved so people started to spend more money on luxuries such as soft drinks.

• The post-war baby boom kids were reaching their teenage years.

There were very big increases in the late 70's. Then, the increase showed signs of leveling off. However, there were large increases again in 1983 and 1984.

How Long Can You Expect to Live?

1. Study the table below. At your birth, how long could you expect to live?

Life Expectancy at Birth

Birth Year	White		Black and Other	
	Male	Female	Male	Female
1920	54.4	55.6	45.5	45.2
1930	59.7	63.5	47.3	49.2
1940	62.1	66.6	51.5	54.9
1950	66.5	72.2	59.1	62.9
1955	67.4	73.7	61.4	66.1
1960	67.4	74.1	61.1	66.3
1965	67.6	74.7	61.1	67.4
1970	68.0	75.6	61.3	69.4
1971	68.3	75.8	61.6	69.7
1972	68.3	75.9	61.5	69.9
1973	68.4	76.1	61.9	70.1
1974	68.9	76.6	62.9	71.3
1975	69.4	77.2	63.6	72.3
1976	69.7	77.3	64.1	72.6
1977	70.0	77.7	64.6	73.1
1978	70.2	77.8	65.0	73.6
1979, preliminary	70.6	78.3	65.5	74.5

Source: United States National Center for Health Statistics.

2. Can males or females expect to live longer?

3. Can whites or blacks and others expect to live longer?

The life expectancies for each group have been placed on the following plot and the points have been connected by a line.

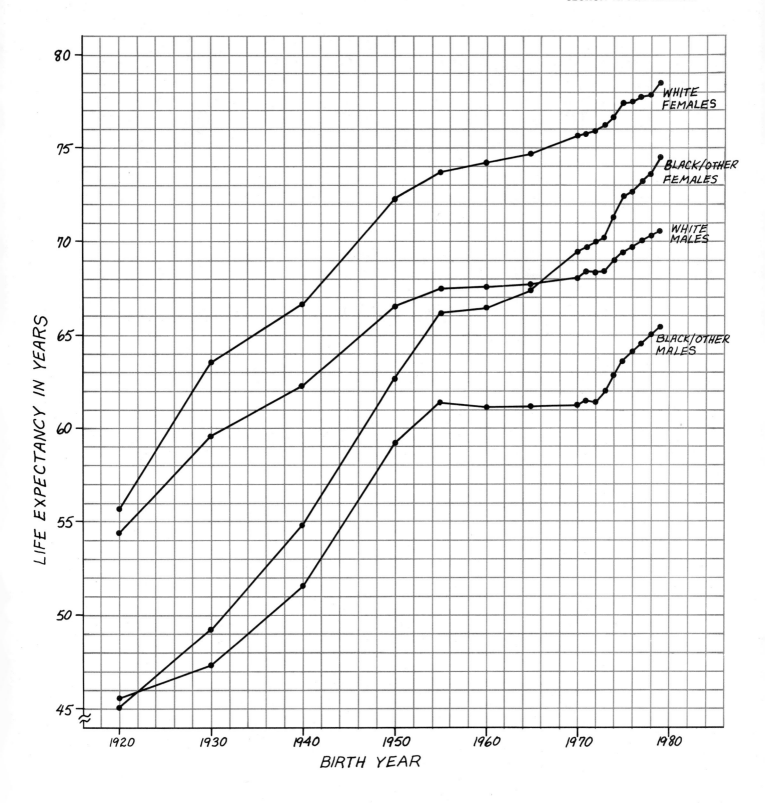

4. Which group born in 1979 could expect the longest life?

5. Which group made the greatest gain in life expectancy in the years from 1920 to 1979?

6. Which group has had the smallest increase in life expectancy since 1920?

7. During which decade did the largest increase in life expectancy occur for black and other females?

8. Within each race, males and females had about the same life expectancy in 1920. Was this still true in 1979?

9. Write a summary of the trends you see in the plot.

Application 25

Speeding

The following table shows average freeway speeds as recorded by highway monitoring devices in California. The newspaper gave no explanation why the average speed is missing for 1971 and 1973.

Year	Average Highway Speed in Miles per Hour
1970	59
1971	—
1972	61
1973	—
1974	55
1975	56
1976	57
1977	57
1978	57
1979	58
1980	56
1981	57
1982	57

Source: *Los Angeles Times*, May 22, 1983.

1. Construct a plot over time of the average speeds.

2. Can you guess what year the 55 miles per hour speed limit went into effect?

3. Some people think drivers are ignoring the 55 miles per hour speed limit. Do you think your plot shows that this is the case?

4. The fatalities in California per 100 million miles driven are shown in the following table. Construct a plot over time of these data.

Year	Fatalities per 100 Million Miles
1970	3.8
1971	3.2
1972	3.2
1973	3.0
1974	2.2
1975	2.2
1976	2.3
1977	2.4
1978	2.6
1979	2.5
1980	2.5
1981	2.4
1982	2.1

Source: *Los Angeles Times*, May 22, 1983.

5. Was there a decrease in fatalities when the 55 miles per hour speed limit took effect?

6. Another way to display these data is with a scatter plot of fatalities against speed. Construct such a plot. Place the values for speed on the horizontal axis. Plot the last two digits of the year instead of a dot.

7. What do you learn from the plot in question 6?

8. Why is the plot in question 6 the best one?

Application 26

Sex Ratio by Age

The following table gives the ratio of males to females at different ages for whites, blacks, and other races in 1980. The sex ratio is computed by dividing the number of males by the number of females.

Sex Ratio by Age (total number male/total number female)

Age	White	Black	Other
0-4	1.054	1.016	1.035
5-9	1.053	1.016	1.036
10-14	1.050	1.011	1.035
15-19	1.037	.995	1.073
20-24	1.009	.913	1.087
25-29	1.003	.877	1.026
30-34	.994	.856	.971
35-39	.983	.832	.972
40-44	.974	.828	.973
45-49	.963	.821	.917
50-54	.939	.808	.878
55-59	.901	.818	.913
60-64	.869	.793	.864
65-69	.804	.745	.863
70-74	.720	.712	.925
75-79	.620	.651	.865
80-84	.524	.599	.730
85-	.429	.500	.642

Source: United States Census Bureau.

1. If there are 750 males and 500 females, what is the sex ratio?
2. If there are 500 males and 700 females, what is the sex ratio?
3. If the sex ratio is 1.000, are there more males than females, fewer males than females, or the same number of males as females?
4. If the sex ratio is 1.213, are there more males, fewer males, or the same number of males as females?
5. If the sex ratio is 0.736, are there more males, fewer males, or the same number of males as females?
6. Is there a higher percentage of males among
   a. 0-4 year old whites, 0-4 year old blacks, or 0-4 year old "others"?
   b. 80-84 year old whites, 80-84 year old blacks, or 80-84 year old "others"?

The following scatter plot shows the curves for whites, blacks, and "others."

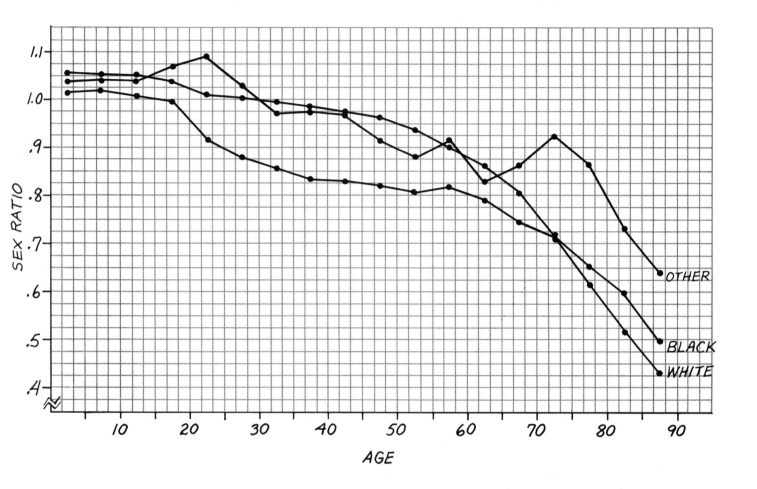

7. Do the three curves look about the same overall?

8. What is one general characteristic of all three curves?

9. What does it mean when the curve is going downhill?

10. Where are the curves closest?

11. a) At what ages do the curves for whites and blacks first start separating?

    b) Can you think of any possible explanations for this?

12. a) How do the white and black curves compare at older ages?

    b) Again, can you think of any possible explanations for this?

13. Write a description of the information you see in this plot. Include any questions the plot suggests to you.

Scatter Plots — Summary

Scatter plots are the best way to display data in which two numbers are given for each person or item. When you analyze a scatter plot, look for the following:

- positive, negative, or no association
- clusters of points
- points that do not follow the general pattern

If you find any of these features, ask yourself what could have caused them.

On time series plots, it is often helpful to connect the points in order to see the trend. Look for places where the general trend seems to change, and try to find possible explanations. If there is more than one time series on a plot, compare them to determine similarities and differences.

Suggestions for Student Projects

Think of a problem that interests you or select one of those below. Collect the data, make the appropriate plot(s), and write a summary of your results. Try to explain any trends or patterns.

1. Did the students who studied the most hours tend to get the higher grades on your last test?

2. Do students who get the most allowance tend to work more hours doing chores at home?

3. Can the students who do the most sit-ups in one minute also do the most push-ups?

4. Investigate whether there are relationships between certain physical characteristics by measuring a group of students. Some possibilities include the following:

    a. height and elbow-hand length

    b. circumference of closed fist and length of foot

    c. hand span and circumference of wrist

    d. weight and waist

    e. circumferences of head and neck

5. Construct a plot over time of the number of absences in your class on each day of the last six weeks. What trends do you see?

VII. LINES ON SCATTER PLOTS

The 45° Line

In the last section we interpreted scatter plots by looking for general relationships of positive, negative, and no association. We also looked for clusters of points that seemed special in some way. This section shows how interpretations of scatter plots are sometimes helped by adding a straight line to the plot. Two different straight lines are used. One is the 45° line going through the points (0, 0), (1, 1), (2, 2), and so forth. The second type is a straight line that is fitted to go through much of the data.

This table lists the number of black state legislators for each state in 1974 and 1984.

Number of Black State Legislators					
	1974	1984		1974	1984
Alabama	3	24	Montana	0	0
Alaska	2	1	Nebraska	1	1
Arizona	2	2	Nevada	3	3
Arkansas	4	5	New Hampshire	0	0
California	7	8	New Jersey	7	7
Colorado	4	3	New Mexico	1	0
Connecticut	6	10	New York	14	20
Delaware	3	3	North Carolina	3	15
District of Columbia	n/a	n/a	North Dakota	0	0
Florida	3	12	Ohio	11	12
Georgia	16	26	Oklahoma	4	5
Hawaii	0	0	Oregon	1	3
Idaho	0	0	Pennsylvania	13	18
Illinois	19	20	Rhode Island	1	4
Indiana	7	8	South Carolina	3	20
Iowa	1	1	South Dakota	0	0
Kansas	5	4	Tennessee	9	13
Kentucky	3	2	Texas	8	13
Louisiana	8	18	Utah	0	1
Maine	1	0	Vermont	0	1
Maryland	19	24	Virginia	2	7
Massachusetts	5	6	Washington	2	3
Michigan	13	17	West Virginia	1	1
Minnesota	2	1	Wisconsin	3	4
Mississippi	1	20	Wyoming	0	1
Missouri	15	15	Total	236	382

Source: Joint Center for Political Studies.

The scatter plot of the 1984 number against the 1974 number follows:

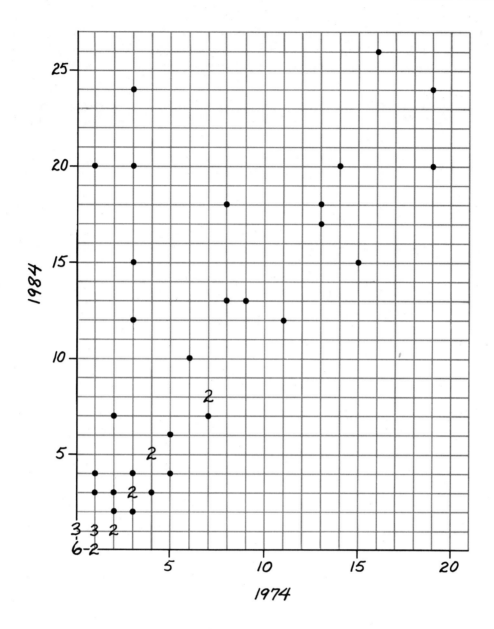

A striking feature of the plot is that the points all seem to lie above an (imaginary) diagonal line. Another feature is that there are many points in the lower left-hand corner. In fact, several states sometimes lie at exactly the same point. For example, Arkansas and Oklahoma both lie at (4, 5). To show this, we placed a 2 at (4, 5).

Discussion Questions

1. Place a ruler on the plot next to the line going through (0, 0), (10, 10), (20, 20), and so forth. For states on this line, the 1984 and 1974 numbers of black legislators are equal. How many points are exactly on this line?

2. If a point is above this line, the number of black legislators in that state in 1984 is larger than the number of black legislators that state had in 1974. Name three states for which this statement is true.

3. How many points fall below this line? What can we say about these states? What is the maximum (vertical) distance any of these is below the line? What does this mean in terms of the number of black legislators in 1974 and 1984?

4. Again, consider states above this line, those where the number of black legislators was larger in 1984 than in 1974. What are the names of the 7 or so states that lie farthest above the line? What do these states have in common?

5. The number of black legislators has generally increased from 1974 to 1984. Does this mean that the percentage of legislators who are black has necessarily increased? (Hint: Is the total number of legislators in a state necessarily the same in 1984 as in 1974?)

In summary, this 45° line (sometimes called the $y = x$ line) divides the plot into two regions. We should try to distinguish the characteristics of the points in the two regions. In this plot the top region contains states where the number of black legislators in 1984 is larger than it was in 1974. Most of the states lie in this region. The points in this region that are farthest from the line are those where the number has increased the most from 1974 to 1984. These states turn out to be states in the deep south. There are only a few points slightly below the 45° line, where the number of black legislators was greater in 1974 than in 1984. These are all states that had only 5 or fewer black legislators in 1974. Almost half the states are in the lower left-hand corner, with 5 or fewer in both years. Two states, Illinois and Maryland, had relatively large numbers in both years.

It would have been helpful to plot each state's abbreviation (such as NY for New York) instead of a dot. However, there wasn't room to do this for the states in the lower left corner.

Application 27

Submarine Sinkings

During World War II, the United States Navy tried to estimate how many German submarines were sunk each month. After the war, the Navy was able to get the actual numbers. The results follow:

Month	U.S. Estimate	Actual Number of Sinkings
1	3	3
2	2	2
3	4	6
4	2	3
5	5	4
6	5	3
7	9	11
8	12	9
9	8	10
10	13	16
11	14	13
12	3	5
13	4	6
14	13	19
15	10	15
16	16	15

Source: Mosteller, Fienberg, and Rourke, *Beginning Statistics with Data Analysis.*

1. Make a scatter plot of the data. Put the U.S. estimate on the horizontal axis.

2. Draw in the line that connects all the points where the number estimated by the U.S. Navy would be the same as the actual number of sinkings.

3. If a point is above the line, does it mean that the U.S. Navy's estimate was too high or too low?

4. Are more points above the line or below it?

5. Did the U.S. Navy tend to underestimate or overestimate the number of submarine sinkings?

6. Which point is farthest from the line? How many units away from the line is it? (Count the units vertically from the point to the line.)

7. How many points are three units or more from the line?

Fitting a Line

Not all ducks look alike, and it turns out that not all species of ducks behave alike, either. In an effort to study possible relationships between looks and behavior of ducks, two scales were created and an experiment performed. A plumage scale was devised to reflect the color and other characteristics of the duck's feathers. The scale ranged from 0 (looks just like a mallard with a green head and white neck-ring) to 20 (looks just like a pintail with a needle tail and neck stripe). Similarly, a behavior scale was devised ranging from 0 (generally congregate in pairs, just like mallards) to 15 (generally congregate in larger groups, just like pintails). The crucial scientific question is: After some interbreeding of mallards and pintails to produce ducks with a variety of looks and behavior, will we be able to predict how the ducks behave from their looks?

An experiment was performed. Mallards were mated with pintails and 11 second generation males were studied. For ease of identification, we have named the ducks. The results follow:

Duck	Plumage	Behavior
Rub	7	3
Stu	13	10
Ugly	14	11
Fred	6	5
Y.U.	14	15
Kold	15	15
Don	4	7
Ole	8	10
Van	7	4
Joe	9	9
Lou	14	11

Source: Richard J. Larsen and Donna Fox Stroup, *Statistics in the Real World.*

Kold Duck looked the most like a pintail. Don Duck looked the most like a mallard. The scatter plot of these data follows:

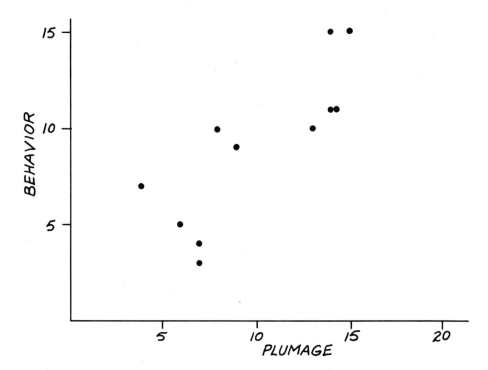

There is a positive association between a duck's plumage rating and his behavior rating. Ducks who look more like pintails tend to act more like pintails.

The same plot with a line through the points follows. This line is called the *fitted line*.

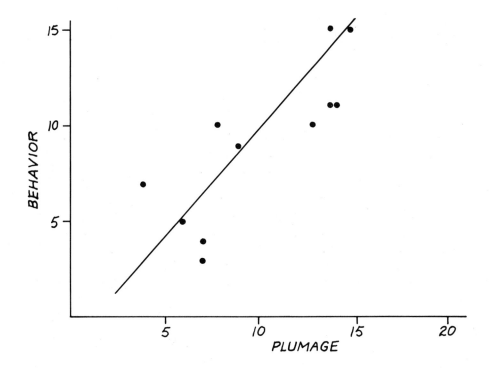

We can use this line to predict the behavior rating of a duck with a given plumage rating. For example, if a duck has a plumage rating of 5, what would you expect for his behavior rating?

113

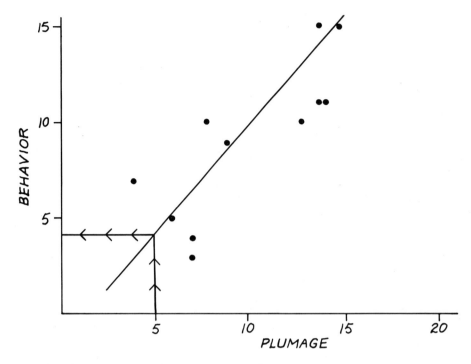

You should expect a behavior rating of 4.

Now we will describe a method for drawing a line through the data in order to predict a duck's behavior rating if we are given a plumage rating.

First, count the total number of points. Draw two vertical dashed lines so there are approximately the same number of points in each of the three strips. The two outer strips should have the same number of points, if possible.

In this case, we have 11 points. We will have four points in each outside strip and three points in the middle.

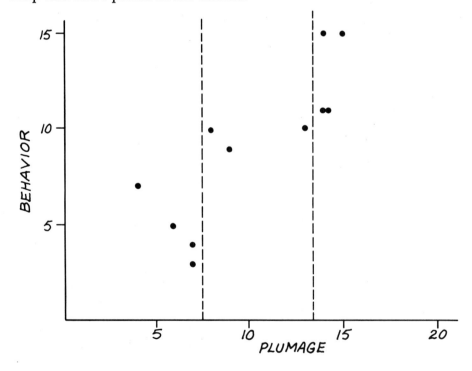

Second, place an X in each strip at the "center" of the points in that strip.

Study the left strip. It has four points. We want to find the median of the plumage ratings and the median of the behavior ratings. The median of the plumage ratings is halfway between the second and third points counting from the left. To find the median of the plumage ratings, place a ruler to the left of the points and move it toward the right until it is halfway between the second and third points. Draw a short vertical dashed line there.

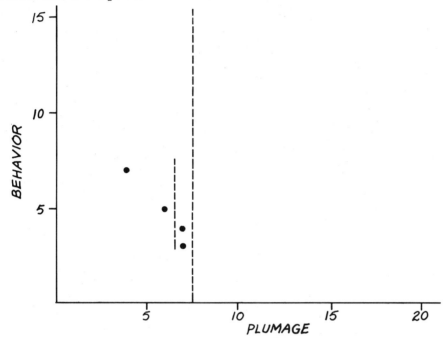

The median of the behavior ratings is halfway between the second and third points, counting from the bottom. Move the ruler up until it is halfway between these points and draw a horizontal dashed line there. The plot is shown as follows:

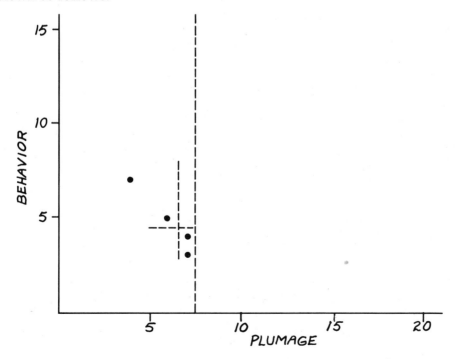

Mark an X where the dashed lines cross.

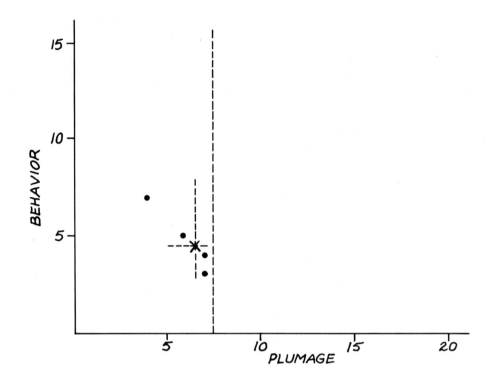

The center strip has three points. The median of the plumage ratings is at the second point, counting from the left.

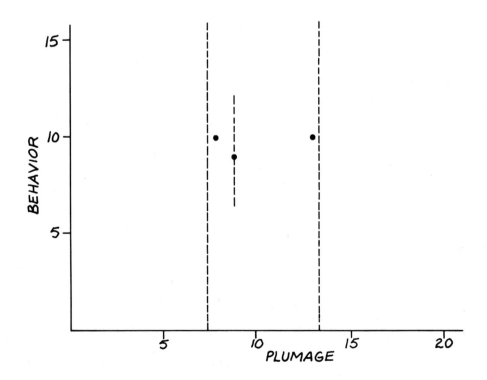

The median of the behavior ratings is at the second point, counting from the bottom.

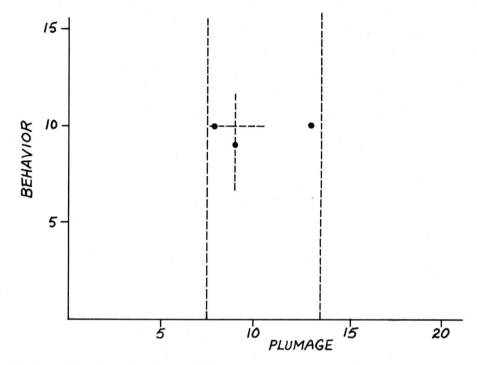

Mark an X where the dashed lines cross.

After the "center" of the right strip is also found, the plot looks as follows:

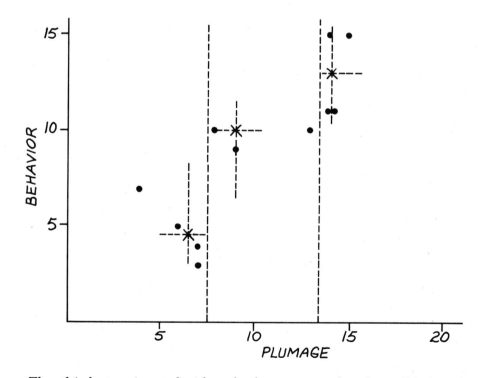

The third step is to decide whether or not the three X's lie close to a straight line. Use your ruler, balanced on its edge, to help decide. For this example, the X's lie approximately on a straight line.

Finally, place your ruler so that it connects the two X's in the outside strips. Now slide the ruler one-third of the way to the middle X and draw the line.

The finished plot including the fitted line is shown below. It is not necessary to include the dashed lines.

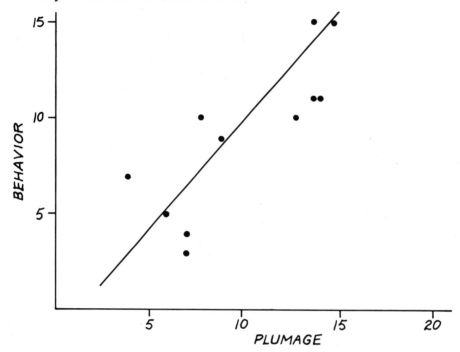

Discussion Questions

1. Which duck behaved the most like a pintail?

2. Which duck behaved the most like a mallard?

3. Why do we need a method for drawing a line? Why can't we just sketch one?

4. If a duck has a plumage rating of 10, what would you expect his behavior rating to be? Use the fitted line to get your answer.

5. If a duck has a plumage rating of 4, what would you expect his behavior rating to be?

6. To judge how much a duck's actual behavior differs from its predicted behavior, we measure the vertical distance from the point to the fitted line. Which duck is farthest from the line, and how many units is he from the line?

7. Which ducks are within two units of the line?

8. You might wonder why the fitted line has been constructed this way. Why have we used medians instead of means to form the X's? Why have we constructed three X's instead of two or four? Why have we constructed the slope of the line by using only the two end X's? After connecting the two end X's, why did we slide the ruler one-third of the way towards the middle X rather than some other fraction? Try to think of reasons for these choices or of alternate reasons for constructing a fitted line in a different way.

Application 28

Smoking and Heart Disease

The following table lists 21 countries with the cigarette consumption per adult per year and the number of deaths per 100,000 people per year from coronary heart disease (CHD).

Country	Cigarette Consumption per Adult per Year	CHD Mortality per 100,000 (ages 35-64)
United States	3900	257
Canada	3350	212
Australia	3220	238
New Zealand	3220	212
United Kingdom	2790	194
Switzerland	2780	125
Ireland	2770	187
Iceland	2290	111
Finland	2160	233
West Germany	1890	150
Netherlands	1810	125
Greece	1800	41
Austria	1770	182
Belgium	1700	118
Mexico	1680	32
Italy	1510	114
Denmark	1500	145
France	1410	60
Sweden	1270	127
Spain	1200	44
Norway	1090	136

Source: *American Journal of Public Health.*

1. In which country do adults smoke the largest number of cigarettes?

2. Which country has the highest death rate from coronary heart disease?

3. Which country has the lowest death rate from coronary heart disease?

4. If we want to predict CHD mortality from cigarette consumption, which variable should be placed on the horizontal axis of a scatter plot?

5. a) Make a scatter plot of the data.

   b) Draw two vertical lines so there are seven points in each strip.

   c) Place an X in each strip at the median of the cigarette consumption and the median of the CHD mortality.

   d) Do the three X's lie close to a straight line?

   e) Draw in the fitted line.

6. a) Which three countries lie the farthest vertical distance from the line?

    b) How many units do they lie from the line?

    c) Considering the cigarette consumption, are these countries relatively high or low in CHD mortality?

7. If you were told that the adults in a country smoke an average of 2500 cigarettes a year, how many deaths from CHD would you expect?

8. If you were told that the adults in a country smoke an average of 1300 cigarettes a year, how many deaths from CHD would you expect?

9. (For class discussion) Sometimes strong association in a scatter plot is taken to mean that one of the variables *causes* the other one. Do you think that a high CHD death rate could cause cigarette consumption to be high? Could high cigarette consumption cause the CHD death rate to be high? Sometimes, though, there is not a causal relationship between the two variables. Instead, there is a hidden third variable. This variable could cause both of the variables to be large simultaneously. Do you think that this might be the situation for this example? Can you think of such a possible variable?

10. (For students who have studied algebra.) Choose two points on the fitted line, and from them find the equation of the line. Express it in the form $y = mx + b$, where y is mortality from coronary heart disease per 100,000 people (aged 35-64) per year, and x is cigarette consumption per adult per year. Using this equation, how many additional deaths per 100,000 people tend to result from an increase of 200 in cigarette consumption? What number of cigarettes per year is associated with one additional death from CHD per 100,000 people per year?

Application 29

Catholic Clergy

Nineteen states have more than 500,000 residents who are Catholic. The following table lists these states, along with the number of priests and nuns in each state.

State	Number of Priests	Nuns
Arizona	412	591
California	4242	6615
Connecticut	1298	2450
Florida	1224	1240
Illinois	4131	8564
Indiana	1229	2515
Iowa	982	2140
Louisiana	1236	1931
Massachusetts	3630	6715
Michigan	1892	4296
Minnesota	1403	3911
Missouri	1660	4049
New Jersey	2784	5102
New York	7334	14665
Ohio	2901	6685
Pennsylvania	4600	12785
Rhode Island	580	1105
Texas	2146	3832
Wisconsin	2167	5176

Source: *The Official Catholic Directory.*

Clearly, the number of priests and nuns varies greatly among these states. This application investigates whether there is any relationship between the number of priests and the number of nuns.

1. Make a scatter plot of the number of nuns on the vertical axis against the number of priests on the horizontal axis.

2. Fit a straight line to the scatter plot.

3. Do you feel that a straight line fits these data well, overall?

4. New York is the state with the largest number of Catholic clergy. Would you say that the two numbers for New York follow the same relationship as do the other states? Give your reasons.

5. Which state has a large number of nuns compared to its number of priests? Which state has a relatively small number of nuns compared to its number of priests?

6. (For students who have studied algebra.) Find the equation of the fitted line. Express it in the form $y = mx + b$, where y is the number of nuns and x is the number of priests. According to this equation, if one state had 100 more priests than a second state, how many more nuns would we expect the first state to have than the second? If there were 100 priests in a state, how many nuns would the equation predict? The moral is: One should be careful using fitted lines for values far to the left or right of the given points.

Application 30

Voting for President

The following table gives the percentage of the vote received by the Democratic candidate in the presidential elections of 1920, 1960, and 1964. The percentages were calculated using only votes for the two major party candidates. The question we want to investigate here is whether the 1964 percentage can be predicted from either the 1920 or the 1960 percentage. Only states in the northeast and midwest are included.

| **Percentage Vote Received by Democrat** | | | |
State	1920	1960	1964
Colorado	38	45	62
Connecticut	35	54	68
Delaware	43	51	61
Illinois	27	50	59
Indiana	42	45	56
Iowa	26	43	62
Kansas	33	39	55
Maine	30	43	69
Maryland	43	54	66
Massachusetts	29	60	76
Michigan	23	51	67
Minnesota	22	51	64
Nebraska	33	38	53
New Hampshire	40	47	64
New Jersey	30	50	66
New York	29	53	69
North Dakota	19	45	58
Ohio	40	47	63
Pennsylvania	29	51	65
Rhode Island	34	64	81
South Dakota	24	42	56
Vermont	24	41	66
West Virginia	44	53	68
Wisconsin	18	48	62

Source: United States Census Bureau.

1. By looking down the columns of percentages, do you think the Democratic or Republican candidate won the election in

   a. 1920?

   b. 1960?

   c. 1964?

2. Make a scatter plot with the 1960 percentages on the horizontal axis and the 1964 percentages on the vertical axis.

3. Is there a positive, negative, or no association? Why?

4. Fit a straight line to the scatter plot. Due to the fact that three states have a 1960 percentage of 45 and four states have a 1960 percentage of 51, you will have to have 9 states in the left group, 5 in the middle group, and 10 in the right group.

5. Which two states lie the farthest vertical distance from the line?

6. Use your line to complete these sentences.

   a. A state with a 50% vote for the Democratic candidate in 1960 would give the Democratic candidate about a _____% vote in 1964.

   b. A state with a 60% vote for the Democratic candidate in 1960 would give the Democratic candidate about a _____% vote in 1964.

   c. As an approximation using the fitted line, the 1964 vote can be estimated by adding about _____% to the 1960 vote.

7. We call the vertical distance of each point from the fitted line the "error." With the exception of the two states in question 5, all the rest of the states give an "error" less than _____.

8. Putting together the information in questions 5, 6, and 7, we can say the following: The 1964 Democratic percentage equals the 1960 Democratic percentage plus _____%, with an error of less than _____% for all these states except for two, which are _____ and _____.

9. Now make a scatter plot with the 1920 percentages on the horizontal axis and the 1964 percentages on the vertical axis.

10. Is there positive, negative, or no association? Why?

11. Divide the plot into three vertical strips and mark the X in each strip. The three X's do not lie close to a straight line, so do not draw one in.

12. Is it possible to predict the 1964 vote if you are given the 1920 vote?

13. Summarize the information from these two scatter plots in a paragraph.

14. What two candidates ran in

   a. 1920?

   b. 1960?

   c. 1964?

Fitting a Line with a More Complicated Example

When the scatter plot has more points on it than in the previous examples, we can still use the method that was described to fit a straight line. However, some parts of the construction and interpretation can be more complicated, so we will now work a larger example.

The following scatter plot shows the weights and heights of 52 men in an office. Notice that in several places there is a 2 in the plot. This means that two men had the same height and weight.

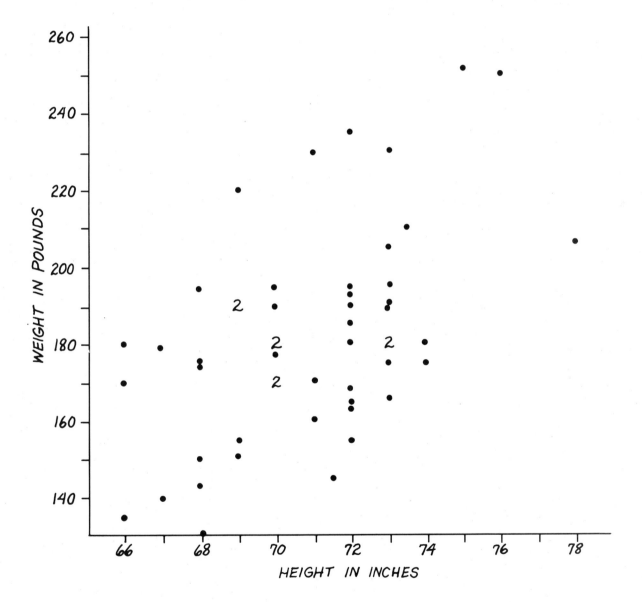

There are 52 points, so to construct the fitted line we would like to divide the points into groups of 17, 18, and 17 points. This division is not possible because different men have the same height. For example, for the left group there are 16 men with heights 69" or less, and 23 men with heights 70" or less. We cannot construct a group with exactly 17 men, so we choose the group with 16 by making the dividing line at 69.5". For the right group, counting in from the right side of the plot shows that 15 men have heights

73" or taller, and 25 men have heights 72" or taller. Similarly, we choose the dividing point to be 72.5", so the right group has 15 points. This choice leaves 21 points in the middle. The dividing lines are shown in the following scatter plot.

Next, we find the centers of the three groups, using the median method. For the left group of 16 points, both the eighth and ninth largest heights are 68", so the median height is 68". For the weights, the eighth largest is 170 and the ninth is 175, so the median weight is 172.5 pounds. These medians give the left X on the scatter plot. For the right group of 15 points, the eighth height is 73" and the eighth weight is 190 pounds. These medians give the right X on the plot. Similarly, the center X is obtained from the 21 points in the center group as before.

The scatter plot with the three X's follows. It is important to stop now and see if the three X's fall reasonably close to a straight line. If they do not, we would not continue to fit the straight line.

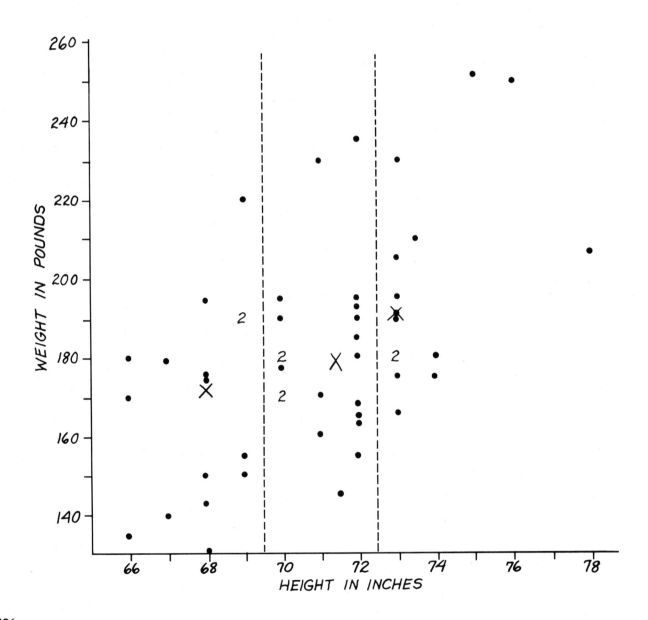

In this case the three X's are close to a straight line, so we continue. Draw the fitted line by first taking a straightedge and placing it along the two end X's. The middle X is below this line. We now slide the straightedge down one-third of the way towards the middle X and draw in the fitted line. This line is shown in the following scatter plot.

The fitted line does not go exactly through any of the three X's, but it goes close to each of them. From this straight line we can predict that a typical weight for a man 66″ tall is 160 pounds, and a typical weight for a man 76″ tall is 197 pounds. For a 10″ increase in height there is a typical increase in weight of 37 pounds, so we could say that on the average for each one inch increase in height there is a 3.7 pound increase in weight. It would be difficult to draw a conclusion like this without fitting a line to the scatter plot.

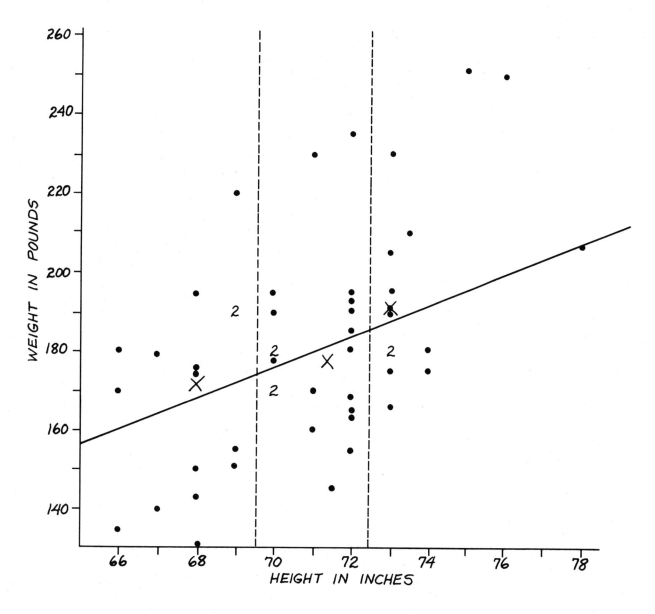

It is also useful to examine the spread of the points about the fitted line. A good way to do this is to add two additional lines that are parallel to the fitted line. We want these new lines to be an equal distance above and below the fitted line. We also want them drawn far enough from the fitted line so that most, but not all, of the points lie between the two new lines. This lets us notice and focus our attention more easily on outlying points or on other unusual features of the data around the edges.

This has been done in the following plot, using lines giving weights that are 30 pounds more, and 30 pounds less, than the predicted weight for each height. The value 30 pounds was chosen by sliding a ruler parallel to the fitted line so that most, but not all, of the men would fall between these additional lines.

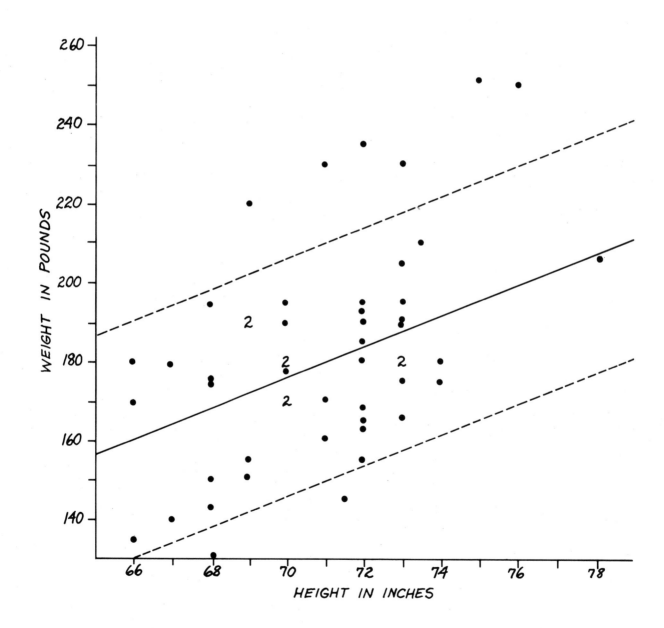

Discussion Questions

1. How many men fall above the top line? Below the bottom line?

2. What percentage of these 52 men would you say are unusually heavy for their height (above the top line)?

3. What percentage of these 52 men would you say are unusually light for their height?

4. Are there more men who are very heavy for their height, or are there more men who are very light for their height? Why do you think this is the case?

5. For those men whose weight is unusually heavy or unusually light for their height, which group has the more extreme values of weight?

6. Consider the man with height 78".

   a. How many men are heavier than he is?

   b. Do you think he is overweight? Why or why not?

1980-84 Rock Hits

The following table lists the top 25 single records from 1980 through 1984 and the number of weeks each of these was in the Top 10 and the Top 40. Is there a close relationship between these two numbers? If we know how many weeks a hit record was in the Top 10, could we accurately predict the total length of time it would remain in the Top 40?

Top Record Hits, 1980-1984

Title — Artist	Number of weeks in	
	Top 10	Top 40
"Physical" — Olivia Newton-John	15	21
"Endless Love" — Diana Ross & Lionel Richie	13	19
"Bette Davis Eyes" — Kim Carnes	14	20
"Every Breath You Take" — Police	13	20
"Billie Jean" — Michael Jackson	11	17
"I Love Rock 'n Roll" — Joan Jett & The Blackhearts	12	16
"Ebony and Ivory" — Paul McCartney & Stevie Wonder	12	15
"Flashdance ... What a Feeling" — Irene Cara	14	20
"Centerfold" — J. Geils Band	12	20
"Lady" — Kenny Rogers	13	19
"Call Me" — Blondie	12	19
"Eye of the Tiger" — Survivor	15	18
"Say Say Say" — Paul McCartney & Michael Jackson	13	18
"(Just Like) Starting Over" — John Lennon	14	19
"When Doves Cry" — Prince	11	16
"Jump" — Van Halen	10	15
"Total Eclipse of the Heart" — Bonnie Tyler	11	18
"Upside Down" — Diana Ross	14	17
"Another Brick in the Wall (part II)" — Pink Floyd	12	19
"Down Under" — Men At Work	10	19
"Rock with You" — Michael Jackson	9	19
"All Night Long (All Night)" — Lionel Richie	13	17
"Maneater" — Daryl Hall & John Oates	13	17
"Magic" — Olivia Newton-John	9	16
"Funkytown" — Lipps, Inc.	9	15

Source: *The Billboard Book of Top 40 Hits*, 1985.

1. Construct a scatter plot, putting weeks in the Top 40 on the vertical axis and weeks in the Top 10 on the horizontal axis.

2. Next divide the data into three groups. There are 25 points, so we would like to have three groups of 8, 9, and 8 points. However, notice that there are many records that are tied with the same Top 10 values.

For the right group, if we include records 14 or more weeks in the Top 10, we would have 6 points. If we include records 13 or more weeks in the Top 10, we would have 12 points. In order to have enough points remaining to put into the other two groups, it seems reasonable to make the right group consist of the 6 records with 14 or more weeks in the Top 10. Decide how to form the left and center groups.

3. Using these three groups, fit the line to these data.

4. If a record stayed in the Top 10 for ten weeks, about how long would it stay in the Top 40?

5. Which records are farthest from the line? Did they spend a relatively long or short time in the Top 40 compared to their time in the Top 10? Can you think of any reasons?

6. Write a paragraph that summarizes these data.

52 Men in an Insurance Office

The following table lists the heights, shoe sizes, and weights for 52 men in an office. These weights and heights were discussed earlier, on pages 125 to 129. Now we will consider shoe size against height to see if this relationship is similar to or different from the relationship with weight and height.

Height	Shoe Size	Weight	Height	Shoe Size	Weight
70	10.5	195	73	10	190
68	10.5	195	70	9.5	180
69	8.5	152	72	9	168
72	10.5	185	72	10	193
72	10	180	74	12	175
73	9.5	189	71	9	160
74	11	180	72	9.5	163
70	10	180	73	10.5	175
72	9.5	155	72	10	235
73	11	180	71	12	230
68	7	150	69	9.5	220
72	10	195	75	12	252
66	7	135	68	10	175
67	8.5	178	76	13	250
68	9	143	69	9	190
69	10	190	70	10	170
70	9.5	170	73	10	230
73	10.5	205	73	11.5	195
73	10	180	72	9.5	190
67	8.5	140	66	8.5	170
72	10	165	68	8.5	130
70	10	190	73	10.5	166
70	9.5	178	78	13	207
73.5	11	210	66	8.5	180
71.5	10	145	71	9	170
68	9	176	69	9	155

1. Construct a scatter plot of shoe size against height. Put height on the horizontal axis. There are several men with exactly the same height and shoe size. For example, 5 men have the same height of 72" and the same shoe size of 10, so there should be a 5 at that position on the plot. At first, you will want to make the scatter plot lightly with pencil so you can change the dots to numerals as necessary.

2. Use the method that was given to fit a line to these points. (Since there are many repeated heights on the horizontal axis, you will want the three groups to have 16, 21, and 15 points, from left to right.) Does the line fit well?

3. What shoe size would you predict for a man 66" tall? For a man 76" tall? About how many additional inches of height are needed for a man's predicted shoe size to increase by one whole size?

4. Draw lines 1-1/2 shoe sizes above and 1-1/2 shoe sizes below the fitted line. Are there many points falling outside this range? Are they primarily above the top line or below the bottom line?

5. Are there any outlying points in the plot that do not follow the relationship given by the fitted line?

6. Compare the plot of shoe size against height with the earlier plot of weight against height. Which plot indicates a closer, tighter relationship? Does this surprise you? Can you think of any explanation for this?

Fitted Straight Lines — Clustering and Curvature

In the previous section there were many scatter plots that can be appropriately fitted with straight lines. However, don't assume that it is always appropriate to fit a straight line to a scatter plot. Sometimes the points simply do not lie near a single straight line. Two possibilities are that the data could be *clustered* into two or more groups in the scatter plot or that the data might fall near a *curved* (not straight) line.

How can we tell if there is clustering or curvature, and what should we do about them? Look at the scatter plot as a whole, as you did in Section VI, to see if you observe clusters or a curved relationship. Sometimes clusters or curvature are more obvious after a straight line has been fitted. Always look at a plot again after fitting a line to see if something is apparent that wasn't before.

In some cases, a straight line fits well within one of the clusters but not to all the data. Then you can use this line for prediction or summary within the range of data corresponding to the cluster, but don't use a single line that is fitted to all the data. Sometimes you might fit two separate straight lines to different parts of the data. These lines can help you see that a single straight line does not fit well and that a curve might be better. Of course, you might decide instead that no straight or curved line fits well and none should be used for prediction or summary. This could be the best answer.

The following two applications have scatter plots containing clustering and curvature. For these plots it is best not to interpret the data in terms of a single straight line fit.

Telephone Office Costs (Clustering)

The following scatter plot involves some engineering data. The horizontal axis gives the number of telephone lines that can be handled by each of 20 telephone switching offices. (A telephone switching office is the place that local telephone calls pass through and one customer is connected to another.) The vertical axis gives an estimate of the total cost of constructing the office. The cost depends on more than just the number of telephone lines. Each point in the scatter plot represents one telephone switching office. The horizontal value is the number of telephone lines into the office and the vertical value is the total cost. We want to study the scatter plot to learn whether or not there is a close relationship between cost and capacity for these switching offices.

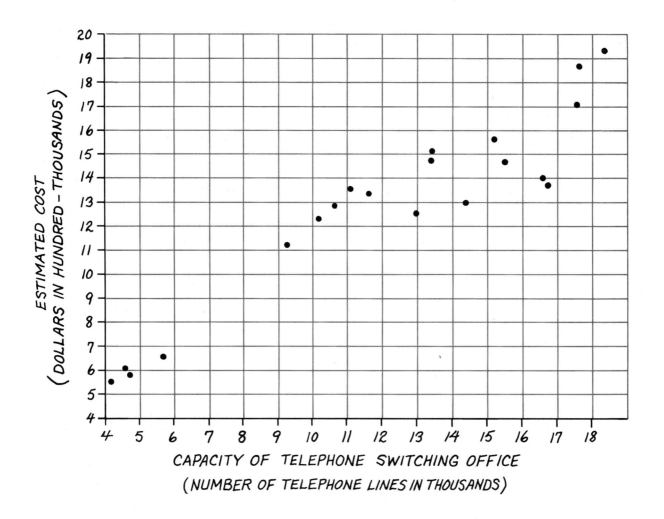

The first general impression is that there is a large gap in the data, giving two separate groups of switching offices. The bottom four offices are all separated by over 3,000 lines from the smallest of the other 16. You might think that the topmost three points should also be treated as a separate cluster. Perhaps they should be, but the gap on the horizontal axis here is definitely smaller, only about 1,000 lines. Thus, as a first step, it seems sensible to treat the data as two clusters rather than one or three.

The data values for the 20 offices are listed in the following table. You will need to construct or trace a scatter plot such as the preceding one to answer the following questions.

Switching Office Capacity (lines)	Estimated Cost	Switching Office Capacity (lines)	Estimated Cost
4,200	$560,000	13,200	$1,470,000
4,600	610,000	13,300	1,510,000
4,700	580,000	14,400	1,300,000
5,700	660,000	15,200	1,580,000
9,300	1,120,000	15,500	1,480,000
10,200	1,230,000	16,700	1,400,000
10,700	1,270,000	16,800	1,370,000
11,100	1,360,000	17,600	1,710,000
11,600	1,340,000	17,700	1,870,000
13,000	1,250,000	18,400	1,930,000

1. For an office with 5,000 telephone lines, what cost would you estimate? Do not fit any straight line. Just scan the plot to get an estimate.

2. Fit a straight line to the cluster of 16 larger offices.

3. For offices of about 18,000 telephone lines, what cost does this line predict?

4. Extend the fitted line to the extreme left of the plot. What would it predict as the cost for an office of size 5,000?

5. How well does the line fit the four observations with small capacity? For what size offices does the fitted line give reasonable estimates of cost?

Tree Age and Diameter (Curvature)

The table below lists 27 chestnut oak trees planted on a poor site with their ages and diameters at chest height. We would like to determine how their size increases with age.

Age in Years	Diameter at Chest Height in Inches
4	0.8
5	0.8
8	1.0
8	2.0
8	3.0
10	2.0
10	3.5
12	4.9
13	3.5
14	2.5
16	4.5
18	4.6
20	5.5
22	5.8
23	4.7
25	6.5
28	6.0
29	4.5
30	6.0
30	7.0
33	8.0
34	6.5
35	7.0
38	5.0
38	7.0
40	7.5
42	7.5

Source: Chapman and Demeritt, *Elements of Forest Mensuration.*

1. Make a scatter plot of these data. We want to predict diameter given age. Which variable will you put on the horizontal axis?

2. Divide the points into three strips. Mark the three X's and draw in the fitted line.

3. Do the three X's lie very close to a single straight line?

4. In the left strip, how many points are

   a. above the line?

   b. below the line?

5. In the center strip, how many points are

    a. above the line?

    b. below the line?

6. In the right strip, how many points are

    a. above the line?

    b. below the line?

There are too many points above the line in the center strip and too many points below the line in both end strips. This means that a single straight line does not fit these data well. A curved line would summarize these data better. There are more complicated statistical methods for fitting a curve to data, but we won't investigate them. You could draw a free-hand curve through the middle of the data.

7. The fact that the points lie on a curved line tells us that trees do not grow at the same rate over their lifetime. Does the diameter increase at a faster rate when the tree is young or old?

Lines on Scatter Plots — Summary

The scatter plot is the basic method for learning about relationships between two variables. Sometimes interpretations are clear simply from studying the scatter plot. This section has dealt with problems where the interpretation becomes clearer by adding a straight line to the plot.

The method of adding the 45° line ($y = x$ line) through the points (0, 0), (1, 1), (2, 2), and so forth and then observing on which side of this line most points lie can assist us in learning whether the variable on the horizontal axis or the variable on the vertical axis is generally larger. This method does not require fitting a line to the data.

In some examples it is helpful to fit a straight line through the central part of the data. We have used a method based on medians. This method is not greatly affected by a few outlying points. If the data follow a straight-line relationship, the method described gives a line that fits the data closely. Moreover, looking at the data in terms of the three X's and the straight line can help us to recognize examples where the data do not fit a single straight line. These situations, such as clustering and curvature, need to be dealt with differently.

The critical feature about the 45° line and the fitted straight line is not just the method of constructing them. As with all the other methods in this book, their purpose is to assist you in the interpretation and analysis of the data. These straight lines can help identify interesting and important data points, find and summarize relationships between the variables, and predict the variable on the vertical axis from the variable on the horizontal axis.

Student Project

1. Take the scatter plots you made on your projects from Section VI and add straight lines when appropriate. Do the lines change any of your interpretations?

VIII. SMOOTHING PLOTS OVER TIME

The following table lists the American League home run champions from 1921 to 1985.

Year	American League	HR	Year	American League	HR
1921	Babe Ruth, New York	59	1957	Roy Sievers, Washington	42
1922	Ken Williams, St. Louis	39	1958	Mickey Mantle, New York	42
1923	Babe Ruth, New York	41	1959	Rocky Colavito, Cleveland	42
1924	Babe Ruth, New York	46		Harmon Killebrew, Washington	
1925	Bob Meusel, New York	33	1960	Mickey Mantle, New York	40
1926	Babe Ruth, New York	47	1961	Roger Maris, New York	61
1927	Babe Ruth, New York	60	1962	Harmon Killebrew, Minnesota	48
1928	Babe Ruth, New York	54	1963	Harmon Killebrew, Minnesota	45
1929	Babe Ruth, New York	46	1964	Harmon Killebrew, Minnesota	49
1930	Babe Ruth, New York	49	1965	Tony Conigliaro, Boston	32
1931	Babe Ruth, New York	46	1966	Frank Robinson, Baltimore	49
	Lou Gehrig, New York		1967	Carl Yastrzemski, Boston	44
1932	Jimmy Foxx, Philadelphia	58		Harmon Killebrew, Minnesota	
1933	Jimmy Foxx, Philadelphia	48	1968	Frank Howard, Washington	44
1934	Lou Gehrig, New York	49	1969	Harmon Killebrew, Minnesota	49
1935	Jimmy Foxx, Philadelphia	36	1970	Frank Howard, Washington	44
	Hank Greenberg, Detroit		1971	Bill Melton, Chicago	33
1936	Lou Gehrig, New York	49	1972	Dick Allen, Chicago	37
1937	Joe DiMaggio, New York	46	1973	Reggie Jackson, Oakland	32
1938	Hank Greenberg, Detroit	58	1974	Dick Allen, Chicago	32
1939	Jimmy Foxx, Boston	35	1975	George Scott, Milwaukee	36
1940	Hank Greenberg, Detroit	41		Reggie Jackson, Oakland	
1941	Ted Williams, Boston	37	1976	Graig Nettles, New York	32
1942	Ted Williams, Boston	36	1977	Jim Rice, Boston	39
1943	Rudy York, Detroit	34	1978	Jim Rice, Boston	46
1944	Nick Etten, New York	22	1979	Gorman Thomas, Milwaukee	45
1945	Vern Stephens, St. Louis	24	1980	Reggie Jackson, New York	41
1946	Hank Greenberg, Detroit	44		Ben Oglivie, Milwaukee	
1947	Ted Williams, Boston	32	1981	Bobby Grich, California	22
1948	Joe DiMaggio, New York	39		Tony Armas, Oakland	
1949	Ted Williams, Boston	43		Dwight Evans, Boston	
1950	Al Rosen, Cleveland	37		Eddie Murray, Baltimore	
1951	Gus Zernial, Chicago-Philadelphia	33	1982	Gorman Thomas, Milwaukee	39
1952	Larry Doby, Cleveland	32		Reggie Jackson, California	
1953	Al Rosen, Cleveland	43	1983	Jim Rice, Boston	39
1954	Larry Doby, Cleveland	32	1984	Tony Armas, Boston	43
1955	Mickey Mantle, New York	37	1985	Darrell Evans, Detroit	40
1956	Mickey Mantle, New York	52			

Source: *The World Almanac and Book of Facts,* 1985 edition.

From this list it is difficult to see any general trends in the number of home runs through the years. To try to determine the general trends, we will make a scatter plot over time of the number of home runs hit by the champions and connect these points.

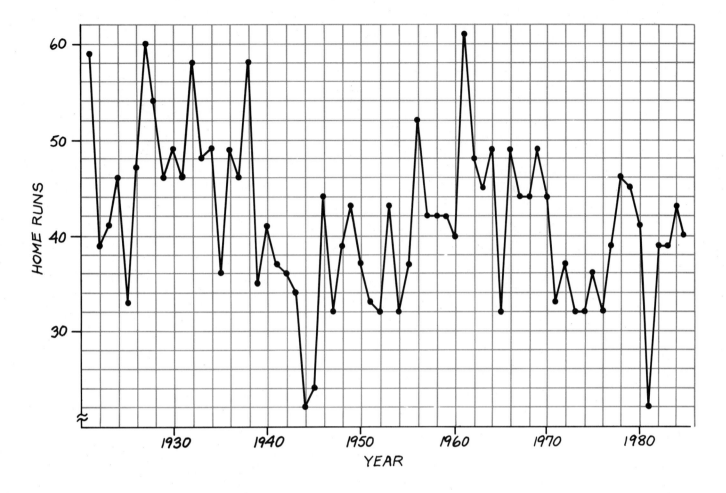

This scatter plot looks all jumbled up! It is impossible to see general trends because of the large fluctuations in the number of home runs hit from year to year. For example, 58 home runs were hit in 1938 compared to only 35 the next year. This variation gives the plot a sawtooth effect. The highs and lows, not the overall pattern, capture our attention. To remove the large fluctuations from the data, we will use a method called *smoothing*.

To illustrate, the smoothed version of the first ten years of the home run champions' data follows.

Year	Home Runs	Smoothed Values
1921	59	59
1922	39	41
1923	41	41
1924	46	41
1925	33	46
1926	47	47
1927	60	54
1928	54	54
1929	46	49
1930	49	46
1931	46	

139

To find the smoothed value for 1924, for example, the 46 home runs for that year are compared to the number of home runs for the year before, 41, and the number of home runs for the following year, 33. The median of the three numbers, 41, is entered into the smoothed values column.

For the first and last years, just copy the original data into the smoothed values column.

The plot of the connected smoothed values follows. Notice what has happened to the large fluctuation between 1938 and 1939. Since this plot is smoother than the previous one, we can see general trends better, such as the drop in the number of home runs in the 1940's.

Discussion Questions

1. Complete the smoothed value column through 1940 for the next ten American League home run champions.

2. Study the smoothed plot of the American League home run champions.

   a. What happened around 1940 that could have affected the number of home runs hit?

   b. Did the increase in the number of games from 154 to 162 in 1961 have an effect on the number of home runs hit?

3. Study the following rule changes. Do any of them seem to have affected the number of home runs hit by the champions?

   1926 — A ball hit over a fence that is less than 250 feet from home plate will not be counted as a home run.

   1931 — A fair ball that bounces over a fence will be counted as a double instead of a home run.

   1959 — New ballparks must have a minimum distance of 325 feet down the foul lines and 400 feet in center field.

   1969 — The strike zone is decreased in size to include only the area from the armpit to the top of the knee.

   1969 — The pitcher's mound is lowered, giving an advantage to the hitter.

   1971 — All batters must wear helmets.

4. In 1981 there was a strike that shortened the season. Can this be seen in the original data? In the smoothed values?

5. Since they were not smoothed, the endpoints may appear to be out of place. The number of home runs hit in 1921 seems too high. Can you determine a better rule for deciding what to write in the smoothed values column for the endpoints?

6. Imagine a curve through the smoothed values. Try to predict the number of home runs hit in 1986.

7. Some students feel that smoothing is not a legitimate method. For example, they do not like changing the original 33 home runs in 1925 to 46 home runs on the plot of smoothed values. Write a description of the trends that are visible in the smoothed plot that are not easily seen in the original plot. Try to convince a reluctant fellow student that smoothing is valuable. Then study the following answer. Did you mention features we omitted?

   The original plot of the time series for home runs gives a very jagged appearance. There were values that were quite large for two years in the 1920's, two years in the 1930's, and also in 1961. Extremely low values occurred in the mid-1940's and in 1981. Using this plot, it is difficult to evaluate overall trends. However, the values in the 1940's and early 1950's seem lower than the values in the late 1920's and 1930's.

   We get a stronger impression of trends from the smoothed plot of the home run data. In particular, for the years from 1927 to 1935, the values are generally higher than at any other time before or since. The only period that was nearly comparable was in the early 1960's. The original data show that the champions causing the earlier values to be large were Babe Ruth, Jimmy Foxx, and Lou Gehrig. In the 1960's, it was Roger Maris and Harmon Killebrew. These players clearly were outstanding home run hitters!

There was a steady decline in home runs from the late 1930's to a low period in the middle 1940's. There were also low periods in the early 1950's and in the early 1970's. It is interesting that these lows coincide roughly with World War II, the Korean War, and the Viet Nam War. These wars might be possible causes for the declines, although we have not proved this simply through observing this association. The values for the years since 1980 are near the middle compared to the whole 65-year series. The smoothed series has removed some of the individual highs (such as Maris' 61 in 1961) and lows (such as the 22 in the strike-shortened 1981 season). Therefore, the longer trends stand out more clearly.

Application 35

Birth Months

The following table gives the number of babies born in the United States for each month of 1984. The numbers are in thousands.

Month	Births (thousands)	Smoothed Values
January	314	
February	289	
March	291	
April	302	
May	296	
June	297	
July	336	
August	323	
September	329	
October	316	
November	292	
December	311	

Source: National Center for Health Statistics.

1. How many babies were born in May 1984?

2. In which month were the most babies born?

The time series plot for these data is given as follows. This plot is a good candidate for smoothing because of the sawtooth effect. This appearance is an indication that some points are unusually large or small.

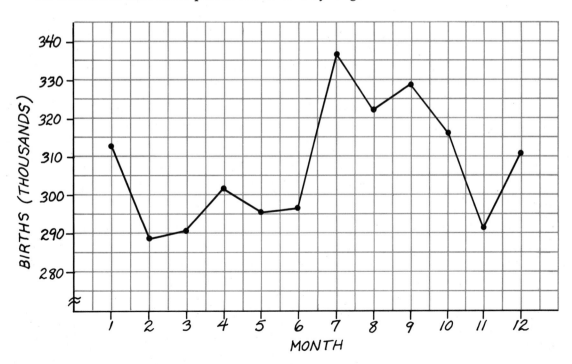

3. Copy and complete the "Smoothed Values" column.

4. Make a scatter plot of the smoothed values.

5. What is the general trend in the number of babies born throughout the year?

Application 36

Olympic Marathon

The following table shows the winning times for the marathon run (slightly more than 26 miles) in the 1896-1984 Olympics. The times are rounded to the nearest minute.

Year	Winner Name, Country	Time		Time in Minutes	Smoothed Values
1896	Loues, Greece	2 hours	59 minutes	179	
1900	Teato, France	3	0	180	
1904	Hicks, U.S.A.	3	29	209	
1908	Hayes, U.S.A.	2	55	175	
1912	McArthur, South Africa	2	37	157	
1920	Kolehmainen, Finland	2	33	153	
1924	Stenroos, Finland	2	41	161	
1928	El Ouafi, France	2	33	153	
1932	Zabala, Argentina	2	32	152	
1936	Son, Japan	2	29	149	
1948	Cabrera, Argentina	2	35		
1952	Zatopek, Czechoslovakia	2	23		
1956	Mimoun, France	2	25		
1960	Bikila, Ethiopia	2	15		
1964	Bikila, Ethiopia	2	12		
1968	Wolde, Ethiopia	2	20		
1972	Shorter, U.S.A.	2	12		
1976	Cierpinski, East Germany	2	10		
1980	Cierpinski, East Germany	2	11		
1984	Lopes, Portugal	2	9		

Source: *The World Almanac and Book of Facts,* 1985 edition.

1. The first Olympic women's marathon was not held until 1984. The winner was Joan Benoit of the United States with a time of 2 hours 25 minutes. What was the first year that a Olympic men's marathon winner was able to beat this time?

2. Find the three years when the Olympics were not held. Why were the Olympics not held in these years?

3. Complete the second to the last column of the previous table by converting each time to minutes. The first ten are done for you.

A plot over time with year on the horizontal axis and time in minutes on the vertical axis is shown as follows:

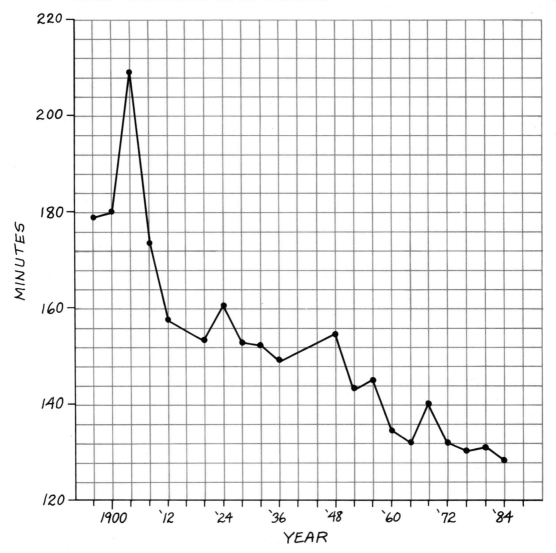

4. What trends do you see in this plot?

5. On the time series plot, which year is farthest from the general trend?

6. Complete the last column of the previous table by smoothing the "time in minutes" column.

7. Construct a plot over time for the smoothed values.

8. Study your plot over time for the smoothed values.

   a. When did the largest drop in time occur?

   b. What do you predict for the winning time in the 1988 Olympic marathon?

   c. Describe the patterns shown on your plot in a short paragraph.

Application 37

Tennis Earnings

The following two tables from *Tennis Championships Magazine* list the top tennis players of each sex and their earnings from tennis tournaments in the first part of 1985.

The Top 32 Women

Name	Birthplace	Height	Weight	Age	Computer Ranking	1985 Earnings
Chris Evert Lloyd	Ft. Lauderdale, FL	5'6"	118	30	1	$652,269
Martina Navratilova	Czechoslovakia	5'7"	145	28	2	994,579
Hana Mandlikova	Czechoslovakia	5'8"	130	23	3	294,872
Pam Shriver	Baltimore, MD	5'11"	130	23	4	244,653
Manuela Maleeva	Bulgaria	5'6"	114	18	5	115,113
Helena Sukova	Czechoslovakia	6'1"	139	20	6	261,512
Zina Garrison	Houston, TX	5'4"	128	21	7	162,732
Claudia Kohde-Kilsch	West Germany	6'0"	140	21	8	181,995
Wendy Turnbull	Australia	5'4"	120	32	9	104,795
Kathy Rinaldi	Stuart, FL	5'5"	110	18	10	120,315
Bonnie Gadusek	Pittsburgh, PA	5'6"	120	21	11	88,097
Steffi Graf	West Germany	5'5"	110	16	12	81,872
Catarina Lindqvist	Sweden	5'5"	125	22	13	107,805
Gabriela Sabatini	Argentina	5'7"	121	15	14	85,405
Carling Bassett	Canada	5'5"	118	17	15	113,173
Barbara Potter	Waterbury, CT	5'9"	135	23	16	82,949
Kathy Jordan	Bryn Mawr, PA	5'8"	130	25	17	149,763
Bettina Bunge	Switzerland	5'7"	120	22	18	72,090
Sylvia Hanika	West Germany	5'8"	128	25	19	32,310
Andrea Temesvari	Hungary	5'11"	125	19	20	49,810
Alycia Moulton	Sacramento, CA	5'11"	145	24	21	58,735
Peanut Louie	San Francisco, CA	5'5"	115	25	22	48,850
Pam Casale	Camden, NJ	5'8"	127	21	23	43,965
Gigi Fernandez	Puerto Rico	5'7"	140	21	24	56,850
Kathleen Horvath	Chicago, IL	5'7"	115	20	25	68,962
Michelle Torres	Chicago, IL	5'5"	107	18	26	10,950
Elise Burgin	Baltimore, MD	5'4"	115	23	27	68,806
Katerina Maleeva	Bulgaria	5'5"	110	16	28	54,897
Rosalyn Fairbank	South Africa	5'8"	140	24	29	81,301
Catherine Tanvier	France	5'8"	116	20	30	45,660
Virginia Ruzici	Romania	5'8"	128	30	31	49,757
Pascale Paradis	France	5'9"	135	19	32	42,017

Source: *Tennis Championships Magazine.*

The Top 32 Men

Name	Birthplace	Height	Weight	Age	Computer Ranking	1985 Earnings
John McEnroe	West Germany	5'11"	165	26	1	$618,852
Ivan Lendl	Czechoslovakia	6'2"	175	25	2	609,283
Mats Wilander	Sweden	6'1"	175	21	3	416,037
Jimmy Connors	Belleville, IL	5'10"	155	32	4	375,291
Kevin Curren	South Africa	6'1"	170	27	5	193,422
Anders Jarryd	Sweden	5'11"	155	24	6	248,133
Yannick Noah	France	6'4"	180	25	7	202,899
Andres Gomez	Ecuador	6'3"	190	25	8	99,794
Boris Becker	West Germany	6'2"	173	17	9	278,207
Joakim Nystrom	Sweden	6'2"	155	22	10	192,583
Stefan Edberg	Sweden	6'2"	158	19	11	169,920
Eliot Teltscher	Palos Verdes, CA	5'10"	150	26	12	81,092
Miloslav Mecir	Czechoslovakia	6'3"	180	21	13	209,172
Johan Kriek	South Africa	5'8"	155	27	14	151,991
Pat Cash	Australia	5'11"	170	20	15	123,244
Tim Mayotte	Springfield, MA	6'3"	180	25	16	255,174
Scott Davis	Santa Monica, CA	6'2"	170	22	17	126,324
Henrik Sundstrom	Sweden	6'2"	160	21	18	140,122
Tomas Smid	Czechoslovakia	6'3"	175	29	19	220,043
Brad Gilbert	Oakland, CA	6'1"	160	24	20	92,667
Martin Jaite	Argentina	5'11"	150	20	21	104,985
David Pate	Los Angeles, CA	6'0"	170	23	22	84,798
Aaron Krickstein	Ann Arbor, MI	5'10"	150	18	23	110,965
Greg Holmes	Covina, CA	5'10"	160	21	24	56,092
Vitas Gerulaitis	Brooklyn, NY	6'0"	155	31	25	54,329
Libor Pimek	Czechoslovakia	6'5"	172	22	26	61,542
Henri Leconte	France	6'1"	160	22	27	101,690
Jose Luis Clerc	Argentina	6'1"	176	27	28	46,356
Jan Gunnarsson	Sweden	6'0"	165	23	29	81,694
Ben Testerman	Knoxville, TN	6'3"	180	23	30	40,557
Sammy Giammalva	Houston, TX	5'10"	165	22	31	78,873
Jimmy Arias	Buffalo, NY	5'9"	145	21	32	79,941

Source: *Tennis Championships Magazine.*

Do this activity in pairs, with one of you taking the data for men and the other the data for women. After you each answer questions separately for your players, you will put your plots together to compare the women's earnings with the men's. You will need to coordinate with your partner so you both use the same size graph paper.

1. Construct a plot over time of the earnings against the computer ranking for your players. Begin by plotting the 32 values as dots; do not connect them with lines. Because the first few men and women earned so much more than the rest, a vertical axis that includes all the earnings would result in most of the earnings being too close together at the bottom. Instead, make the vertical axis from $0 to $400,000. For those

players who earned more than this, just write in their numbers at the top.

2. In the earlier examples, to get the smoothed earnings we constructed a column of smoothed values and then plotted them. This time we will save a step and do this directly on the plot. For each rank, plot an X at the median of the three earnings from that rank, the next lower rank, and the next higher rank. (You might also want to use a different color from the dots for the X's to help distinguish the actual earnings from the smoothed earnings.)

3. Connect the X's by lines. This gives a smooth curve relating the 1985 earnings to the computer rankings.

4. Name any players that have earned a relatively large amount, or a relatively small amount, considering their ranking. Can you think of any reasons for this to happen?

5. The earnings generally decrease as the computer ranking increases. Do the earnings decrease more quickly for the very top ranked players or for the lower ranked players?

6. Give an estimate of how much money you would expect the player who is fifth ranked in 1986 to earn in the corresponding part of 1986.

To answer the remaining questions, work with your partner so you have plots for both men and women.

7. Is smoothing more helpful for the men's data or the women's data to get a useful picture of how earnings relate to rank?

8. Which top tennis players earn more, men or women? To compare the earnings, it helps to place the two plots on top of each other and hold them up to a light. Write a paragraph summarizing how the women's and men's earnings compare.

Advanced Smoothing (Optional)

Often the smoothing method we have just used will give a smooth curve. Sometimes, however, it will still have fluctuations in it that can hide overall trends. In these cases, we will want to smooth the data a little bit more.

For example, in the plot of smoothed values for the American League home run leaders on page 140, the points for the years 1927, 1928, 1944, and 1945 are separated from the general trend. They still give that sawtooth appearance that obscures the overall pattern. A simple method for further smoothing is described in the following paragraphs.

One result of what we did to the first ten years of American League home run data was to make some short strings where adjacent values are equal. For example, the smoothed values for 1922 to 1924 are all 41. One possibility is to treat such "horizontal ties" as single points, and then do the smoothing a second time.

To illustrate, the data for the first ten years, the first smoothed values, and the second smoothed values are listed in the following table.

Year	Home Runs	First Smoothed Values	Second Smoothed Values
1921	59	59	59
1922	39	41	46
1923	41	41	46
1924	46	41	46
1925	33	46	46
1926	47	47	47
1927	60	54	49
1928	54	54	49
1929	46	49	49
1930	49	46	

To find the second smoothed values, we use only the first smoothed values. For the first year, 1921, the value is simply retained. For 1922, we treat the three adjacent 41's as a single value and find the median of 59, 41, and 46, which is 46. For 1923 and 1924, we have the median of 59, 41, and 46 again. For 1925, use the median of 41, 46, and 47. For 1926, use the median of 46, 47, and 54. Use the median of 47, 54, and 49 for 1927 and 1928. For 1929, use the median of 54, 49, and 46.

The plot of the second smoothed values follows. Notice that these smoothed values show the overall trends somewhat more clearly than the earlier smoothed values. Almost all the points that lie far away from the others have been smoothed away. It is now easy to imagine a smooth curve that connects most of the points.

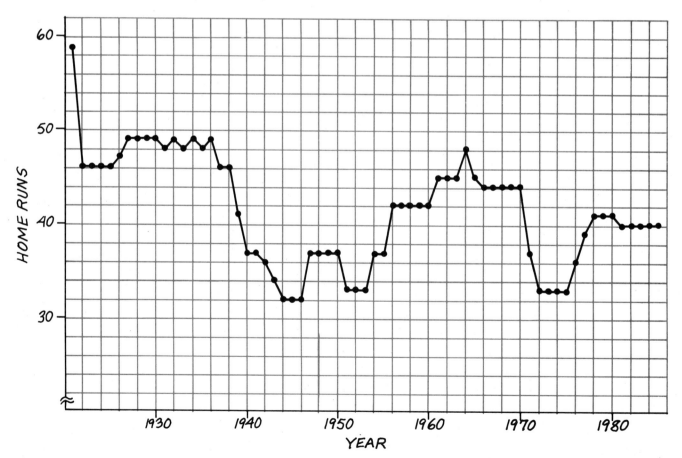

Discussion Questions

1. Complete the next ten values in the second column of smoothed values for the American League home run champions.

2. Which period had the most home runs? Who was responsible for this occurrence?

3. When were the periods of fewest home runs? What was happening during these years?

4. Compare the original home run champions' data to the smoother curve just shown. Which champions differed the most from the value of the overall trend when they played?

This same smoothing process can be repeated to get third smoothed values that are even smoother than the second ones. Using the second smoothed values and the same exact method that was used to calculate the second smoothed values from the first smoothed values, you can calculate the third smoothed values. The effect will be to remove even more of the "bumpiness." For these particular data, the third smoothed values will remove the small peak in 1947-1950 and lower the peak in 1964.

National League Home Run Champions (Optional)

The following table lists the National League home run champions.

	National League		
Year		HR	First Smoothed Values
1921	George Kelly, New York	23	23
1922	Rogers Hornsby, St. Louis	42	41
1923	Cy Williams, Philadelphia	41	41
1924	Jacques Foumier, Brooklyn	27	39
1925	Rogers Hornsby, St. Louis	39	27
1926	Hack Wilson, Chicago	21	30
1927	Hack Wilson, Chicago Cy Williams, Philadelphia	30	30
1928	Hack Wilson, Chicago Jim Bottomley, St. Louis	31	31
1929	Charles Klein, Philadelphia	43	43
1930	Hack Wilson, Chicago	56	43
1931	Charles Klein, Philadelphia	31	38
1932	Charles Klein, Philadelphia Mel Ott, New York	38	31
1933	Charles Klein, Philadelphia	28	35
1934	Rip Collins, St. Louis Mel Ott, New York	35	34
1935	Walter Berger, Boston	34	34
1936	Mel Ott, New York	33	33
1937	Mel Ott, New York Joe Medwick, St. Louis	31	33
1938	Mel Ott, New York	36	31
1939	John Mize, St. Louis	28	36
1940	John Mize, St. Louis	43	34
1941	Dolph Camilli, Brooklyn	34	34
1942	Mel Ott, New York	30	30
1943	Bill Nicholson, Chicago	29	30
1944	Bill Nicholson, Chicago	33	29
1945	Tommy Holmes, Boston	28	28
1946	Ralph Kiner, Pittsburgh	23	28
1947	Ralph Kiner, Pittsburgh John Mize, New York	51	40
1948	Ralph Kiner, Pittsburgh John Mize, New York	40	51
1949	Ralph Kiner, Pittsburgh	54	47
1950	Ralph Kiner, Pittsburgh	47	47
1951	Ralph Kiner, Pittsburgh	42	42

Source: *The World Almanac and Book of Facts,* 1985 edition.

Year	National League	HR	First Smoothed Values
1952	Ralph Kiner, Pittsburgh Hank Sauer, Chicago	37	42
1953	Ed Mathews, Milwaukee	47	47
1954	Ted Kluszewski, Cincinnati	49	49
1955	Willie Mays, New York	51	49
1956	Duke Snider, Brooklyn	43	44
1957	Hank Aaron, Milwaukee	44	44
1958	Ernie Banks, Chicago	47	46
1959	Ed Mathews, Milwaukee	46	46
1960	Ernie Banks, Chicago	41	46
1961	Orlando Cepeda, San Francisco	46	46
1962	Willie Mays, San Francisco	49	46
1963	Hank Aaron, Milwaukee Willie McCovey, San Francisco	44	47
1964	Willie Mays, San Francisco	47	47
1965	Willie Mays, San Francisco	52	47
1966	Hank Aaron, Atlanta	44	44
1967	Hank Aaron, Atlanta	39	39
1968	Willie McCovey, San Francisco	36	39
1969	Willie McCovey, San Francisco	45	45
1970	Johnny Bench, Cincinnati	45	45
1971	Willie Stargell, Pittsburgh	48	45
1972	Johnny Bench, Cincinnati	40	44
1973	Willie Stargell, Pittsburgh	44	40
1974	Mike Schmidt, Philadelphia	36	38
1975	Mike Schmidt, Philadelphia	38	38
1976	Mike Schmidt, Philadelphia	38	38
1977	George Foster, Cincinnati	52	40
1978	George Foster, Cincinnati	40	48
1979	Dave Kingman, Chicago	48	48
1980	Mike Schmidt, Philadelphia	48	48
1981	Mike Schmidt, Philadelphia	31	37
1982	Dave Kingman, New York	37	37
1983	Mike Schmidt, Philadelphia	40	37
1984	Mike Schmidt, Philadelphia Dale Murphy, Atlanta	36	37
1985	Dale Murphy, Atlanta	37	37

Source: *The World Almanac and Book of Facts,* 1985 edition.

1. Which player hit the largest number of home runs in a season?

2. Which player was champion for the most seasons?

A plot over time of the number of home runs follows:

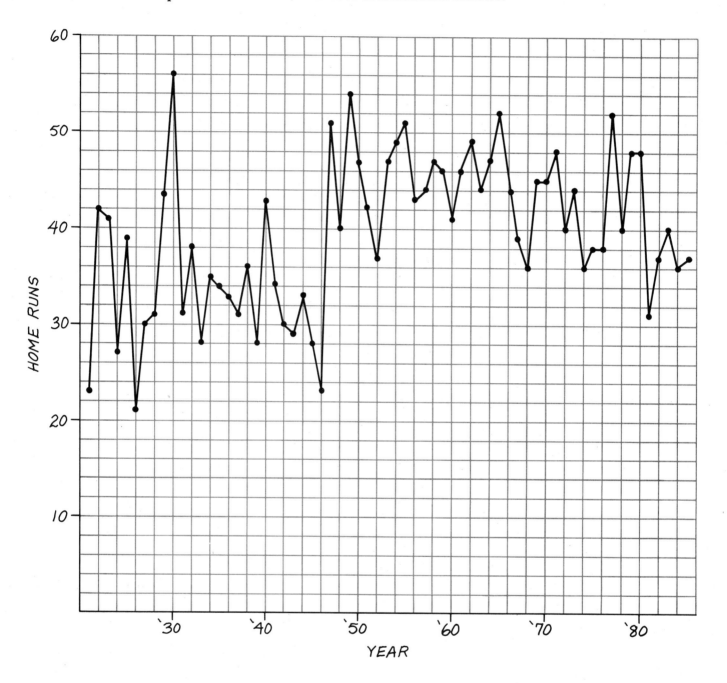

3. From this plot, it is easy to spot unusually high or low years. Which years stand out as the most unusual?

A plot over time of the smoothed values follows:

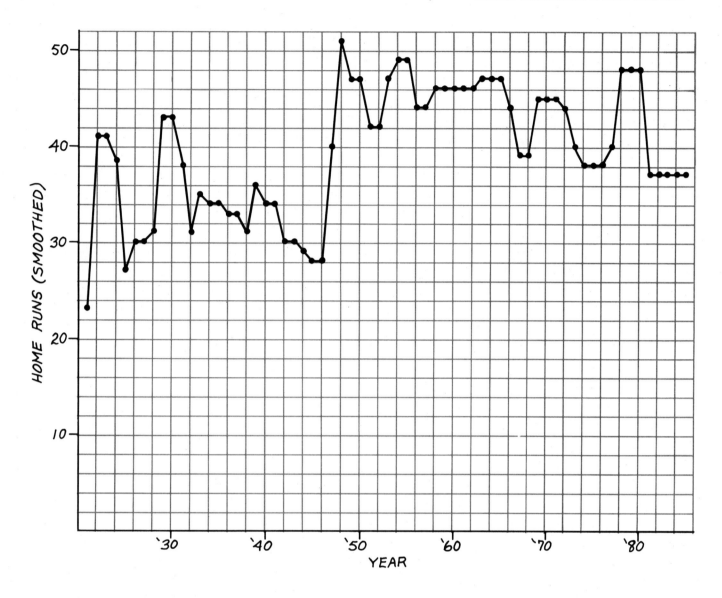

4. Is there a dip in the early 1940's (during World War II) as there was for the American League?

5. Are there any other especially noticeable trends in this plot?

6. This is an example where a second smoothing might be useful for spotting overall trends. Using the method described just before this application, use the column of first smoothed values and add a column of second smoothed values.

7. Construct a plot over time using the second smoothed values.

8. What has been happening to the number of home runs since 1950?

9. How did the numbers of home runs in the 1920's and 1930's compare to the numbers in the 1960's and 1970's?

10. Do you think that the second smoothed value for 1921 is reasonable? Try to invent a method to smooth endpoints.

11. When did the largest increase in home runs occur?

12. What do you think was the winning number of home runs in 1986?

13. For which year is the actual data value the farthest above the second smoothed value? For which year is the data value the farthest below the second smoothed value?

14. Compare the second smoothed curve for the American League home runs with the second smoothed curve for the National League. What is one way that these curves are similar? What is one way that they are different?

15. Since 1960, are the trends in both leagues about the same?

Smoothing Plots Over Time — Summary

Smoothing is a technique that can be used with time series data where the horizontal axis is marked off in years, days, hours, ages, and so forth. We can use medians to obtain smoothed values, and these smoothed values can remove much of the sawtooth effect often seen in time series data. As a result, a clearer picture of where values are increasing and decreasing emerges.

Many students feel uncomfortable with smoothing. Try to think of it in the same way you think about computing, say, a mean. When you average your test scores in math, the original scores disappear and you are left with one number that summarizes how well you did overall. It is a similar idea with smoothing. Some of the original data disappear and you are left with a summary of overall trends.

Suggestions for Student Projects

1. If any of the scatter plots from your projects in Section VI were plots over time, smooth those plots. Does this show any of the trends more clearly than before?

2. Collect some time series data that interest you and analyze these data according to the methods of this section. Your topic might be one of the following:

    • the number of student absences in your class or school for each day of the last few months

    • daily sales in the school cafeteria during the last few months

    • the daily temperature maximums, minimums, or ranges as reported in the local newspaper

    • sports records for your school

3. A variation of the procedure for smoothing is to replace each value with the median of that value and the *two* values on either side. For example, in the American League home run data, the smoothed value for 1924 would be 41, which is the median of 39, 41, 46, 33, and 47. These are the number of home runs hit in 1922, 1923, 1924, 1925, and 1926. Use this method of "smoothing by medians of five values" on the American League home run data. Discuss the advantages and disadvantages over the usual method.

IX. REVIEW OF ALL TECHNIQUES

It might be helpful to reread the review of one variable techniques in Section V before reading this section.

Two Variable Techniques

Suppose that we have measured the cumulative grade point average and the SAT score for each senior in a school. We want to learn how grade point averages and SAT scores are related. This is called a *two variable* situation since we have two values, grade average and test score, for each person.

The basic display for this situation is the scatter plot (Section VI). From a scatter plot you can determine if there is positive, negative, or no association between the variables. You can also determine whether or not the data separate into several clusters of points and whether or not there are any outlying points that do not follow the general pattern. If you notice one of these features, try to find possible reasons for it as part of your interpretation. Often in scatter plots, one of the two variables is time. In these situations we have a plot over time (Section VI).

After constructing and studying a scatter plot, the relationship between the variables may be clear. If so, there is no need to supplement the scatter plot. However, important yet subtle interpretations, concerning both general relationships and specific data points, can often be brought out by adding an appropriate straight line to the scatter plot (Section VII). For plots over time, smoothing can help to show long-run underlying trends, as well as departures of specific points from these trends (Section VIII).

The following applications will help you to see the relative advantages and disadvantages of the statistical methods described in Sections I-VIII. No new techniques are given. These applications will take more time and thought than previous ones as you will have to decide which plot is the best.

There are no right or wrong answers to many of the questions. Your teacher will expect you to make plots that are appropriate and to write thoughtful and complete comments about the characteristics of the data shown in the plot.

Presidential Autographs

The following table lists the U.S. presidents. With each is the lowest price you could expect to pay for his autograph (a plain signature).

Washington, George	$450	Arthur, Chester A.	$30
Adams, John	300	Cleveland, Grover	26
Jefferson, Thomas	400	Harrison, Benjamin	28
Madison, James	100	McKinley, William	38
Monroe, James	75	Roosevelt, Theodore	32
Adams, John Q.	80	Taft, William H.	28
Jackson, Andrew	150	Wilson, Woodrow	38
Van Buren, Martin	65	Harding, Warren G.	28
Harrison, William H.	80	Coolidge, Calvin	28
Tyler, John	60	Hoover, Herbert	28
Polk, James K.	60	Roosevelt, Franklin	33
Taylor, Zachary	60	Truman, Harry	39
Fillmore, Millard	50	Eisenhower, Dwight D.	28
Pierce, Franklin	50	Kennedy, John F.	80
Buchanan, James	50	Johnson, Lyndon B.	35
Lincoln, Abraham	350	Nixon, Richard M.	50
Johnson, Andrew	50	Ford, Gerald	28
Grant, U. S.	40	Carter, James E.	25
Hayes, Rutherford B.	30	Reagan, Ronald W.	25
Garfield, James	38		

Source: *The Official Price Guide to Paper Collectibles, 1985.*

1. Which president's autograph costs the most?

2. Which president's autograph costs the least?

3. Theodore Roosevelt became president in 1901, and all those preceding him in this list were president before 1900. We want to compare the prices of autographs for those who were president before 1900 with the prices for those who were president since 1900. Use any two of the three types of plots — line, stem-and-leaf, or box — to make this comparison.

4. Which plot do you prefer? Why?

5. From this plot, estimate the median prices of autographs of presidents before 1900 and the median prices of autographs of presidents after 1900.

6. Do you think that presidents' autographs become more valuable as they get older? Construct the appropriate plot over time. If it seems to be helpful, make a plot of the smoothed values.

7. Write a summary of the information that you have learned about presidential autographs.

Application 40

Least and Most Expensive Cities

The following table lists some major world cities. With each are the cost in dollars of one night for a single room in a good mid-range hotel and the cost of dinner for one including wine and a tip in a good restaurant.

CITY	HOTEL	DINNER
Athens	$23.73	$10.79
Caracas	24.82	10.95
New Delhi	34.18	12.70
Frankfurt	33.59	5.60
Hong Kong	45.86	19.11
Johannesburg	36.04	22.52
Lisbon	28.90	5.62
London	67.39	19.97
Madrid	30.81	6.56
Manila	81.80	27.27
Mexico City	46.82	13.38
Nairobi	22.22	5.93
New York	60.00	20.00
Paris	74.18	30.91
Rio de Janeiro	46.41	14.97
Rome	43.67	17.47
Stockholm	50.69	19.01
Sydney	54.11	17.75
Tokyo	48.24	16.35
Toronto	50.26	13.78
Vienna	39.77	10.60
Zurich	45.89	13.77

Source: Murray J. Brown, "Hotel and Dining Prices in Cities," *Los Angeles Times*, November 13, 1983.

1. Which city has the most expensive dinner? Which has the least expensive hotel?

   To answer the following questions, you will have to decide which type of plot must be constructed and then construct it.

2. In which city is the cost of dinner relatively expensive compared to the cost of a hotel?

3. If the cost of a hotel room in a particular city is $50, what would you expect the cost of a dinner to be?

4. Write a description of the information displayed in your plot.

Application 41

Who Was the Greatest Yankee Home Run Hitter?

The following table lists four of the greatest New York Yankees' home run hitters with the number of home runs each hit while a Yankee.

Babe Ruth		Lou Gehrig		Mickey Mantle		Roger Maris	
Year	Home Runs	Year	Home Runs	Year	Home Runs	Year	Home Runs
1920	54	1923	1	1951	13	1960	39
1921	59	1924	0	1952	23	1961	61
1922	35	1925	20	1953	21	1962	33
1923	41	1926	16	1954	27	1963	23
1924	46	1927	47	1955	37	1964	26
1925	25	1928	27	1956	52	1965	8
1926	47	1929	35	1957	34	1966	13
1927	60	1930	41	1958	42		
1928	54	1931	46	1959	31		
1929	46	1932	34	1960	40		
1930	49	1933	32	1961	54		
1931	46	1934	49	1962	30		
1932	41	1935	30	1963	15		
1933	34	1936	49	1964	35		
1934	22	1937	37	1965	19		
		1938	29	1966	23		
		1939	0	1967	22		
				1968	18		

Source: *Macmillan Baseball Encyclopedia*, 4th edition.

1. Study these records. Which player appears to be the greatest home run hitter? Why did you choose this player?

2. Your task now is to rank the four players. You may wish to compute means, medians, or quartiles, or make line plots, stem-and-leaf plots, box plots, plots over time, or smoothed plots over time.

   How did you rank the four players? Describe your reasons and include your plots.

Application 42

Yankees Versus Mets

New York City has two baseball teams, the Yankees and the Mets. The following table gives the attendance and final standing for both teams each year since the Mets began play in 1962. There are no questions for this application. Your assignment is to make the plots you think are appropriate and interesting. Then write a report about your discoveries.

Here is a possible question to get you started: In a year when attendance for the Yankees is high does Mets attendance also tend to be high?

	YANKEES			METS	
Finish	Attendance	Year	Attendance	Finish	
Second	2,214,587	1985	2,751,437	Second	
Third	1,821,815	1984	1,829,482	Second	
Third	2,257,976	1983	1,103,808	Sixth	
Fifth	2,041,219	1982	1,320,055	Sixth	
First	1,614,533	1981	701,910	Fifth	
First	2,627,417	1980	1,178,659	Fifth	
Fourth	2,537,765	1979	788,905	Sixth	
First	2,335,871	1978	1,007,328	Sixth	
First	2,103,092	1977	1,066,825	Sixth	
First	2,012,434	1976	1,468,754	Third	
Third	1,288,048	1975	1,730,566	Third	
Second	1,273,075	1974	1,722,209	Fifth	
Fourth	1,262,077	1973	1,912,390	First	
Fourth	966,328	1972	2,134,185	Third	
Fourth	1,070,771	1971	2,266,680	Third	
Second	1,136,879	1970	2,697,479	Third	
Fifth	1,067,996	1969	2,175,373	First	
Fifth	1,125,124	1968	1,781,657	Ninth	
Ninth	1,141,714	1967	1,565,492	Tenth	
Tenth	1,124,648	1966	1,932,693	Ninth	
Sixth	1,213,552	1965	1,768,389	Tenth	
First	1,305,636	1964	1,732,597	Tenth	
First	1,308,920	1963	1,080,108	Tenth	
First	1,493,574	1962	922,530	Tenth	

Source: *Newark Star-Ledger*, April 7, 1985.

ACKNOWLEDGMENTS

Grateful acknowledgment is made to the following publishers, authors, and institutions for permission to use and adapt copyrighted materials.

Addison-Wesley Publishing Company for data on page 111 on World War II submarine sinkings, from Mosteller, Fienberg, and Rourke, *Beginning Statistics with Data Analysis*, © 1983, Addison-Wesley, Reading, Massachusetts. Pg. 79, Table 3-3. Reprinted with permission.

American Public Health Association for data on page 119 on coronary heart disease, from "Cigarette Smoking Related to Geographic Variations in Coronary Heart Disease Mortality and to Expectation of Life in the Two Sexes," Risteard Mulcahy, J.W. McGiluary, and Noel Hickey, in *American Journal of Public Health,* vol. 60, 1970.

Ballantine Books for data on page 158 on the value of presidential autographs, from *The Official Price Guide to Paper Collectibles,* edited by Thomas E. Hudgeons, © 1985, Ballantine Books, New York, NY 10022.

Beverage World for data on page 18 on U.S. soft drink consumption. Reprinted by permission from *Beverage World,* March 1978.

R. R. Bowker Company for data on page 32 on sales of children's books, from *Eighty Years of Best Sellers,* A. P. Hackett and J. H. Burke. Copyright © 1977, R. R. Bowker Company, New York, NY 10017.

Murray J. Brown for data on page 159 on least and most expensive cities, from "Hotel and Dining Prices in Cities" in the *Los Angeles Times,* November 13, 1983. Reprinted by permission of the author.

Peter H. Brown for the "Dumbing for Dollars" chart on page 90, adapted from an article in the *Los Angeles Times,* January 20, 1985. Reprinted by permission of the author.

Consumers Union for data on page 7 from "Nutritional Information for Fast Foods" in *Consumer Reports;* for data and excerpts on pages 36–37 from "How Does Your Allowance Compare to Others," and for data on page 45 from "Motocross Bike Ratings," both in *Penny Power;* also, for data on page 95 from "Walkaround Stereos" in the *1985 Buying Guide Issue.* Copyright 1979, 1983, 1985 by Consumers Union of the United States, Inc., Mount Vernon, NY 10553. Reprinted by permission from *Consumer Reports,* September 1979, *Penny Power,* February/March 1983, and the *1985 Buying Guide Issue.*

Consumers Union of the United States, Inc., Mount Vernon, NY 10553. Reprinted by permission from *Consumer Reports,* September 1979, *Penny Power,* February/March 1983, and the *1985 Buying Guide Issue.*

Highway Loss Data Institute for data on page 65 on automobile safety records. Copyright Highway Loss Data Institute, Washington, DC 20037.

Joint Center for Political Studies for data on page 108 on the number of black state legislators. Reprinted by permission.

P. J. Kenedy & Sons for data on page 121 on the Catholic clergy, from *The Official Catholic Directory 1985,* published by P. J. Kenedy & Sons, New York, NY 10022.

Los Angeles Times for data on page 3 on top 10 record albums, from "The King of Hearts vs. the Queen of Tarts," Robert Hilburn, copyright 1985, *Los Angeles Times.* Reprinted by permission. For data on page 41 on record album ratings, from "The Pop Meter," copyright 1985, *Los Angeles Times.* Reprinted by permission. For data on pages 69–70, from "Barring L.A. Students from Extracurricular Activities," copyright 1983, *Los Angeles Times.* Reprinted by permission. For data on page 83 on the Celtics-Lakers game, from "The Day in Sports," copyright 1985, *Los Angeles Times.* Reprinted by permission. For data on page 103 on highway speeds, from "Speeding on the Freeways," copyright 1983, *Los Angeles Times.* Reprinted by permission.

Macmillan Publishing Company for data on page 112 on duck plumage and behavior. Reprinted with permission of Macmillan Publishing Company from *Statistics in the Real World: A Book of Examples*, Richard J. Larsen and Donna Fox Stroup. Copyright © 1976 by Macmillan Publishing Company. For data on page 160 on Yankee home run hitters. Reprinted with permission of the publisher from *Macmillan Baseball Encyclopedia*, 4th ed., edited by Joseph L. Reichler. Copyright © 1969, 1974, 1976, 1979 Macmillan Publishing Company.

National Council of Teachers of Mathematics for data on page 79 on letter frequencies, from *Student Math Notes*, copyright © 1983, National Council of Teachers of Mathematics, Reston, VA 22011.

National Soft Drink Association for data on page 98 on U.S. soft drink consumption, from *Sales Survey of the Soft Drink Industry, NSDA 1984*, copyright National Soft Drink Association, Washington, DC 20036.

Newspaper Enterprise Association, Inc. for data on page 1 on 1984 Winter Olympic medal winners; for data on pages 20–21, 138, and 152–53 on National League and American League home run leaders; for data on pages 27 and 29 on heights of buildings in San Francisco and Los Angeles; and for data on page 145 on Olympic marathon times; from *The World Almanac and Book of Facts*, 1985 edition, copyright © Newspaper Enterprise Association, Inc., 1984, New York, NY 10166.

A. C. Nielsen Company for data on page 55 on television ratings, from "Prime Time Network Television Rankings, April 29–May 5, 1985." Copyright © A. C. Nielsen Company, New York, NY 10104.

Record Research for data on pages 46, 50–54, and 130 on number 1 hit records, from *The Billboard Book of Top 40 Hits*, Joel Whitburn. Copyright © 1985, Record Research Inc., P.O. Box 200, Menomonee Falls, WI 53051.

Roller Skating Rink Operators Association for data on page 61 on numbers of roller skating clubs. Copyright © 1978, Roller Skating Rink Operators Association, Lincoln, NE 68501.

The Star-Ledger for data on page 161 on the Yankees and the Mets, from April 7, 1985 edition. Copyright © 1985 *The Star-Ledger*, Newark, NJ 07101.

Williams Press for data on page 136 on tree age and diameter, from Chapman and Demeritt, *Elements of Forest Mensuration*, 2nd ed., copyright © 1936, Williams Press, Albany, NY 12204.

H. O. Zimman, Inc. for data on pages 147–48 on the top-ranked women and men tennis players, from *Tennis Championships Magazine*, Special U.S. Open edition, copyright 1985, H. O. Zimman, Inc., Lynn, MA 01901.

Exploring Probability

Exploring Probability was prepared under the auspices of the American Statistical Association—National Council of Teachers of Mathematics Joint Committee on the Curriculum in Statistics and Probability.

This book is part of the Quantitative Literacy Project, which was funded in part by the National Science Foundation.

Exploring Probability

Claire M. Newman
Queens College

Thomas E. Obremski
University of Denver

Richard L. Scheaffer
University of Florida

DALE SEYMOUR PUBLICATIONS

Cover Design: John Edeen and Francesca Angelesco
Technical Art: Colleen Donovan
Illustrations: Deborah Morse
Editing and Production: Larry Olsen

This publication was prepared as part of the American Statistical
Association Project—Quantitative Literacy—with partial support of the
National Science Foundation Grant No. DPE-8317656. Any opinions,
findings, conclusions, or recommendations expressed in this publication
are those of the authors and do not necessarily represent the views of the
National Science Foundation. These materials shall be subject to a
royalty-free, irrevocable, worldwide, non-exclusive license in the United
States Government to reproduce, perform, translate, and otherwise use
and to authorize others to use such materials for Government purposes.

ISBN 0-86651-333-7
Order Number DS01701

DALE
SEYMOUR
PUBLICATIONS
P.O. BOX 10888
PALO ALTO, CA 94303

CONTENTS

PREFACE

This is the second in a series of publications produced by the ASA-NCTM Joint Committee on the Curriculum in Statistics and Probability. The series includes *Exploring Data, The Art and Techniques of Simulation,* and *Exploring Surveys and Information from Samples.* These four units cover the basic concepts of statistics and probability. The approach emphasizes use of real data, active experiments, and student participation. There are no complicated formulas or abstract mathematical concepts to confuse or distract you.

Exploring Probability covers elementary probability by using only counting skills and some knowledge of fractions. Complicated counting algorithms such as combinations and permutations are not introduced here. The unit provides the background for the many practical applications of probability discussed in *The Art and Techniques of Simulation.*

The material is designed to give you a working knowledge of basic probability.

I. INTRODUCTION

In our daily conversations, it is common to speak of events in terms of their chances of occurring. We speak of the chance that our team will win the big game, the chance that we will get an A in mathematics, or the chance of being elected to a school office. The word *probability* is sometimes used in place of the word *chance*. Then we might speak of the probability of getting a hit in a baseball game or the probability that our new puppy will be born male.

The terms *chance* and *probability* are usually applied to those situations for which we cannot completely determine the outcome in advance. We are doubtful of what will happen. We do not know if our team will win or lose, so we talk about the team's chance of winning. We are not sure if we will get an A in mathematics, so we talk about our chance of getting an A. In other words, we are *uncertain* about what will actually happen when we use the term *chance*. There are, however, situations for which we know the outcomes in advance. We are sure that the sun will rise tomorrow and that school will begin again next fall. We say that we are *certain* about such events. All of us have often heard such statements as "I am certain that I will pass this year" or "I am certain that I can find my way home."

Sometimes we are not certain about how a situation will turn out, but we think the chances are good that a particular outcome will occur. We may call such an outcome *likely* or *highly likely*. If I am confident about knowing the answers to the questions on a math test, I could say that it is likely that I will pass the test. If you are fairly sure that you will go to a movie next Saturday, then you could say that you are likely to attend a movie. However, if we think the chances that an event will occur are low, then we may call such an event *unlikely*. If your team is missing two of its star players, then it may be unlikely that it will win. So, *likely* refers to those events that have high probability of occurring, and *unlikely* refers to those events that have low probability of occurring.

The concept of chance, or probability, is widely used in the natural and social sciences because few results in these areas are known in advance absolutely. Most events are reported in terms of chances—for example, the chance of rain tomorrow, the chance that you can get home from school or work safely, the chance that you will live past the age of 60, the chance of getting a certain disease (or recovering from it), the chance of inheriting a certain trait, and the chance of a candidate winning an election.

Of what use are these probabilities? Perhaps the most important use is to help us make decisions as we go through life. If a student knows that his or her chance of getting an A in mathematics is low, then he or she may decide to study harder. If a certain medicine has only a low chance of curing an illness you may have, then you will probably not waste your money on that particular medicine. If rain is likely, you will be inclined to carry an umbrella or take your raincoat, but if rain is unlikely you will probably not bother with these extra articles. Businesses and industries make important decisions using similar reasoning. For example, insurance companies are interested in the probability of auto accidents among persons in certain age groups, and industries are interested in the probability that a new product will make a profit or the probability that an item can be manufactured without defects in workmanship.

To introduce you to some situations involving probability, think about each of the following events. How likely is each to occur? Use the accompanying scale to assign a number from 0 to 1 to each event, with 0 representing *impossibility* and 1 representing *certainty*.

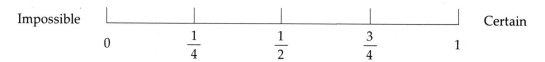

1. You will be absent from school at least one day during this school year.

2. You will have cereal for breakfast one day this week.

3. You will have cereal for lunch one day this week.

4. It will snow in your town in July.

5. It will rain sometime in July in your town.

6. The sun will rise tomorrow.

7. A person can live without water for two months.

8. A Democrat will win the next presidential election.

9. The next baby born in your local hospital will be a boy.

10. You will get an A in your next math test.

Now that you have given some thought to probable and improbable events, we shall explore a more systematic approach to probability in the next section.

Application 1

___

The Spinner

1. A spinner is divided into areas labeled *red* and *white*, as in the accompanying diagram.

   a. If you were to spin the spinner, would you be just as likely to obtain red as white? If not, which color is more likely to occur? Why?

   b. Are you certain of getting at least one red in 100 spins?

   c. Is it very likely that you will not spin any reds in 100 spins?

   d. Is it possible never to spin a red in 100 spins?

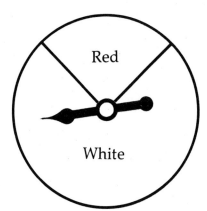

2. Think about events that may occur in your life.

   a. List three events that are certain.

   b. List three events that are impossible—that is, they cannot occur.

   c. List three events that are highly likely.

   d. List three events that are unlikely.

II. EXPERIMENTING WITH CHANCE

We have seen that, in our daily experiences, there are many situations that involve chance outcomes. These are situations for which we do not know the outcome in advance, but we may be able to list possible outcomes. We will now investigate some simple situations of this type by actually observing how often specific outcomes occur. Our goal is to assign *numbers* to various events of interest. These numbers will represent the *chances*, or *probabilities*, of the events we study.

Think about the following simple situation. An official is to toss a coin at the start of a football game to determine who gets first chance to receive the ball. Will the coin come up heads *(H)* or tails *(T)*? We cannot know the outcome in advance, but we do know that there are only two possible outcomes. We can study the possible outcomes of this coin-tossing experiment by actually tossing a coin repeatedly and observing what happens. Throughout our discussion of probability, the term *experiment* will refer to any activity we use to produce observable data. Any *set* of the possible outcomes of an experiment is called an *event*. Let us conduct an experiment to see how coin-tossing works.

Application 2

Tossing a Coin

Toss a coin 50 times. Record the results in the accompanying table.

	Tally	Total
Heads		
Tails		
Total		50

1. Calculate the fraction of tosses that were heads. Use the formula

$$\text{fraction of heads} = \frac{\text{total number of heads}}{\text{total number of tosses}}$$

2. Calculate the fraction of tosses that were tails.

3. Compare your results with those of other students in the class. Do you find some variation in the results?

4. Are the results of this experiment what you would have expected to observe?

5

The fraction of heads obtained in the coin-tossing experiment is called the relative frequency. The relative frequency can now be used to *estimate* the *chance*, or *probability*, of observing a head in the future. We will say that this fraction is an *estimate* of the probability of obtaining a head, based on the 50 tosses we observed. We may have counted 16 heads in 50 tosses. Our estimate of the probability of heads is then $\frac{16}{50}$. You may have obtained a different number of heads. Your estimate of the probability of observing a head is then different from $\frac{16}{50}$. Upon checking with other students in the class, you may find a large number of different estimates of the probability of observing a head.

Estimates of probabilities usually change from experiment to experiment. However, if each student in the class had tossed the coin a *large* number of times (say, 1,000), then the estimates of the probability of heads would not vary quite so much. All estimates, in that case, should be quite close to one another, and any one of them would provide a good estimate of the probability of observing a head.

You have, no doubt, already suspected that the fraction of heads observed in coin-tossing should be close to $\frac{1}{2}$. There are, however, many situations in which an estimate of probability is nearly impossible without some experimentation. Suppose you want to know the probability that a car approaching a specific intersection near your home will turn left. You must observe a number of cars and count the number of left turns. These observations of cars make up the experiment in this case. If, out of 50 cars observed, 20 turn left, then $\frac{20}{50}$ = 0.40 (or 40 percent) is the relative frequency or fraction of left turns. The relative frequency is used as the estimate of the probability that a car will make a left turn. If 200 cars go through this intersection tomorrow, you would *expect* 40 percent of them (80 cars) to turn left.

For some problems, the experiment has already been conducted, and we have only to look at the data. Suppose Joe is coming up to bat in a baseball game. What is the chance he will get a hit? Here we need to observe the fraction of times he has gotten a hit in the past, but this information is already collected and summarized in his batting average. If Joe has been to bat 10 times and has 3 hits, then his batting average is $\frac{3}{10}$ = 0.300. We say he is "hitting 300." This is really a probability measure. Joe's chance of getting a hit his next time at bat is 0.3. In other words, we expect Joe to get a hit on 30 percent of his official turns at bat. If Joe comes to bat 10 times in the next two games, we expect him to get 3 hits. Of course, he may get no hits or many more than 3 hits, but we expect him to average about 3 hits for every 10 times at bat.

It should now be clear that the probability of an event, *E*, can be estimated by

$$P(E) = \frac{\text{the number of observations favorable to } E}{\text{the number of observations in the experiment}}$$

To review, if 50 tosses of a coin result in 16 observations of heads, then the estimate of the probability of observing a head on a future toss is $\frac{16}{50}$ = 0.32, or 32 percent.

Now try the following Applications, which are designed to help you become more familiar with probability experiments and how they are used.

Application 3

The Spinner

Construct a spinner like the one shown below, with eight sectors of equal size. (A larger version of this spinner base is provided at the end of the book. A pointer can be made by spinning a paper clip around a pencil point.) Number each sector and color it yellow, red, or blue as shown. Spin the spinner 30 times and record the *color* on which the spinner lands each time. If the spinner lands on a line, spin again.

	Red	Blue	Yellow
Number Observed			

Use your data to answer the following questions.

1. Would you say that yellow is more or less likely than red? Why?

2. Would you say that blue is more or less likely than red? Why?

3. Estimate the probability of the spinner landing on yellow the next time it is spun.

4. Estimate the probability of the spinner landing on blue the next time it is spun.

5. If you spin this spinner 90 more times, about how many times would you expect it to land on blue?

6. Combine your numbers with those of the rest of the class, and write down the total number of reds, blues, and yellows seen by the entire class. Now, answer questions 1 through 5 again.

Keep your spinner and these results for further experiments.

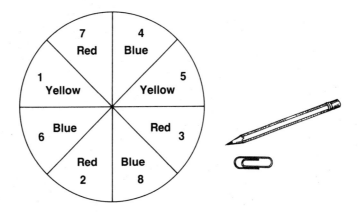

Application 4

Thumbtack Toss

Place 20 identical thumbtacks in a paper cup. Shake the cup and roll (gently) the tacks onto the desk. Count the number of tacks pointing up (the point does not touch the desk) and the number pointing down (the point touches the desk). Record the data in the boxes below. (*Note:* To keep the tacks under control, place them in a clear plastic cup and cover the top with clear plastic held by a rubber band. Shake the cup and turn it upside down on a desk. You can count the number of tacks pointing up or down by looking through the clear plastic.)

Number of tacks pointing up	
Number of tacks pointing down	
Total	20

Use your data to answer the following questions.

1. Is "point up" more likely or less likely than "point down"?

2. If one tack is to be tossed onto the desk, estimate the probability that it will point up.

3. If a cup containing 100 tacks has its contents rolled onto the desk, how many tacks would you expect to point down?

4. Combine your results with those of four other students so that you have data on 100 tacks. Answer questions 1, 2, and 3 again. Are there any differences from your earlier answers?

Application 5

Tossing a Die

Work with a partner as a team. Toss a standard six-faced die (*die* is the singular of *dice*) 60 times and observe the number of dots on the top face. One person should toss the die, and one should record the results in the accompanying table.

	No. of ⚀	No. of ⚁	No. of ⚂	No. of ⚃	No. of ⚄	No. of ⚅
Tally						
Total						

Use your data to answer the following questions.

1. Did you get all six numbers? Would you expect that, for 60 tosses, each number would come up at least once? Explain.

2. Estimate the probability of tossing a 5 with your die.

3. Estimate the probability of tossing a 4 with your die.

4. Are the answers to questions 2 and 3 nearly equal?

5. Estimate the probability of tossing an even number with your die. How does this answer compare with the answer to question 3?

6. Estimate the probability of tossing a number larger than 4.

7. If you tossed your die 100 more times, about how many 4's would you expect to see among the 100 tosses?

Now, ten teams should enter their results on the Combined Data Table, on page 10.

Combined Data Table							
Team	No. of ⚀	No. of ⚁	No. of ⚂	No. of ⚃	No. of ⚄	No. of ⚅	Total No. of Tosses
A							
B							
C							
D							
E							
F							
G							
H							
I							
J							
Total							600

8. Estimate the probability of tossing a 5, using the combined data. How does your answer compare with the answer for question 2?

9. Estimate the probability of tossing a 4, using the combined data. How does this answer compare with the answer for question 3?

10. Estimate the probability of tossing an even number, using the combined data. How does this answer compare with the answer for question 5?

Application 6

Guessing Numbers

Get your pencil ready to write down a number. Ready? Without hesitating, write down a number from 1 to 4.

Fill in the boxes below with the number of students in your class who responded 1, 2, 3, and 4.

Number of Students Choosing Each Number

1	2	3	4

1. What is the total number of responses for your class?

2. Which number was written down most frequently?

3. Studies have shown that, from among the numbers 1, 2, 3, 4, the number 3 is chosen most frequently. If we want to estimate the probability that a person not in your class would choose number 3, how would we use the information in the boxes to do so?

4. Now estimate the probability of students writing down the responses 1, 2, and 4.

Counting Students

For this study, we will provide the data. You may want to conduct a similar study by interviewing the students in your school. Suppose a group of 20 students randomly selected from your school contains 12 girls and 8 boys. (You can select 20 students at random by placing the names of all students in a box, mixing them, and drawing 20 names.) Four of the girls and three of the boys live within easy walking distance of the school. The data may be displayed as follows:

	Girls	Boys	Total
Lives within walking distance	4	3	7
Does not live within walking distance	8	5	13
Total	12	8	20

What does the number 5 in the table mean? It means that, of the 20 students, there are 5 boys who do *not* live within walking distance of the school.

Another student, not among those interviewed, is assigned a locker next to yours.

1. Estimate the probability that this student is a girl.

2. Estimate the probability that this student lives within walking distance of school.

3. A reasonable answer to question 1 is $\frac{12}{20}$ or $\frac{3}{5}$, since there are 12 girls and 20 students in the sample. Now find the probability that the person named is a girl who lives within walking distance of school. (*Hint:* What does the number 4 represent in the table?)

4. Suppose there are 1,000 students in the school. How many would you expect to live within walking distance of the school?

5. If the person assigned a locker next to yours is known to be a girl, estimate the probability that she lives within walking distance of school.

Application 8

Generating Your Own Data

Select the names of two popular movies. Call one movie A, and the other, B. Now interview a number of students in your school and find out how many have seen each movie. (The interviewed students should be randomly selected from all students in the school, as described in Application 7.) Record the numbers in the following table:

	Seen B	Not Seen B	Total
Seen A			
Not Seen A			
Total			

Now select another student in your school whom you have not yet interviewed. Based on the data you have for the students you have interviewed,

1. Estimate the probability he or she has seen A.

2. Estimate the probability he or she has seen B.

3. Estimate the probability he or she has seen neither.

4. Among a group of 100 students from your school, none of whom were interviewed by you, how many students would you expect to have seen both movies?

Application 9

Causes of Fires

The data for this experiment are provided below. These are real data, and you may construct a similar experiment by looking for graphs and other data displays in a newspaper or magazine.

Number of Fires of Various Types Among 100 Typical Home Fires	
Cause of Fire	Number Reported
Heating system	22
Cooking	15
Electrical system	8
Smoking	7
Appliances	7
Other	41

Source: National Fire Incident Reporting Service, 1978.

Suppose a fire starts in a home down the street from where you live. Using the table above, estimate the probability that:

1. It is a cooking fire.

2. It started in the electrical wiring.

3. It was *not* caused by smoking.

4. It was caused by the heating system or appliances.

5. It was caused by someone cooking or smoking.

6. Can we estimate the probability that the fire was caused by lightning?

Application 10

Accident Statistics

The following table lists the total number of accidental deaths in the United States in 1979 and the number of fatal motor-vehicle accidents.

Accidental Deaths in the United States, 1979		
	All Types	Motor Vehicle
All ages	105,312	53,524
Under 5	4,429	1,461
5 to 14	5,689	2,952
15 to 24	26,574	19,369
25 to 44	26,097	15,658
45 to 64	18,346	8,162
65 to 74	9,013	3,171
75 and over	15,164	2,751
Male	74,403	39,309
Female	30,909	14,215

Source: *The World Almanac & Book of Facts,* 1979 and 1984 edition, copyright © Newspaper Enterprise Association, Inc. 1978 and 1983, New York, NY 10166.

You are told that a certain person recently died in an accident. Estimate the probability that:

1. It was a motor-vehicle accident.

2. The person was male.

3. It was a motor-vehicle accident, assuming that the person was a male.

4. It was a motor-vehicle accident, assuming that the person was between 15 and 24 years of age.

5. It was a female who was involved in an accident that was not a motor-vehicle accident.

Application 11

Smoking Data

The accompanying graphs give information about smoking among males and females in 1965 and 1980.

1. Suppose you were to meet Ms. J by chance for the first time. What is your estimate of the probability that:

   a. she does not smoke?

   b. she has never smoked?

   c. she has smoked sometime in her life?

2. Suppose a man had been randomly selected during the year 1965 as part of an experimental study. What is your estimate of the probability that he was a smoker? Is it more or less likely that such a selection would produce a smoker today?

3. Construct two probability questions of your own that can be answered using the graphs.

Quitting Proves Hard

Among Males

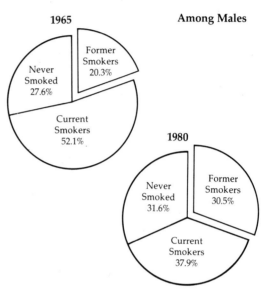

Among Females

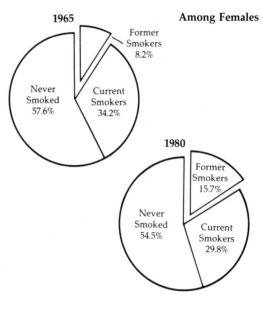

Source: Public Health Service; *The New York Times*, Dec. 25, 1984. Copyright © 1984 by The New York Times Company. Reprinted by permission.

Application 12

Marital Status of the Unemployed

Marital Status of the Unemployed, 1956 and 1982

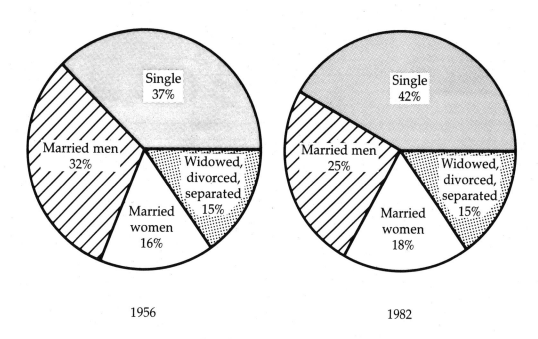

1956   1982

Source: "Workers Without Jobs: A Chartbook on Unemployment,"
Bureau of Labor Statistics, 1983.

The above graphs show the marital status of the unemployed for 1956 and 1982.

1. If you had met an unemployed worker in 1956, what was the probability that this person would have been a married woman? What is the probability that an unemployed worker in 1982 was a married woman? Can you suggest reasons for the change?

2. Suppose your city had 1,000 unemployed workers in 1982. How many would you expect to have been:

    a. married men?

    b. single?

    c. married women?

The Adult Population of the United States

The following data from the U.S. Census Bureau show the percentages of the adult population under age 65 by age classes. The data are for 1981.

Adult Population of the U.S. by Age Classes	
Age Class	Percentage of Adult Population Under Age 65
18–24	21
25–34	28
35–44	19
45–64	32

Use the data to answer the following questions.

1. If you meet a stranger known to be between 18 and 64 years old, what is your estimate of the probability that the stranger is:

   a. between 18 and 24 years old?

   b. over 34 years old?

   c. under 35 years old?

2. If a large firm employs 10,000 workers between the ages of 18 and 64, how many of them would you expect to be:

   a. between 18 and 24 years old?

   b. over 34 years old?

III. KNOWING OUR CHANCES IN ADVANCE

In the coin-tossing experiment in Application 2, you no doubt expected to obtain heads on about $\frac{1}{2}$ of the tosses. This seems reasonable, since there are only two possible outcomes to each toss of the coin, and these outcomes seem to be equally likely. In fact, we say that the *probability* of a head occurring on a toss of a coin is $\frac{1}{2}$, and we write this expression as

$$P(H) = \frac{1}{2}$$

Of course, the probability of a tail occurring is also $\frac{1}{2}$.

In the case of tossing a die, there are six equally likely outcomes. Thus, the probability of observing a 3 on a single toss of a die is $\frac{1}{6}$. Suppose we are interested in the event "observe an even number." Three of the six possible outcomes are favorable to this event, namely, the outcomes 2, 4, and 6. Therefore, the probability of observing an even number is $\frac{3}{6}$ or $\frac{1}{2}$.

Whenever we have an experiment with equally likely outcomes, we may define the probability of an event, E, as

$$P(E) = \frac{\text{number of outcomes favorable to } E}{\text{total number of possible outcomes}} = \frac{f}{n}$$

We use this definition, $P(E) = \frac{f}{n}$, *only* when we are dealing with *equally likely outcomes*. It will not work with outcomes that are not equally likely. For example, the thumbtack toss of Application 4 shows that the two possible outcomes "tack points up" and "tack points down" are not equally likely. Therefore, the probability of the tack pointing down is *not $\frac{1}{2}$*.

The probabilities determined by the rule given in this section are called *theoretical* probabilities because they are determined by what should happen, ideally, in situations with equally likely outcomes. The key to finding these theoretical probabilities is to list *all* possible equally likely outcomes. Then the theoretical probability of any event can be found by simply counting the number *(f)* of outcomes favorable to an event E, counting the total number *(n)* of equally likely outcomes, and using the formula $P(E) = \frac{f}{n}$.

The *theoretical probability* of observing a head in a toss of a coin is $\frac{1}{2}$. But when we actually toss a coin (see Application 2) 50 times, we usually do not get exactly 25 heads. The relative frequency of heads for the 50 tosses of a coin (obtained experimentally) will vary from student to student—and the relative frequency is the *estimated probability* of observing a head. If, however, the number of tosses were 1,000 instead of 50, the relative frequency should be quite close to $\frac{1}{2}$ and should vary little from student to student. The *theoretical probability* of $\frac{1}{2}$ can be used to predict what will happen in the *long run*. The theoretical probability is roughly the same as the estimated probability obtained from a large number of tosses of the coin. If we can determine the theoretical probability of an event, we generally use it as the measure of that event's probability. When we cannot determine the theoretical probability, we estimate the probability by conducting an experiment and determining the relative frequency of the desired event.

The following Applications allow you to use the definition of theoretical probability and to explore the relationship between theoretical and estimated probability.

Application 14

The Spinner Revisited

Obtain the spinner you used in Application 3. The eight numbered sections should be of approximately equal size. Thus, the eight possible numbered outcomes should be equally likely. Using our definition of theoretical probability:

1. Find *P(spinner landing on 3)*.

2. Find *P(spinner landing on an even number)*.

3. Find *P(spinner landing on blue)*.

Spin the spinner 40 times and record the frequency of outcomes in the boxes below.

	1	2	3	4	5	6	7	8	Total
Number of Times Observed									40

4. Find the fraction of 3's observed in the total sample of 40 spins. Compare this relative frequency with your answer to question 1.

5. Find the fraction of even numbers observed in the sample. Compare the result with your answer to question 2.

6. Find the relative frequency of blues observed in the sample. Compare this fraction with your answer to question 3.

7. Questions 4, 5, and 6 give estimates of probabilities. How do you think such estimates would compare with the theoretical probabilities in questions 1, 2, and 3 if we had data on 4,000 spins instead of 40 spins?

Application 15

Play Your Cards Right

Obtain a standard deck of 52 playing cards. Mix them well and count out 25 cards WITHOUT LOOKING AT THEM. Put aside the remaining cards. You are going to perform an experiment to estimate the probability of drawing a club, a diamond, a heart, and a spade from your deck of 25 cards.

   A. Mix the 25 cards well. Draw one card. Record its occurrence in the appropriate box below.

   B. Replace the card and shuffle the deck of 25 cards.

   C. Draw another card and record its suit.

   D. Repeat the above steps until you have recorded a total of 25 draws.

Clubs	Diamonds	Hearts	Spades	Total
				25

Use your data to answer the following questions.

   1. What is your estimate of the probability of drawing a club from the deck of 25 cards?

   2. What is your estimate of the probability of drawing a diamond from the deck of 25 cards?

   3. What is your estimate of the probability of drawing a heart from the deck of 25 cards?

   4. What is your estimate of the probability of drawing a spade from the deck of 25 cards?

   5. Now look at your 25 cards. Count the number of cards in each suit.

   6. What is the theoretical probability of obtaining a club? a diamond? a heart? a spade?

   7. How do these theoretical probabilities compare with the estimated probabilities obtained in the experiment?

   8. Suppose you had recorded a total of 2,500 draws (instead of 25) in your experiment. How would the estimated probabilities compare with the theoretical probabilities then?

Birthdays

If it is not the month of January, take the January page from a large calendar and cut out all of the 31 numbers. Be sure the cut-out numbers are all close to the same size. Place them in a large container and shake them up. Suppose one number is picked out of the container. Before actually selecting a number, find the probability that:

1. The number is 17.

2. The number is an odd number.

3. The number is a one-digit number.

Now draw a number from the container and write it down. Return the number to the container, shake it up, and draw again. Repeat this process 20 times.

4. Find the fraction of odd numbers among the 20 numbers selected. Compare your answer with your answer to question 2.

5. Find the fraction of one-digit numbers among the 20 numbers selected. Compare your answer with your answer to question 3.

6. What is your birth month and birthday? For example, if your birthday is August 12, August is the month and 12 is the day of the month. What is the probability that one number selected from the container matches your birthday?

All the students in your class should have the same answer to the above question, namely, $\frac{1}{31}$. Why is this so?

7. Why is it important to the Application that all the cut-out numbers be about the same size?

Application 17

Experiment in ESP

Do you have ESP (extrasensory perception)? Try this experiment and see.

A. Make a set of 40 cards of the same size using four different symbols, so that you have ten cards for each symbol. They might look like this:

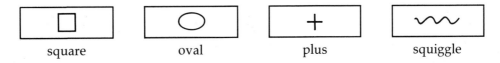

      square   oval   plus   squiggle

B. Choose a partner. Ask him or her to face away from you (or blindfold him or her).

C. Mix the cards well.

D. Turn over a card and concentrate on the symbol it shows.

E. Ask your partner to read your mind and tell you what is written on the card.

F. Record the answer *without* telling him or her whether or not it is correct.

G. Repeat the procedure and tally the results until you have recorded a total of 20 answers.

Right Answer	Wrong Answer	Total

1. Do you think your partner has ESP? Why or why not?

2. If your partner is just guessing, what is the probability of his or her guessing correctly on any one trial?

3. If you were to run this experiment again for 100 trials, about how many answers do you predict would be correct?

Random Numbers

1. Suppose the ten digits from 0 through 9 are written on ten poker chips, one number per chip. The chips are then placed in a box and mixed. You reach into the box and pull out one chip. What is the probability that the number on the chip is:

    a. a 1?

    b. even?

    c. greater than 7?

    d. divisible by 3? (Zero is divisible by 3.)

2. Suppose you pull out a chip that is *not* zero. (If the first chip you pull out is zero, replace the chip and repeat the process until you obtain a chip that is *not* zero.) Write down the number on your chip, put your chip back into the box, mix the chips, and then draw another one. Write the number on this second chip to the right of the first one, forming a two-digit number. What is the probability that the two-digit number:

    a. ends in a 3?

    b. is even? (Zero is an even number.)

Numbers selected in this way are called *random numbers*. Each number has the same probability of being selected. Random numbers are often used in selecting random samples. Suppose you have ten close friends. You could randomly select one of them to attend a ball game with you by numbering them from 0 through 9 and then choosing the one whose number is the same as the number you selected in question 1. We will use random numbers in future Applications.

Application 19

A Random Number Table

You should complete Application 18 before attempting this one. Suppose the experiment in Application 18 is repeated many times, and the resulting numbers are written in table form. The result would be a random number table. Such a table with 250 single-digit entries is shown below. The numbers are separated into five-column groups for ease of reading.

03222	39951	12738	50303	25017
87002	61789	96250	99337	14144
68840	94259	01961	42552	91843
88323	28828	64765	08244	53077
55170	71062	64159	79364	53088
84207	52123	88637	19369	58289
00027	43542	87030	14773	73087
33855	00824	48733	81297	80411
50897	91937	08871	91517	19668
21536	39451	95649	62556	23950

1. How many 1's would you expect to see in such a table?

2. How many even digits would you expect to see in such a table?

3. How many digits greater than 7 would you expect to see in such a table?

4. How many digits divisible by 3 would you expect to see in such a table?

5. Count the number of 1's, the number of even digits, the number of digits greater than 7, and the number of digits divisible by 3 in the table shown above. Are the frequencies close to what you expected?

IV. COMPLEMENTARY EVENTS AND ODDS

1. Complementary Events

Very often, when we consider an event and its probability, we are also interested in knowing the probability that the event will not occur. For each event, E, there exists the complement of that event, *not E* (which we will write as E'). We shall see that the probability of E and the probability of E' always have the same relationship to each other.

Study the probability of each event E below, and compare it with the probability of the event E' (that E will not occur). Each of these examples comes from an experiment discussed in the previous sections.

Experiment	E	$P(E)$	E'	$P(E')$
Toss of one coin	Head	$\frac{1}{2}$	Not a head	$\frac{1}{2}$
Spin of the spinner	Blue	$\frac{3}{8}$	Not blue	$\frac{5}{8}$
Toss of one die	Four	$\frac{1}{6}$	Not a four	$\frac{5}{6}$
Toss of one die	Greater than four	$\frac{2}{6}$	Less than or equal to four	$\frac{4}{6}$

Notice that $\frac{1}{2} + \frac{1}{2} = 1$, $\frac{3}{8} + \frac{5}{8} = 1$, $\frac{1}{6} + \frac{5}{6} = 1$, and $\frac{2}{6} + \frac{4}{6} = 1$. The sum of the two probabilities is always 1. That is, for each pair of complementary events,

$$P(E) + P(E') = 1$$

As another example, suppose the record of a weather station shows that its weather predictions have been accurate 89 times in the past 120 days. What is an estimate of the probability that its next forecast will be incorrect? Let C be the event "the forecast is correct," and let C' be the event "the forecast is incorrect." Then, $P(C) = \frac{89}{120}$. Since $P(C) + P(C') = 1$, $\frac{89}{120} + P(C') = 1$. It follows that

$$P(C') = 1 - \frac{89}{120} = \frac{(120 - 89)}{120} = \frac{31}{120}$$

In each case, we are dealing with a pair of fractions whose denominators are the same. The sum of the two numerators is always equal to that denominator.

$$\frac{1}{2} + \frac{1}{2} = 1 \quad \text{and} \quad 1 + 1 = 2$$
$$\frac{3}{8} + \frac{5}{8} = 1 \quad \text{and} \quad 3 + 5 = 8$$
$$\frac{1}{6} + \frac{5}{6} = 1 \quad \text{and} \quad 1 + 5 = 6$$
$$\frac{89}{120} + \frac{31}{120} = 1 \quad \text{and} \quad 89 + 31 = 120$$

In the spinner experiment, the probability of landing on yellow is $\frac{2}{8}$. What is the probability of not landing on yellow?

2. Odds

The numerators of each probability pair can be compared by means of a ratio. In the case of the toss of a die, we may say that the odds *in favor* of obtaining a 4 are 1:5, and the odds *against* obtaining a 4 are 5:1. Notice the order in which the probability numerators occur in each ratio. From $P(4) = \frac{1}{6}$ and $P(not\ 4) = \frac{5}{6}$, we obtain the odds *in favor* as 1:5 and the odds *against* as 5:1. In the spinner experiment, $P(blue) = \frac{3}{8}$ and $P(not\ blue) = \frac{5}{8}$. Therefore, the odds in favor of the spinner landing on blue are 3:5, whereas the odds against landing on blue are 5:3.

In the weather station example, what are the odds in favor of an accurate weather prediction? In the toss of a die, what are the odds against tossing a number greater than 4?

Observe that the odds in favor of obtaining a head in the toss of one coin are 1:1. In general, what does it mean to say that the odds in favor of an event are 1:1?

Application 20

Finding the Key

Suppose you have eight keys on your key ring. One opens the front door to your house, and one opens the back door. The other six will not help you get into your house. You come home after dark and randomly select a key.

1. What are the odds against the key opening your front door?

2. What are the odds against the key opening the back door?

3. What are the odds in favor of the key opening a door of your house?

4. You can rule out one key because it is much too small to be a house key, and you can tell that by touching it. Now answer questions 1, 2, and 3 again. Did the removal of one key change the odds considerably?

Application 21

Where the Students Go to School

Pupil Enrollment in Public and Private Schools of the United States (in millions)		
Year	Public Schools	Private Schools
1980	40.9	5.3
1983	39.5	5.7

Source: U.S. Department of Education

Suppose you meet a new friend who attends school in the United States.

1. What is your estimate of the probability that he or she attends public school?

2. What would have been your estimate in 1980?

3. Estimate the odds in favor of a pupil attending private school in 1983. Do the same for 1980.

29

Favorite Sports

A Lou Harris poll of April, 1981, obtained the following results for the question "What is your favorite sport?"

Sport	Percent
Football	36
Baseball	21
Basketball	12
Tennis	5
Auto Racing	5
Golf	4
Boxing	4
Others	13

Source: Reprinted by permission of Tribune Media Services.

If you meet a new friend today:

1. What is the probability that the friend's favorite sport is basketball?

2. What is the probability that the friend's favorite sport is *not* football?

3. What are the odds in favor of the friend's favorite sport being baseball?

4. What are the odds against the friend's favorite sport being tennis?

V. COMPOUND EVENTS

Sometimes an event consists of two or more simple events that are considered together as a single event. For example, an outcome from the toss of two coins (two heads, for example) may be thought of as a single event, even though it consists of outcomes on two different coins. Such an event is called a compound event.

Application 23

Tossing Two Coins

A. Select two coins of different denominations (say, a nickel and a quarter).

B. Toss the two coins 50 times. Tally the result of each toss in the boxes below.

Two Heads	One Head and One Tail	Two Tails	Total
			50

1. In what fraction of the tosses did you obtain two heads? Two tails? One head and one tail?

2. Were these results expected? Why or why not?

3. Using the results of this experiment, are the three events "two heads," "two tails," and "one head and one tail" equally likely events?

4. What is your estimate of the probability of obtaining a head and a tail on the toss of two coins?

---

1. Listing Equally Likely Outcomes

Let us work out the theoretical probability of each of the events in the two-coin experiment. First, it is important to be sure that all the possible outcomes of such an experiment are known and that they are equally likely outcomes. Only then can we use the formula to calculate the theoretical probability of various events.

In the case of the two-coin experiment, either coin may fall heads *(H)* or tails *(T)*. To keep track of exactly what may happen, it is convenient to work with different kinds of coins—say, a quarter and a nickel. The quarter can come up heads or tails. If the quarter comes up heads, the nickel can come up heads or tails. Similarly, if the quarter comes up tails, the nickel can be either heads or tails. This situation can be shown by means of the accompanying *tree diagram.*

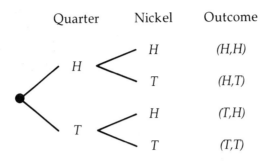

Quarter	Nickel	Outcome
H	H	(H,H)
	T	(H,T)
T	H	(T,H)
	T	(T,T)

It is convenient to think about such compound events in sequence—as though one thing follows the other. In this case, the first thing (toss of the quarter) can happen in two ways, the second thing (toss of the nickel) can happen in two ways, and the first thing followed by the second thing can happen in 2×2 or 4 ways. There are four branches of the tree, and each branch corresponds to exactly one of the four equally likely outcomes. Thus we see that *(H,T)* and *(T,H)* are two distinctly different outcomes. The outcomes would be different even if the two coins were the same kind (both quarters, for example).

The probability of the event E, obtaining one head and one tail on the toss of two coins, can now be calculated by using the formula $P(E) = \frac{f}{n}$.

$$P(E) = \frac{2}{4} = \frac{1}{2}$$

In other words, it is expected that roughly 50 percent of the time the toss of two coins will result in one head and one tail. Look back at the two-coin experiment. Did you find that about one half (or 50 percent) of the tosses resulted in one head and one tail? Were you close? It is unlikely that the result was exactly one half. After all, the theoretical probability of one half is what we expect in the long run. How might you continue the two-coin experiment to obtain a fraction closer to one half?

Application 24

Die and Coin

Suppose you roll a die and then toss a coin. What are the possible outcomes? Complete the tree diagram on page 33 to show the possible outcomes.

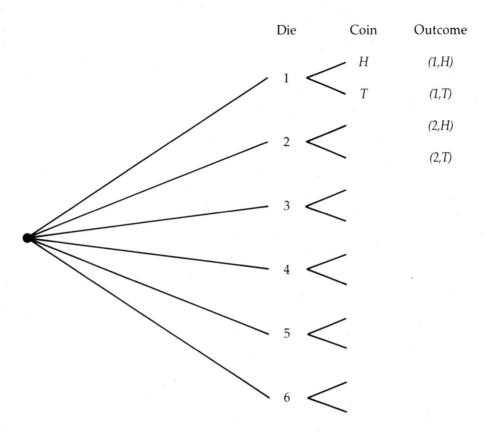

1. How many ways can the die fall?

2. How many ways can the coin fall?

3. How many outcomes are there for the compound experiment "roll a die and then toss a coin"?

4. Do you notice a relationship among your answers to questions 1, 2, and 3?

5. Are the outcomes equally likely?

6. What is the probability of rolling a 4 on the die and tossing a head on the coin?

Consider an experiment that involves tossing two distinguishable dice, say, one red die and one white die. Construct a tree diagram and use it to show that there are 6 × 6 or 36 ways that two dice can fall.

There are other ways of listing the equally likely outcomes in a two-part experiment. For example, a table can be used to display the 36 distinct ordered pairs that represent the 36 possible outcomes of the two-dice experiment.

Red Die

	1	2	3	4	5	6
1	(1,1)	(1,2)	(1,3)	(1,4)	(1,5)	(1,6)
2			(2,3)		(2,5)	
3		(3,2)			(3,5)	
4					(4,5)	
5					(5,5)	
6					(6,5)	

White
Die

Notice that (3,2) and (2,3) represent different outcomes. The ordered pair (3,2) represents a 3 on the white die and a 2 on the red die, whereas (2,3) represents a 2 on the white die and a 3 on the red die. Complete the table by recording an ordered pair in each cell of the table.

It is also possible to use an array of points to represent outcomes in a two-part experiment. The accompanying diagram shows a 6 × 6 array of 36 dots (points). The points on the axes are used for reference so that the ordered pair corresponding to each point can be read easily. Points A and B have been named (2,3) and (3,2), respectively. What ordered pairs are represented by points C and D? Locate the point representing the ordered pair (6,6) and label it M.

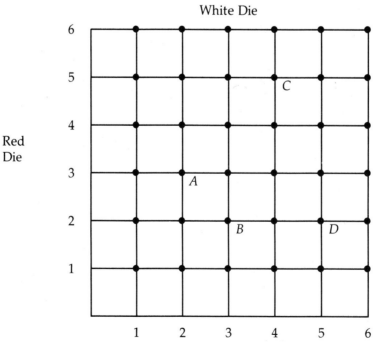

34

Application 25

Two-Dice Experiment

Use the accompanying 6 × 6 array of points to represent the 36 possible outcomes in a two-dice experiment.

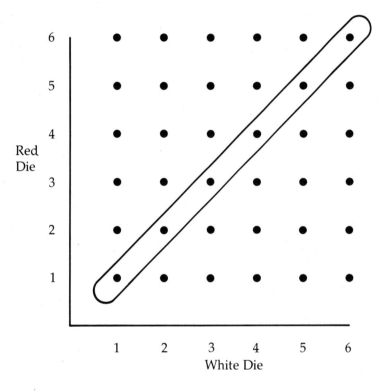

1. A ring has been placed around the points (1,1), (2,2), (3,3), (4,4), (5,5), and (6,6). Calculate the probability of obtaining "doubles" (the same number on each die).

2. Draw a ring around the points that represent the event "the sum of the numbers on the two dice is 8." [Remember that (2,6) and (6,2) are two different favorable outcomes.]

3. Calculate the probability of obtaining a sum of 8 on the toss of two dice.

4. What is the probability of obtaining a sum that is *not* 8?

5. What is the probability of obtaining a sum of 8 and the same number on each die?

6. Suppose that the two dice show the same number. What is the probability that their sum is 8?

2. Multiplication Principle

By using a tree diagram for each of the compound experiments discussed in the previous section, we can list all the equally probable outcomes and determine the total number of outcomes by counting the number of branches of the tree. The results, summarized in the accompanying table, show that the number of branches in a tree diagram can be calculated easily by using multiplication.

Compound Experiment	Number of Outcomes of First Experiment	Number of Outcomes of Second Experiment	Total Number of Outcomes
Toss of two coins	2	2	$2 \times 2 = 4$
Roll of die and toss of coin	6	2	$6 \times 2 = 12$
Toss of two dice	6	6	$6 \times 6 = 36$

Sometimes it is not necessary to construct a complete tree diagram. Instead, multiplication can be used to calculate the total number of outcomes without listing all of them. This Multiplication Principle can be stated as a general rule. If one thing can be done m ways, and a second thing n ways, then there are $m \times n$ ways of doing both things. Thus, for example, if there are three ways of traveling from City A to City B (auto, train, plane) and two ways of traveling from City B to City C (boat, plane), then there are 3×2 or 6 ways of traveling from City A to City C with a stopover in City B.

Application 26

On Your Own

1. Spinner A is divided into six equal sectors, numbered 1, 2, 3, 4, 5, 6. Spinner B is divided into eight equal sectors, numbered 1, 2, 3, 4, 5, 6, 7, 8. In a certain game, spinner A is spun and then spinner B is spun.

    a. How many outcomes are possible?

    b. Are the outcomes equally likely?

    c. What is the probability of spinning a 3 on spinner A and an 8 on spinner B?

2. A certain restaurant offers select-your-own sandwiches. That is, a person may select one item from each of the categories listed:

Bread	Filling	Extras
White Wheat	Tuna Chicken Cheese	Sprouts Lettuce

    a.   Using a tree diagram, list all possible sandwiches that can be ordered.

    b.   Would you expect the choices of a sandwich to be equally likely for most customers?

3.   A certain General American model car can be ordered with one of three engine sizes, with or without air conditioning, and with automatic or manual transmission.

    a.   Show, by means of a tree diagram, all the possible ways this model car can be ordered.

    b.   Suppose you want the car with the smallest engine, air conditioning, and manual transmission. A General American agency tells you there is only one of the cars on hand. What is the probability that it has the features you want, if you assume the outcomes to be equally likely?

4.   Jennifer dresses in a skirt and a blouse by choosing one item from each category. Show, by means of a tree diagram, all the outfits she can make.

Skirts	Blouses
Tan Plaid Gray Striped	White Pink Red

3. Multiplying Probabilities: Independent and Dependent Events

Consider the two events *(A)* it rains on Saturday and *(B)* you go to a movie on Saturday. Are *A* and *B* independent? That is, does either event affect the other? If you intend to go to a movie on Saturday, rain or no rain, then *A* and *B* may be independent. If, however, you plan to attend a movie in the afternoon only if you cannot go swimming, then *A* and *B* may be dependent. In this case, your probability of event *B* will change, depending on the outcome of event *A.*

Whenever two coins are tossed, either coin may fall heads or tails, and the way one coin falls does not depend on what happens to the other. The outcome for the nickel is not affected by the outcome for the quarter, and vice versa. In other words, the coin tosses are independent of each other, and the two tosses are said to be *independent events*. Each of the compound events we have been discussing consists of two independent events. The "roll of die" and "toss of coin" are independent events. If we roll two dice, the "roll of the white die" and the "roll of the red die" are independent events.

In a two-coin experiment, the number of equally likely outcomes can be calculated by means of a tree diagram or by using the Multiplication Principle. That is, since each coin has two possible outcomes, the two coins have 2×2 or 4 outcomes. In calculating the probability of each of the four equally likely outcomes, we can use the definition $P(E) = \frac{f}{n}$ and obtain $\frac{1}{4}$. Notice also that the probability of obtaining heads on the nickel is $\frac{1}{2}$, the probability of obtaining heads on the quarter is $\frac{1}{2}$, and the product of these individual probabilities, $\frac{1}{2} \times \frac{1}{2}$, gives us the same result, $\frac{1}{4}$.

Let us see whether this multiplication of probabilities works for other pairs of independent events. Suppose a die is rolled and a coin is tossed, and we are interested in the outcome "roll a 4 on the die and toss heads on the coin." In Application 24, there are 6×2 or 12 equally likely outcomes, and $(4,H)$ is one of them. Thus $P(4,H) = \frac{1}{12}$. Notice that $P(4) = \frac{1}{6}$, $P(H) = \frac{1}{2}$, and $\frac{1}{6} \times \frac{1}{2} = \frac{1}{12}$. In other words, $P(4,H) = P(4) \times P(H)$ for these two independent events.

In the case of the toss of two dice, the probability of each of the 36 equally likely outcomes is $\frac{1}{36}$. The probability of obtaining a 2 on the white die is $\frac{1}{6}$, the probability of obtaining a 6 on the red die is $\frac{1}{6}$, and the probability of obtaining $(2,6)$ is $\frac{1}{36}$. Once again, $\frac{1}{6} \times \frac{1}{6} = \frac{1}{36}$, and $P(White\ 2) \times P(Red\ 6) = P(2,6)$. This property is a natural outgrowth of tree diagrams and the Multiplication Principle. For any two independent events, A and B,

$$P(A\ and\ B) = P(A) \times P(B)$$

In the spinner question in Application 26 (question 1, part c), the probability of obtaining a 3 on Spinner A is $\frac{1}{6}$ (there are six equal sectors), and the probability of obtaining an 8 on Spinner B is $\frac{1}{8}$ (there are eight equal sectors). *Spin A* and *spin B* are two independent events. Therefore, the formula $P(A\ and\ B) = P(A) \times P(B)$ should give the required probability. That is, $P(3,8) = \frac{1}{6} \times \frac{1}{8}$. There are 6×8 or 48 equally likely outcomes for *spin A* and *spin B*, and $(3,8)$ is one of them. Therefore, $P(3,8) = \frac{1}{48}$ is correct.

Often, however, events are not independent. Suppose a box contains 3 red marbles and 2 blue marbles, all of the same size. A marble is drawn at random. The probability that it is red is $\frac{3}{5}$. If you pick a marble, replace it, and randomly pick again, the probability of picking a red marble remains $\frac{3}{5}$. However, suppose you pick a red marble, do not replace the marble, and then pick another marble. What is the probability of picking a red marble then?

To keep track of the different marbles, let us use r_1, r_2, and r_3 to identify the red marbles, and b_1 and b_2 to identify the blue marbles. Assuming that a red marble has been picked on the first draw, only the following situations could exist:

Select r_1	Leave r_2, r_3, b_1, b_2
Select r_2	Leave r_1, r_3, b_1, b_2
Select r_3	Leave r_1, r_2, b_1, b_2

There would be only two red marbles left, and the bag would now contain only four marbles. The probability of obtaining a red marble on the second draw, assuming that the first pick is a red, is $\frac{2}{4}$ or $\frac{1}{2}$. The second draw is clearly dependent on the first. Check to see that, if the first marble is blue and it is not replaced, the probability of obtaining a red marble on the second draw would then be $\frac{3}{4}$.

Your favorite baseball team is about to play a double header (two games in a row). If your team has won 60 percent of its games in the past, can we simply multiply 0.6 times 0.6 to estimate the probability of the team winning both games? The answer is yes, if we assume the outcomes of the two games to be independent. We often assume events to be independent so that we can approximate probabilities. In the case of your team's double header, the assumption of independent outcomes is probably not far from the truth and gives us an easy way to estimate the probability of the team winning both games.

Application 27

Are They Independent?

In each question below, state whether you think the pairs of events are independent or dependent.

1. *A:* Fred plays with his home video game about one hour a day.

   B: Fred will score more than 2,000 points the next time he plays Pacman.

2. *A:* The Dallas Cowboys will win the Super Bowl this year.

   B: Mount St. Helens will erupt again this year.

3. *A:* Lucy will get an A on her next spelling quiz.

   B: Lucy got an A on her last spelling quiz.

4. *A:* It will snow tonight.

   B: Fred's school bus will be late tomorrow morning.

5. *A:* The next child born in your county will be a boy.

   B: The last child born in your county was a boy.

Marbles in a Box

A box contains 3 red marbles and 2 blue marbles, indistinguishable except for color. A marble is drawn at random, and, without replacing it, another marble is drawn. Complete a tree diagram for this experiment.

First Pick   Second Pick

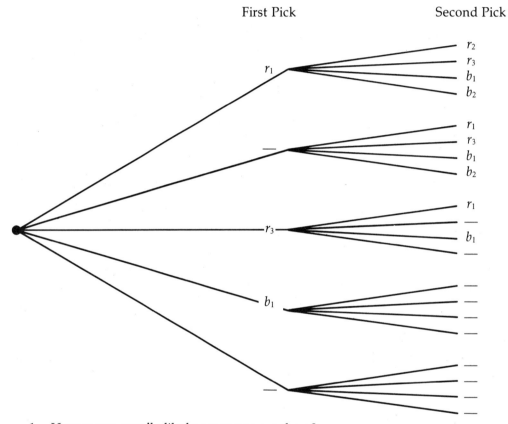

1. How many equally likely outcomes are there?

2. Place an asterisk next to those picks that show two successive red marbles. How many of these outcomes are there?

3. a. Compute the probability of drawing two red marbles.

    b. About what percentage of the time can you expect to draw two blue marbles?

    c. Do you have a better chance of drawing a blue marble first and then a red marble or a red marble first and then a blue marble—or are these equally likely events?

    d. What is the probability of drawing a red marble and a blue marble?

Consider the probability of drawing two red marbles from the box of marbles in Application 28. Using the tree diagram or the Multiplication Principle, we see that there are 5×4 or 20 equally likely outcomes. Of these, there are 3×2 or 6 outcomes showing two red marbles. Therefore,

$$P\text{(two reds)} = \frac{3 \times 2}{5 \times 4} = \frac{6}{20} = \frac{3}{10}$$

Here, too, the probabilities can be multiplied if we are careful to observe how the second draw depends on the first draw. We can see that

$$P\text{(red on first draw)} = \frac{3}{5}$$

and

$$P\text{(red on the second draw, given that a red was taken out on the first draw)} = \frac{2}{4} = \frac{1}{2}$$

The probability of observing two reds can be written as:

$$P\text{(two reds)} = P\text{(red on the first draw)} \times P\text{(red on the second draw,}$$
$$\text{given that a red was taken out on the first draw)} = \frac{3}{5} \times \frac{2}{4} = \frac{6}{20} = \frac{3}{10}$$

In the case of the 3 red marbles and 2 blue marbles, verify that

$$P\text{(two blues)} = \frac{2}{5} \times \frac{1}{4} = \frac{2}{20} = \frac{1}{10}$$

$$P\text{(blue first, red second)} = \frac{2}{5} \times \frac{3}{4} = \frac{6}{20} = \frac{3}{10}$$

$$P\text{(red first, blue second)} = \frac{3}{5} \times \frac{2}{4} = \frac{6}{20} = \frac{3}{10}$$

Drawing a red marble and a blue marble consists of two separate compound events: *(blue first, red second)* or *(red first, blue second)*. The tree diagram for Application 28 shows that there are a total of 12 outcomes in which either draw is red and the other draw is blue. Thus, the probability of drawing a red marble and a blue marble is $\frac{12}{20} = \frac{3}{5}$.

Application 29

___

On Your Own

1. To prevent cable damage as the result of an overload of circuits, an electric company has installed two special switching devices that work automatically and independently to shut off the flow of electricity when the demand for electricity is too great. Experience shows that the first switch has not worked 25 percent of the time and the second switch has not worked 30 percent of the time. (This can be interpreted to mean that the probability that the first switch will fail is $\frac{25}{100}$, and the probability that the second switch will fail is $\frac{30}{100}$.)

a.   What is the probability that both switches will fail to work the next time there is an overload?

b.   Approximately what percent of the time do both switches fail?

2.   A standard deck of 52 playing cards has 4 suits and 13 cards in each suit. The 52 cards of a deck are displayed in the accompanying array of dots.

Spades   .   .   .   .

Hearts   .   .   .   .

Diamonds   .   .   .   .

Clubs   .   .   .   .
           2   3   4   5   6   7   8   9   10   J   Q   K   A

a.   A card is drawn at random. What is the probability that the card is:

(i) a heart?   (ii) an ace?   (iii) the ace of hearts?

b.   Suppose the card is replaced and another card is drawn. What is the probability that the card is:

(i)   a heart, if the first card was a heart?
(ii) an ace, if the first card was an ace?
(iii) the ace of hearts, if the first card was the ace of hearts?

c.   Suppose the card is not replaced and another card is drawn. What is the probability that the second card is:

(i)   a heart, if the first card was a heart?
(ii) an ace, if the first card was an ace?
(iii) the ace of hearts, if the first card was the ace of hearts?

d.   If two cards are drawn, what is the probability that they are:

(i)   two aces?
(ii) any pair?
(iii) the jack of diamonds followed by the king of clubs?

4. Adding Probabilities

Consider the experiment of a single toss of a standard die. There are six equally likely outcomes: 1, 2, 3, 4, 5, 6. Suppose we define certain events as follows:

A   observe a 2
B   observe a 6
C   observe an even number
D   observe a number less than 5

Each event is a set of one or more of the possible outcomes listed above. That is,

A   = {2}
B   = {6}
C   = {2,4,6}
D   = {1,2,3,4}

Events C and D are shown in the accompanying diagram.

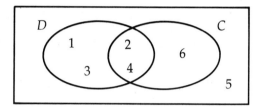

Since the six possible outcomes are equally likely, $P(A) = \frac{1}{6}$ and $P(B) = \frac{1}{6}$. But, what about the probability of observing a 2 or a 6? Two of the six equally likely outcomes are included in the event "observe a 2 or a 6," and so

$$P(\text{observe a 2 or a 6}) = P(A \text{ or } B) = \frac{2}{6}$$

In this case,

$$
\begin{aligned}
P(A \text{ or } B) &= P(A) + P(B) \\
&= \frac{1}{6} + \frac{1}{6} \\
&= \frac{2}{6} \\
&= \frac{1}{3}
\end{aligned}
$$

Will this be true for any two events? Consider the events C and D, as defined above. It is important to recognize that the event (C or D) includes all the outcomes in C or D or both. That is,

$$
\begin{aligned}
P(C \text{ or } D) &= P(\text{observe an even number or a number less} \\
&\qquad \text{than 5}) \\
&= P(\text{observe 2, 4, 6 or observe 1, 2, 3, 4})
\end{aligned}
$$

Every outcome except 5 is included in (C or D). Thus, there are exactly five *different* favorable outcomes, even though the outcomes 2 and 4 are listed twice. Thus,

$$P(C \text{ or } D) = \frac{5}{6}$$

But, $P(C) + P(D) = \frac{3}{6} + \frac{4}{6}$, and this sum is $\frac{7}{6}$, not $\frac{5}{6}$. So, $P(C\ or\ D) \neq P(C) + P(D)$. In fact, $P(C) + P(D)$ cannot represent a probability at all since $\frac{7}{6}$ exceeds 1.

A little investigation will explain what seems to be an inconsistency. Although there are three outcomes in C and four outcomes in D, there are a total of five outcomes in either C or D or both. The outcomes 2 and 4 are contained in both C and D, and care must be taken to count each outcome exactly once. By calculating $P(C) + P(D)$, the probabilities for these two outcomes are added twice. To arrive at the correct result, the probability of this overlap, the event C *and* D, must be subtracted. That is,

$$P(C\ or\ D) = P(C) + P(D) - P(C\ and\ D)$$
$$= \frac{3}{6} + \frac{4}{6} - \frac{2}{6}$$
$$= \frac{5}{6}$$

This result agrees with the probability we originally computed for the event C *or* D and leads to the Addition Rule for any event of the form C *or* D:

$$P(C\ or\ D) = P(C) + P(D) - P(C\ and\ D)$$

The Addition Rule will work for any two events linked by *or*. Consider the events A and B described above. Does $P(A\ or\ B) = P(A) + P(B) - P(A\ and\ B)$? In this case, it is impossible to observe the event A *and* B (a 2 and a 6 at the same time). Therefore, $P(A\ and\ B) = 0$, making $P(A\ or\ B) = P(A) + P(B)$, or $\frac{1}{3}$, as before.

Consider another example of the use of the Addition Rule. Two symptoms of a common disease are a fever (F) and a rash (R). A local doctor reports that, out of a typical group of ten people with the disease, two will have the fever alone, three will have the rash alone, and one will have both symptoms. The accompanying diagram shows this situation. (The integers in the diagram represent the number of people in each set.)

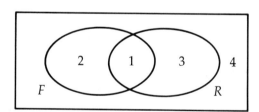

For a randomly selected person with the disease, $P(F) = \frac{3}{10}$, $P(R) = \frac{4}{10}$, $P(F\ and\ R) = \frac{1}{10}$, and $P(neither\ symptom) = \frac{4}{10}$. What is the probability that this person will have at least one symptom—that is, either one or both of the symptoms, the fever *or* the rash $(F\ or\ R)$? Now,

$$P(F\ or\ R) = P(F) + P(R) - P(F\ and\ R)$$
$$= \frac{3}{10} + \frac{4}{10} - \frac{1}{10}$$
$$= \frac{3}{5}$$

This calculation can be verified by looking at the diagram to see that six out of ten cases fall inside at least one of the sets identifying *F or R*. It is also interesting to notice that "at least one" means "not none." As we have seen, *P(neither symptom)* = $\frac{4}{10}$. Therefore, *P(not neither symptom)* = $1 - \frac{4}{10}$, or $\frac{6}{10}$. The double negative "not neither" is equivalent to "at least one."

In the previous examples, it was possible to find the probabilities without using the Addition Rule. Is the rule really necessary? In some cases it is. One such situation follows.

A computing center has two mainframe computers that operate independently. Let *A* denote the event that computer I is in operation at a randomly selected instant, and let *B* denote a similar event for computer II. Suppose *P(A)* = 0.9 and *P(B)* = 0.8. When you call the computer center from your terminal, what is the probability that at least one computer is running? The event *at least one computer is running* is *A or B*. Using the addition rule for *P(A or B)*, we have

$$P(A \text{ or } B) = P(A) + P(B) - P(A \text{ and } B)$$

Since the computers operate independently,

$$P(A \text{ and } B) = P(A) \times P(B)$$
$$= (0.9)(0.8)$$
$$= 0.72$$

Then,

$$P(A \text{ or } B) = 0.9 + 0.8 - 0.72$$
$$= 0.98$$

Note that the probability that at least one computer is in operation is greater than either *P(A)* or *P(B)*. Why is this a reasonable result?

Sometimes the interpretation of numbers in tables requires the correct addition and subtraction of probabilities. The table below shows the race and location of residence of 203,000,000 Americans.

Where Americans Live (in millions)			
	White (W)	Nonwhite (N)	Total
Urban (U)	101	17	118
Suburban (S)	28	3	31
Rural (R)	49	5	54
Total	178	25	203

Source: *The World Almanac & Book of Facts*, 1979 and 1984 edition, copyright © Newspaper Enterprise Association, Inc. 1978 and 1984, New York, NY 10166.

Suppose a pollster chooses a person at random from the U.S. population. What is the probability that he or she is from an urban or suburban area? Now,

$$P(U \text{ or } S) = P(U) + P(S) - P(U \text{ and } S)$$

But, since a person cannot be from both an urban and a suburban area, $P(U \text{ and } S) = 0$. Thus,

$$P(U \text{ or } S) = P(U) + P(S) - 0$$
$$= \frac{118}{203} + \frac{31}{203}$$
$$= \frac{149}{203}$$

What is the probability that the randomly selected person is from an urban or suburban area if he or she is known to be white? Looking at the column for White,

$$P(\text{urban white or suburban white}) =$$
$$P(\text{urban white}) + P(\text{suburban white}) - P(\text{urban and suburban white})$$
$$= \frac{101}{178} + \frac{28}{178} - 0$$
$$= \frac{129}{178}$$

What is the probability that the randomly selected person is either white or from an urban area? Once again the Addition Rule applies. Noting that 101,000,000 are both white *and* live in an urban area,

$$P(W \text{ or } U) = P(W) + P(U) - P(W \text{ and } U)$$
$$= \frac{178}{203} + \frac{118}{203} - \frac{101}{203}$$
$$= \frac{195}{203}$$

Now try some of the following Applications on your own.

Application 30

Using the Addition Rule

1. Refer to the two-dice experiment in Application 25. Calculate each probability in two ways, by counting dots and by using the Addition Rule.

   a. What is the probability of obtaining a sum of 8 or doubles?

   b. What is the probability of obtaining a sum of 7 or a sum of 11?

   c. What is the probability of obtaining at least one 6?

2. Refer to the standard deck of 52 playing cards described in Application 29, question 2. Use the Addition Rule to calculate the following probabilities.

   a. What is the probability that a card drawn at random is a heart or a spade?

   b. What is the probability that a card drawn at random is a heart or an ace?

   c. What is the probability that a card drawn at random is a red king or a diamond?

Application 31

Who Sees the Advertisement?

An advertising firm reports that a certain advertisement on regional radio and television is heard by 30 percent of the regional population on radio and is viewed by 20 percent of the population on TV. Only 5 percent of the regional population hear the ad on both radio and TV. These data are displayed in the figure below.

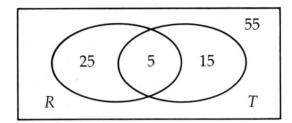

R = Radio, T = Television

Note that 25 percent hear the ad on radio only, and 15 percent see it on TV only.

A customer walks into the store that is sponsoring the advertisement. Find the probability that the customer:

1. has seen the ad on TV.

2. has seen the ad on TV *and* heard it on radio.

3. has neither seen nor heard the ad.

4. has either heard the ad on radio *or* seen it on TV.

What Is the Most Important Subject?

A Gallup youth survey (*Gainesville Sun*, February 13, 1985; The Associated Press) asked a sample of high school juniors and seniors the following question:

What course or subject that you have studied in high school has been the best for preparing you for your future education or career?

Among the males, 30 percent answered "mathematics." Among the females, only 19 percent gave this answer. Answer the following questions under the assumption that approximately 50 percent of the high school juniors and seniors are male. We will let M denote male, F denote female, and A denote the mathematics answer. Thus, MA will denote that a student is male and answered "mathematics."

For a randomly selected high school junior or senior, find the probability that:

1. The student answered "mathematics," given that she is female *(A given F)*.

2. The student is a female and answered "mathematics" *(FA)*.

3. The student answered "mathematics" *(A)*. (Note that $A = MA$ or FA.)

4. The student was male, given that the student answered "mathematics" *(M given A)*. [*Hint:* This is the ratio of the number of males who answered "mathematics" to the total number who answered "mathematics."]

Application 33

How Americans Get to Work

According to a recent survey (*Gainsville Sun*, February 25, 1985), 64 percent of Americans get to work by driving alone. Other methods for getting to work are listed in the table below.

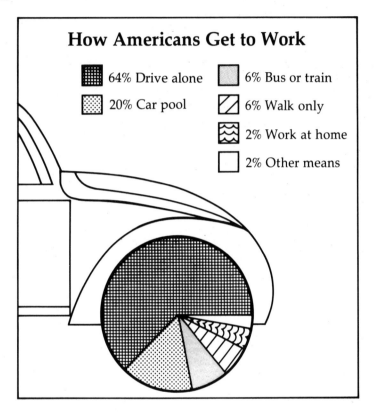

1. What is the probability that a randomly selected worker drives alone or in a car pool to get to work?

If two workers, *A* and *B*, are selected independently, what is the probability that:

2. both drive alone?

3. *A* drives alone and *B* walks?

4. *B* drives alone and *A* walks?

5. one of the two drives alone and the other walks?

6. exactly one of the two drives alone?

7. at least one of the two drives alone? [*Hint:* "At least one" means "exactly one of the two *or* both."]

Measuring Association

Foresters and biologists are often interested in studying how two species of plants (or animals) either mingle with each other or separate from each other. Suppose that we are studying two species of trees, A and B, that are both growing in a forest. One method of measuring their association is to randomly sample a tree, observe its species, and then observe the species of its nearest neighbor. This process is repeated for many trees. The data are then recorded as shown below. (The data represent experiments in two different forests.) Use these data to answer the questions below.

Species of Nearest Neighbor

	A	B	Total
A	30	10	40
B	5	55	60
Total	35	65	100

Species of Sampled Tree

Forest I

Species of Nearest Neighbor

	A	B	Total
A	5	35	40
B	30	30	60
Total	35	65	100

Forest II

1. For a randomly selected tree from Forest I, find the probability that:

   a. It is of species A.

   b. It has a neighbor of species A, given that it was observed to be of species A.

   c. Both it and its neighbor are of species A.

   d. Both it and its neighbor are of the same species.

2. Answer question 1, parts a through d, for a randomly selected tree from Forest II.

3. Do you think the probability found in question 1, part d, measures association? Explain.

4. Which forest seems to have more mixing of the species? Which forest seems to have more separation of the species? Discuss how you formulated your answers.

VI. SUPPLEMENTARY APPLICATIONS

The following Applications review the ideas presented in the first five sections of this book.

Application 35

___

Counting M&Ms

Open a bag (any size) of M&M candies. Make a list of all of the colors represented (dark brown, light brown, yellow, etc.). Next to each color listed, write the number of candies in the bag that are that color (example: yellow, 4; light brown, 7). Be sure to save this list for later.

1. How many M&Ms were there all together?

2. If we put all the candies back into the bag and select one from the bag without looking, what color is it most likely to be? What color is it least likely to be?

3. Is your answer to question 1 an even number or an odd number? If it is an odd number, select one M&M from the bag and eat it!

4. You should now have an even number of M&Ms. Randomly divide them into two piles of equal size. How many are there in each pile? (*Random* means that the M&Ms should be divided into two piles without paying attention to the colors.)

5. Without looking at the piles, which pile is likely to have more yellow candies?

6. Now take turns matching one M&M from pile 1 with one of the same color from pile 2. Remove the two candies of the same color and eat them. There will be some candies in each pile that have no color match in the opposite pile. Look at their colors. Can you explain why these colors are left?

7. Look back to question 5 above. If the division into two piles was carried out randomly, then neither pile is more likely to have more yellow candies. Can you explain why?

If you had reached into the original bag of M&Ms and selected one at random (without looking at the color),

8. Find *P(selecting a yellow)*.

9. Find *P(selecting a brown)*.

10. Find *P(selecting a blue)*.

11. Are the answers to questions 8, 9, and 10 theoretical or estimated probabilities?

The Labor Force

Selected Characteristics of the Civilian Labor Force
and the Unemployed, 1982

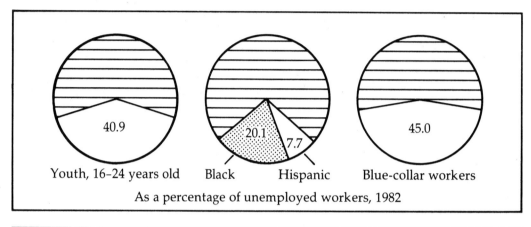

As a percentage of unemployed workers, 1982

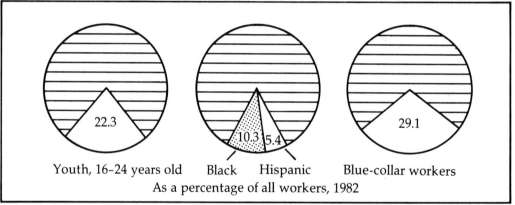

As a percentage of all workers, 1982

Source: "Workers Without Jobs: A Chartbook on Unemployment,"
Bureau of Labor Statistics, 1983.

Use the data in the graphs above to answer the following questions.

1. If you meet an unemployed worker, what is the probability that he or she is black?

2. If you meet a worker, what is the probability that he or she is black?

3. If you meet an unemployed worker, what are the odds in favor of him or her being between 16 and 24 years old?

4. If you meet a worker, what are the odds in favor of him or her having a blue-collar job?

Application 37

Using Random Numbers

Suppose Bob, Mary, Tom, Bill, and Alice are nominated for school safety patrol, but only two are to be chosen. The teacher could randomly choose two from this group of five by:

A. assigning each student a different number from 1 to 5.

B. entering the random number table at any place and reading right, left, up, or down until two numbers between 1 and 5 are found.

C. choosing the two people whose numbers are found in the table.

For example, if we begin in the lower right corner of the random number table in Application 19 and read to the left, the numbers are 0, 5, 9, 3, 2. The first two digits between 1 and 5 are 5 and 3. Thus, students having those two numbers would be selected.

Suppose the five students are numbered from 1 to 5 in the order in which their names appear above. Two students are selected by entering the random number table given in Application 19 at a random point and reading the numbers until the first two distinct digits between 1 and 5 appear. The two students with those numbers are selected.

1. Draw a tree diagram to represent the outcomes of this selection process. The first column of branches should indicate the five possibilities for the first selection. The second column of branches should indicate the possibilities for the second selection.

2. How many possible paths are on the tree?

3. Are the possible outcomes equally likely?

4. What is the probability that Mary and Tom are selected (in either order)?

5. What is the probability that two boys are selected?

6. What is the probability that at least one boy is selected?

7. What are the odds against selecting two girls?

8. What are the odds in favor of selecting at least one girl?

Choosing Students

Five students, Art, Bonnie, Carol, Doug, and Ed, volunteer to sell refreshments at the faculty–student basketball game, and only three students are needed. In order to select three students, the following procedure is to be used. Each of the ten possible selections of three students (listed below) is written on a piece of paper, and then one piece of paper is selected at random.

Art, Bonnie, Carol	Art, Bonnie, Doug	Bonnie, Carol, Doug
Art, Bonnie, Ed	Art, Carol, Doug	Bonnie, Carol, Ed
Art, Carol, Ed	Art, Doug, Ed	Bonnie, Doug, Ed
	Carol, Doug, Ed	

1. What is the probability that Art is selected?

2. What is the probability that Doug is *not* selected?

3. What is the probability that both Art and Ed are selected?

4. If Bonnie is selected, what is the probability that Carol is *not* selected?

5. What is the probability that either Bonnie or Carol is selected?

Application 39

Getting a Hit

Mickey Ruth is coming up to bat. The record of outcomes for his last 100 times at bat is shown in the accompanying table. Use these data to answer the following questions.

Home runs	4
Triples	1
Doubles	9
Singles	16
Walks	8
Sacrifices	2
Outs	60
Total	100

1. What is the probability that Mickey will get a hit on his next time at bat?

2. What is his batting average? (The batting average does not count walks or sacrifices as official times at bat.)

3. What is the probability that he will get a home run on his next time at bat?

4. How many walks can he be expected to get out of his next 15 times at bat?

5. What is the probability that he will *not* get a walk on his next time at bat?

6. If he gets a hit, what is the probability that it will be a single?

7. What are the odds against his getting a hit on his next time at bat?

8. What are the odds in favor of his getting an extra-base hit on his next time at bat?

Suppose Mickey Ruth comes up to bat twice in a game.

9. What is the probability that he gets two hits?

10. What are the odds in favor of him getting at least one hit?

Application 40

Chances of Failing

The diagram below shows the following information. In a certain class of 180 students, all of whom took both English and history, 15 failed history, 10 failed English, and 5 failed both. Find the probability that a student chosen at random from this class:

1. failed history and passed English.

2. failed English and passed history.

3. failed both subjects.

4. failed at least one subject.

5. failed neither subject.

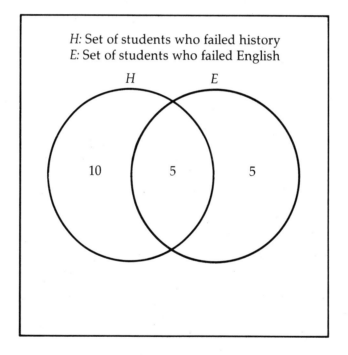

H: Set of students who failed history
E: Set of students who failed English

Application 41

Who Buys the Records?

A Gallup youth survey of 1983 reports that the percentage of teenagers who own over 50 records has decreased from 24 percent in 1981 to 13 percent in 1983. The percentage who own 20 or fewer records increased from 38 percent to 45 percent during the same period. (Source: The Associated Press.)

Suppose there were 1,000 teenagers in your school in 1981.

1. How many would you expect to own over 50 records?

2. How many would you expect to own 20 or fewer records?

3. Answer questions 1 and 2 for a school of 1,000 teenagers in 1983.

4. Does the information from the survey suggest that fewer records were sold in 1983 than in 1981?

5. Suppose you met a teenaged friend in 1983. What are the odds in favor of this friend owning over 50 records?

Probability in the Courtroom

A California court convicted a couple of a crime because the couple had six characteristics observed by witnesses of the crime. The prosecution's case relied heavily on the probabilities of these events, which were approximated as follows:

Characteristic	Probability
Black man with beard	$\frac{1}{10}$
Man with moustache	$\frac{1}{4}$
Woman with blond hair	$\frac{1}{3}$
Woman's hair in ponytail	$\frac{1}{10}$
Interracial couple	$\frac{1}{1,000}$
Driving yellow car	$\frac{1}{10}$

The prosecution argued that the probability of any one couple having all these characteristics was

$$\frac{1}{10} \times \frac{1}{4} \times \frac{1}{3} \times \frac{1}{10} \times \frac{1}{1,000} \times \frac{1}{10} = \frac{1}{12,000,000}$$

Therefore, the couple found to have these characteristics must be guilty.

A higher court overturned this conviction. Would you side with the lower court or higher court? Why? (See *Time*, April 26, 1968, p. 41, for more details.)

Application 43

Straight or Curly Hair?

Two parents with wavy hair can produce a child with hair that is straight, wavy, or curly. Genetic theory states that the odds in favor of such a child having straight hair are 1:3, the odds in favor of wavy hair are 1:1, and the odds in favor of curly hair are 1:3.

Suppose two parents with wavy hair have one child. What is the probability that the child has:

1. straight hair?

2. wavy hair?

3. hair that is not curly?

4. Are the stated odds consistent? That is, can all three statements on odds be true?

Suppose two parents with wavy hair have two children. What is the probability that:

5. both have straight hair?

6. at least one has straight hair?

7. Suppose your school contains 100 students whose parents both have wavy hair. How many of those students would you expect to have curly hair?

Estimating an Area

The square below measures 2 inches on each side, and the circle has a radius of $\frac{1}{2}$ inch. Therefore, the area of the square is 4 square inches, and the area of the circle is $\frac{1}{4} \pi$ square inches.

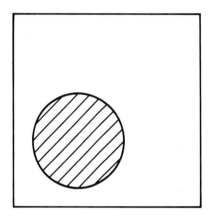

Place the square on a dart board and toss a dart into the square from 8 to 10 feet away. This approximates locating a random point inside the square. Repeat the process until at least 20 darts have landed inside the square. The probability that a dart landing inside the square also lands inside the circle is given by the area of the circle divided by the area of the square.

1. What is the probability of a dart landing inside the circle, given that it has landed inside the square? (Compute this theoretically.)

2. Among the darts landing inside the square, what fraction land inside the circle, for your experiment?

3. Is the experimental proportion in question 2 close to the theoretical probability in question 1?

4. Try the experiment again, and answer questions 2 and 3.

We can use the fraction of darts (random points) falling inside the shaded area to estimate the fractional part of the square covered by that shaded area. In the case of the circle, we knew the area, but for other shapes we might not. Consider the figure on page 61. The area of the square is 4 square inches.

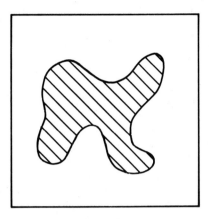

5. Toss darts at the figure from a distance of 8 to 10 feet until at least 20 darts hit inside the square. Of the darts inside the square, how many are inside the shaded area? Calculate the fraction of darts inside the square that are also inside the shaded area. This is an estimate of the fractional part of the square covered by the shaded area.

6. Since the area of the square is 4 square inches, find an estimate of the area of the shaded region.

7. Use this method to estimate an area, or areal proportion, of interest to you. Examples might be the proportion of your state covered by water or the proportion of green in a color photograph.

SPINNER BASE

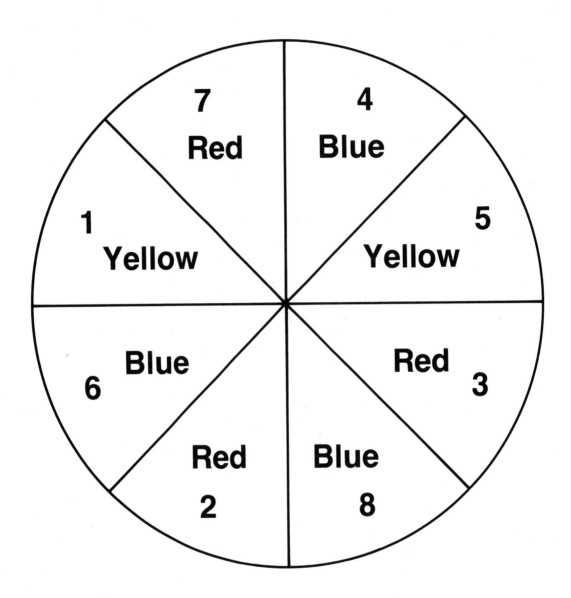

OUTCOMES FOR TOSSING TWO DICE

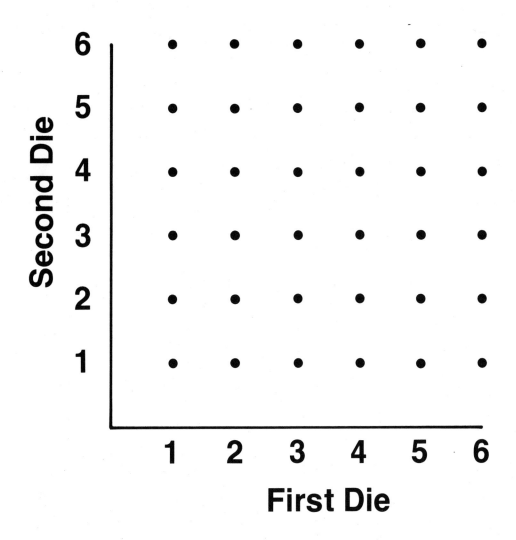

The Art and Techniques of Simulation

The Art and Techniques of Simulation was prepared under the auspices of the American Statistical Association—National Council of Teachers of Mathematics Joint Committee on the Curriculum in Statistics and Probability.

This book is part of the Quantitative Literacy Project, which was funded in part by the National Science Foundation.

The Art and Techniques of Simulation

Mrudulla Gnanadesikan
Fairleigh Dickinson University

Richard L. Scheaffer
University of Florida

Jim Swift
Nanaimo School District
Nanaimo, British Columbia, Canada

DALE SEYMOUR PUBLICATIONS

Cover: John Edeen and Francesca Angelesco
Technical Art: Colleen Donovan
Cartoonist: Barry Geller
Editing and Production: Larry Olsen

This publication was prepared as part of the American Statistical Association Project—Quantitative Literacy—with partial support of the National Science Foundation Grant No. DPE-8317656. Any opinions, findings, conclusions, or recommendations expressed in this publication are those of the authors and do not necessarily represent the views of the National Science Foundation. These materials shall be subject to a royalty-free, irrevocable, worldwide, nonexclusive license in the United States Government to reproduce, perform, translate, and otherwise use and to authorize others to use such materials for Government purposes.

ISBN 0-86651-336-1

Order Number DS01704

DALE
SEYMOUR
PUBLICATIONS
P.O. BOX 10888
PALO ALTO, CA 94303

CONTENTS

PREFACE

This is the third in a series of publications produced by the ASA-NCTM Joint Committee on the Curriculum in Statistics and Probability. The others are *Exploring Data, Exploring Probability,* and *Exploring Surveys and Information from Samples.* These four units cover the basic concepts of statistics and probability. The approach emphasizes use of real data, active experiments, and student participation. There are no complicated formulas or abstract mathematical concepts to confuse or mislead you.

The Art and Techniques of Simulation builds on the material in *Exploring Probability* and shows how practical problems, from the simple to the complex, can be solved, at least approximately, by using simple simulations. Many of the Applications herein are readily adapted to the computer, but all can be done without access to a computer.

I. INTRODUCTION

Simulation is a procedure developed for answering questions about real problems by running experiments that closely resemble the real situation. Many of you may have worked through the unit on probability and done experiments to estimate probabilities. You have also found probabilities by collecting data and observing the values of the variables. This unit will build on the experience you got from the previous units dealing with both probability and exploring data. It will show you how to find probabilities for complex events and how to understand the behavior and estimate the outcomes of real processes.

Suppose we want to find the probability that a three-child family contains exactly one girl. We can find a theoretical answer for this probability if we know something about the rules of probability. We could also estimate this probability if we could observe a large number of three-child families and count the number that contain exactly one girl. But what if we cannot compute the theoretical answer and do not have the time to locate three-child families for observation? The best plan, in this case, might be to *simulate* the outcomes for three-child families.

One way to accomplish this for our example is to toss coins to represent the three births. A head could represent the birth of a girl. Then, observing exactly one head in a toss of three coins would be similar, in terms of probability, to observing exactly one girl in a three-child family. We could easily toss the three coins many times to estimate the probability of seeing exactly one head. The result gives us an estimate of the probability of seeing exactly one girl in a three-child family. This is a simple problem to simulate, but the idea is very useful in complex problems for which theoretical probabilities may be nearly impossible to obtain.

Simulation is a technique that evolved as people tried to find ways to answer questions about the behavior of complex processes under varying conditions. For instance, in the process of designing the electronic guidance systems of a space shuttle, scientists would be interested in the probability of system failure for various possible designs. One way of estimating this probability would be actually to build the systems and test them in real flight conditions, but this would be very time consuming and expensive. Another way of estimating this probability is to simulate the performance of the guidance systems on a computer. The systems can then be observed through many simulated tests quite quickly, and the probabilities of failure can be estimated quite well. The simulations allow the scientist to choose the design that has the smallest probability of failure.

Simulations can also be used to help determine the outcomes of business ventures. Suppose you wanted to set up a lemonade stand but wanted to do so only if it were profitable. You could experiment with different prices per glass of lemonade and different lemonade mixtures while conducting your business, but you might use up your whole summer before you settled on the best price and best mixture. A better way to proceed would be to collect some data on important variables and simulate the performance of your lemonade stand. For example, you could ask some of your friends if they would pay 30 cents per glass as opposed to 20 cents per glass. You could also let them taste two different mixtures to see which one they preferred. The chance of selling a glass of lemonade might be affected by the weather, so you might want to estimate the proportion of sunny days in the summer for your location. This information could then be used to simulate the performance of your lemonade business. The simulation could allow you to estimate, for example, your chances of selling a glass of mixture A for 30 cents on a sunny day. You could also estimate your expected profits for a month.

This unit will provide an introduction to simulation techniques. It will begin with simple models for obtaining an estimate of the probability of an event and then progress toward answering more complex questions, such as "How much money can I expect to make from my lemonade stand?" The approach will *not* be computer dependent, although computer programs make the actual simulations somewhat easier to perform.

II. A SIMULATION MODEL

We will now look at one simulation problem in great detail. We will set up an eight-step process that will carry us through this problem. The same eight-step process should be used in all the Applications in this book.

Step 1   State the problem clearly.

It is important that the problem be stated so that all necessary information is given and the objective of the simulation is clear.

Example: Mary has not studied for her history exam. She knows none of the answers on a seven-question true–false exam, and she decides to guess at all seven. Estimate the probability that Mary will guess the correct answers to four or more of the seven questions.

Step 2   Define the key components.

The outcomes of most real situations we study will be made up of a series of key components. It is important to define these components clearly since they form the basis of our simulation.

Example: Answering the seven questions on Mary's exam forms the seven key components in this case. We must first simulate the answering of one question and then repeat that simulation six more times for the remaining questions.

Step 3   State the underlying assumptions.

Most real problems require some simplifying assumptions before a solution can be found. These assumptions should be clearly stated.

Example: We assume that Mary's guessing makes her equally likely to answer true or false on each question. Thus, Mary has a probability of one half of guessing the correct answer to any one question. We also assume that her guesses are independent—that is, her answer to any one question is not affected by her answers to previous questions.

Step 4   Select a model to generate the outcomes for a key component.

We model a key component by choosing a simple device to generate chance outcomes with probabilities to match those of the real situation.

Example: Since the probability that Mary guesses the correct answer on any one question is one half, we can model her answering a single question by tossing a coin and letting a head (H) stand for "correct answer" and a tail (T) stand for "incorrect answer."

Step 5   Define and conduct a trial.

A trial consists of a series of key component simulations that stops when the situation of interest has been simulated once.

Example: Mary is to guess seven answers in a row. Therefore, tossing a fair coin seven times simulates her answering one complete exam.

Step 6 Record the observation of interest.

Recall the objective of the simulation from step 1. Now, record the information necessary to reach that objective. In most cases, we will record whether the trial was favorable to an event of interest. In some cases, other numerical outcomes will be noted.

Example: After the coin is tossed seven times, we observe the number of heads. If the number of heads is four or more, then the trial is favorable to the event "Mary answers four or more questions correctly." We usually want to keep a record of the outcome for each trial.

Step 7 Repeat steps 5 and 6 a large number of times (at least 50).

The accurate estimation of a probability requires the experiment to contain many trials. If the experiment is done by hand, then 50 trials may be enough. If the experiment is done by computer, then 1,000 or more trials can be run. (When conducting the experiments by hand, divide the work so that no one student does more than about five trials.)

Example: Toss the coin seven more times and record the number of heads. Repeat this process for 50 trials of seven coin tosses.

Step 8 Summarize the information and draw conclusions.

We can now estimate the probability of an event of interest, *E*, by looking at

$$\frac{\text{the number of trials favorable to } E}{\text{the total number of trials in the experiment}}$$

Other summary statistics can be calculated. For example, we might be interested in the average value of some numerical outcomes.

Example: We can now estimate the probability that Mary correctly answers four or more questions by looking at

$$\frac{\text{the number of trials containing four or more heads}}{\text{the total number of trials in the experiment}}$$

We can also calculate the average number of correct answers per trial and use this as an estimate of the expected number of correct answers when guessing on a seven-question true–false exam.

Table 1 shows the results of a computer simulation of the true–false exam, with 100 trials. Table 1 was obtained by using a computer program written for Apple II computers. A listing of this program is shown on page 5. Your instructor can supply you with computer programs to work all of the Application problems in this book.

SIMPRO1

Program to Simulate Trials with Repeated Coin Tosses

```
10    PRINT "PROGRAM TO SIMULATE TRIALS WITH REPEATED"
20    PRINT "COIN TOSSES IN EACH TRIAL"
30    PRINT
40    PRINT "YOU WILL HAVE TO ENTER THE NUMBER OF"
50    PRINT "KEY COMPONENTS IN EACH TRIAL AND THE"
60    PRINT "NUMBER OF TRIALS."
70    PRINT
80    INPUT "ENTER THE NUMBER OF KEY COMPONENTS";N
90    PRINT
100   INPUT "ENTER THE NUMBER OF TRIALS";NT
110   PRINT
120   DIM T$(NT,N),C(2 * N)
130   PRINT "RESULTS OF";NT;"TRIALS AND THE NUMBER OF HEADS"
140   FOR I = 1 TO NT
150   LET NH = 0
160   FOR J= 1 TO N
170   LET X = RND (1)
180   IF X < .5 THEN 220
190   T$ (I,J) = "H"
200   NH = NH + 1
210   GOTO 230
220   T$ (I,J) = "T"
230   IF J = N THEN 260
240   PRINT T$ (I,J);
250   GOTO 270
260   PRINT T$ (I,J);" ";NH,
270   NEXT J
280   C(NH + 1) = C(NH + 1) + 1
290   NEXT I
300   PRINT
310   PRINT
320   PRINT "# OF HEADS", "# OF TRIALS"
330   FOR K= 1 TO N + 1
340   PRINT K - 1,C(K)
350   NEXT K
360   END
```

Table 1
Computer Simulation for 100 Trials of Tossing a Coin 7 Times,
with Number of Heads Noted in Second Column

TTTTTHT	1	TTTTTTH	1	TTTHHHH	4	HHTTTHH	4
HTTTTHT	2	TTHHTTT	2	HTTHTHH	4	HHHTTTT	3
THHTTTT	2	THHHTTT	3	HHHHTHH	6	TTHHHHT	4
HHHHHTH	6	HTTTHHT	3	HTHHTHT	4	TTTTHHT	2
HTHHHHH	6	THTTHTT	2	HTTHHTH	4	TTHTHHH	4
TTHHHHH	5	THHHTTT	3	TTHHTHH	4	HHTHTTT	3
HTHHHHT	5	THTTHTH	3	HHHTHHT	5	HHTHTTT	3
THTTHHH	4	TTTHHHH	4	HHTTHHH	5	HHHHHHT	6
HHHHHTT	5	HTTTTHH	3	HTTHHHT	4	HHHTTTH	4
TTTHTHH	3	HHHHHTT	5	THTHTHT	3	TTHTTTH	2
HTHHTHT	4	HHHHTHT	5	HTTTHHT	3	HTHHHHT	5
HHHTTHH	5	HTTHTTT	2	HHTTTTH	3	HHTTHHH	5
TTTHHTH	3	HTTHHTH	4	HTTHTTT	2	THTTHTT	2
HHTTHTH	4	THHTTHT	3	THTHTTH	3	HTHTHHT	4
TTTTTHH	2	TTHHHTT	3	HTTTHTH	3	TTHTTTH	2
HTTTTTT	1	HHTHTTH	4	THHTHTH	4	HHHTTTT	3
THHTHHH	5	HHTHTTT	3	HHTTHTT	3	TTTTTTH	1
TTTTTHT	1	THTHHHT	4	TTTTHTT	1	TTHHHTM	4
THHTHHT	4	TTHHTTH	3	HTTHTHH	4	THTTHHT	3
HHHHTHH	6	HHTTTTT	2	TTHHHHT	4	HHHHTHT	5
HTHTHHH	5	HTHHTTT	3	HTHHHTT	4	HHTHTHT	4
HTHHTHH	5	HTHTHTT	3	HTTTTHT	2	HHTTTHH	4
HHHTTHH	5	HTHTTHH	4	HTTHTHH	4	THTHHTT	3
HTTHHTH	4	HTTTHHH	4	TTTHTTH	2	TTHHTHH	4
THHTHHT	4	TTTTHTT	1	HTTTTHT	2	TTHHTHT	3

Table 2
Summary of Table 1 Outcomes for Number of Heads Occurring per Trial
in 100 Trials of 7 Coin Tosses

Number of Heads per Trial	Number of Trials (7 Coin Tosses) with This Outcome	Estimated Probability
0	0	$\frac{0}{100}$
1	7	$\frac{7}{100}$
2	15	$\frac{15}{100}$
3	26	$\frac{26}{100}$
4	32	$\frac{32}{100}$
5	15	$\frac{15}{100}$
6	5	$\frac{5}{100}$
7	0	$\frac{0}{100}$

In Table 1, the numbers next to the outcomes of the seven key components show the number of heads and make the counting of heads easier. We see from the table that the first trial resulted in TTTTTHT. One head in the trial corresponds to Mary guessing only one answer correctly. Table 2 contains a summary of the numerical outcome of interest— the number of heads. We see that, in 100 trials, one head occurred 7 times, two heads occurred 15 times, and so on. The probability that Mary guesses four or more answers correctly is estimated by

$$\frac{(32 + 15 + 5 + 0)}{100} = \frac{52}{100} = 0.5, \text{ approximately}$$

You may be interested in knowing how close your simulation results are to the theoretical probabilities. The mathematical formula for these probabilities, in the case where each key component has only two possible outcomes denoted as *yes* and *no*, is as follows:

Let n = number of key components in each trial
k = number of *yes*es observed
p = probability of getting a *yes* as the outcome of a key component

Then, the probability of getting k *yes*es in n repeats of the key component is given by the formula

$$\frac{n(n-1)\,(n-2)\ldots(n-k+1)}{k(k-1)\,(k-2)\ldots 2 \times 1} \times p^k(1-p)^{n-k}$$

For example, the theoretical probability of seeing exactly $k = 4$ heads in a series of $n = 7$ coin tosses is

$$\frac{7\,(6)\,(5)\,(4)}{4\,(3)\,(2)\,(1)} \left(\frac{1}{2}\right)^4 \left(\frac{1}{2}\right)^3 = 35 \left(\frac{1}{2}\right)^7 = \frac{35}{128} = 0.27$$

which is close to our simulated result of $\frac{32}{100} = 0.32$.

The average number of correct guesses for the seven-question exam is calculated from the formula

$$\frac{\text{number of trials favorable to } E}{\text{total number of trials}} =$$

$$\frac{1(7) + 2(15) + 3(26) + 4(32) + 5(15) + 6(5) + 7(0)}{100} = 3.48$$

Thus, we expect Mary to guess three or four answers correctly on a seven-question true–false exam.

In performing a large simulation using a coin-tossing model, it may be too time consuming actually to toss the coins the required number of times. In that case, Table 3 can be used. This table shows the results of 2,000 coin tosses. Just enter the table at any point and read up, down, left, or right to obtain random results for the required number of tosses.

We used a coin to generate the outcomes of our experiment because we wanted a device that would generate two outcomes with equal frequency. You do not have to use a coin. You can set up your own scheme for simulating results of a trial that can have only two possible outcomes. For example, you could use a die as your device. Since a toss of a die can result in six outcomes, three of them even and three of them odd, you could have the even numbers represent the result of your event of interest. You could also make your own spinner. The main thing to watch for is that the outcomes have an equal chance of occurring.

Here are two more examples of how to use the eight-step process.

Table 3
2,000 Tosses of a Coin

TTHTH	THHTH	THHTT	TTHTH	THHTT	HHTHT	HTHTH	TTTHT	TTHTT	HHTTH
THHTT	HHTHH	HTTTH	TTHHT	HHHTH	HHTTH	HTHHT	HTHHT	THTTT	TTTHT
TTHTT	HTTTT	TTTHH	TTTTH	HHHTH	HHHTH	HTHTH	HHTTT	THTTT	HTHHH
THHHH	THTTT	TTHHH	HHHTH	HTTTH	HTHHH	TTTTT	HTHTH	THTTT	HHTHH
HHHTH	THTHH	THHHH	HHTTT	HTHHH	THTTH	HHTTH	HTHHH	HTHTH	THTHH
THTTH	THHTT	THHHT	TTTHH	HTTTH	THTHH	HTHTH	TTTHT	TTHHT	THTTT
HHHTH	THHTH	HHHTT	TTHHT	TTHHH	HHHTT	HTHTT	HHTTT	TTHHT	HTTTT
TTTTT	HTHHH	HTHHT	HTTHH	HTHHT	HTHHH	HTTHT	HTTTH	TTTHT	THTHT
HTTTT	TTTTT	THHTH	HHHTT	HTTHH	HTTHT	HHHTT	HHHTT	TTTHT	TTHHT
THTHT	THTHT	HHHTT	HTTHT	TTTTT	THHHH	THTTH	THHTH	HHTTH	HHTTT
THHHT	HHHTH	HTTTT	TTTTH	HHTTH	THTHH	TTTHT	THHHT	TTTTT	HTHTT
TTHHT	THHTT	THTHH	THHHH	THHTH	TTTTH	TTTHH	HHTHT	HHTHH	THHHH
HTHTT	THTHH	TTHTT	THHHH	HTHTH	HHTHT	HHHTH	HHHTH	HTHTH	THHTT
TTHHH	TTHHT	HHHHT	HTTTH	HHHHH	TTHTH	HTHHH	TTHTT	HHTHH	HTHTH
HTTHT	HTHHH	THTHH	THTHT	HTHTH	TTTTH	HHTTT	HTHHH	HHTHH	THTTH
THTTH	TTTTT	TTTTH	TTTTH	TTHHT	HTHTT	HTTTT	THHTT	THTHT	TTHTT
HTHTT	HHTHH	HHHTT	TTHTH	HHTHT	HHHTH	TTHHH	HTHHH	HHHHT	THHTH
HHTTT	HTHHT	THHTT	HTTTT	THTTH	TTHHT	TTTTT	HHHHH	HHHHH	HTTTT
HHHTH	TTHTT	TTTTH	HHTHT	HTTTH	TTHTH	THHHT	THHHH	TTTHT	TTHHT
HTHTH	THTHH	THHHT	THTTH	HHTHT	THTHH	THHTH	THTHH	THHHH	HTTTH
HTTTT	TTHHH	TTHHT	HHHTH	THTTH	THTTT	HTTHT	HTTTT	TTTHH	HTHTT
HHTHH	THHHT	HTHTH	THHTH	HTHHT	HTTTH	TTHHT	TTTTT	HHTTT	HTTHH
TTTTT	HHTTH	THTTT	HHHHT	THHHT	THTHH	TTTHT	HHHTT	HTTHT	HHTTH
HHTTH	TTTTT	HHTHT	HTTHH	THHTT	HHHTT	HHTHH	THTHT	THTTH	HTTHH
HHHHT	HTHHH	HTTTH	HHHHH	HHHTH	HHHTT	TTTHT	TTTHT	HTTTH	HHHTT
HTHHT	TTHHH	HTTHH	HHTHH	HTHTT	HTTTT	THTHT	HHHHT	THTTH	THTHT
TTHTT	HHTTH	HTTTT	TTHTT	THHHT	THTTT	HHHTT	HHHHH	TTHTT	HHHHH
THTHH	HTHTT	HTTTH	THHHH	THHHT	THTTH	HHHTH	THHHH	TTTTH	HHHTH
TTHTT	HTHHH	TTHHT	TTTTH	TTTTT	TTTTH	TTHTT	HHHHH	HTTTT	HHTTH
HTHHH	HHTHT	THHTT	HTHHT	THTTT	THTTT	TTHHT	THTHH	TTHHT	TTHTT
THHHT	TTHHT	HHTTH	HHTHH	THHHH	THTHH	THHHH	TTHTT	HTTTH	HTHHT
HTHTT	HTHHH	THHTT	HTTTT	TTTTT	TTTHT	THTTT	TTTTT	THHTT	THTHT
HTTHT	THHHT	HTTTH	THTHT	HTHHH	TTTTT	THHHT	TTTTT	THHHH	HHHHH
HTTTH	HHHHH	THTHT	HTHHT	HHHTT	TTHHT	THTHT	THHHH	THTHH	HTTTT
HTHHT	TTTTH	HHTHH	HHTTH	TTTHH	HTHTT	THTHT	TTHHT	TTHTH	HTHTT
TTTTH	HTHTT	TTTHT	HHTHH	HHHHH	HHTHT	THTTT	HTTHT	HTHHT	THTTH
TTTTT	TTTTH	HHHHH	TTTHT	HHTTH	TTTHH	HHTTH	HTTTT	HTHHH	HHTHH
TTHHH	TTHHT	THHHH	HTHTH	HTTTT	THTHT	HTHTH	HHHHT	THTHT	TTTHH
HTHHH	HTTHH	HHHTH	HTHHH	THTTH	THHHH	HHTTH	THTHH	HTTHH	TTHTT
HHTTT	THHTT	THHHT	HTTTT	THTHT	THHHT	TTHHH	HHHHT	HTHTT	HTTTT

Example 1

Step 1   State the problem clearly.

What is the probability that a three-child family will contain exactly one girl?

Step 2   Define the key components.

A key component is the birth of one child, which may be either a boy or a girl.

Step 3   State the underlying assumptions.

We assume that the probability of the birth of a female child is one half and that the sex of a child is independent of the sex of any other child.

Step 4   Select a model to generate the outcomes for a key component.

We will toss a coin and let heads correspond to a female birth. (We could also use a die and let an even number correspond to a female birth, or we could use a random number table and let digits 0 through 4 correspond to a female birth.)

Step 5   Define and conduct a trial.

We will toss a coin three times to represent a three-child family. The first trial (set of three coin tosses) turned out to be HHT, which corresponds to two girls and one boy being born into the family.

Step 6   Record the observation of interest.

We are interested only in whether or not exactly one girl was born into the three-child family. The first trial (HHT) was *not* favorable to the event of interest.

Step 7   Repeat steps 5 and 6 until 50 trials are reached.

The results of 50 trials are shown below. Asterisks mark those trials favorable to the event "exactly one girl."

HHT	THH	HHH	THT*	HTT*
TTT	THT*	HTH	THH	HTH
HHH	HHH	HHT	THH	HTH
HTT*	HHH	HTH	HHT	THH
HHH	THT*	TTT	TTT	TTH*
HTT*	HTH	HTT*	THT*	THH
HHT	HHT	HTT*	HHH	HHH
TTT	THT*	HTH	TTT	TTT
TTH*	HHT	HTH	TTT	HHT
THH	THT*	HTT*	THT*	HHH

Step 8   Summarize the information and draw conclusions.

There are 15 trials favorable to the event of interest. Therefore, the probability of seeing exactly one girl in a three-child family is estimated to be $\frac{15}{50}$ = 0.30.

Example 2

Step 1   State the problem clearly.

Our new neighbor has two children, but I do not know their sex. However, I am told that there is at least one girl in the family. What is the probability that there are two girls in the family?

Step 2   Define the key components.

A key component is the birth of a child, which may be either a boy or a girl.

Step 3   State the underlying assumptions.

We assume that the probability of the birth of a female child is one half and that the sex of one child is independent of the sex of the other child.

Step 4   Select a model for a key component.

We will toss a coin and let heads correspond to a female birth.

Step 5   Define and conduct a trial.

We toss a coin twice since there are two children in the family. However, if two tails come up, we do *not* count the toss as a trial. At least one head must appear because we *know* that there is at least one girl in the family. Our first trial was HT, which we can keep in our simulation because an H occurred.

Step 6   Record the observation of interest.

The observation in this example is simply whether or not two heads (two girls) appear on the trial. The first trial (HT) was *not* favorable to this event.

Step 7   Repeat steps 5 and 6 until 50 trials are reached.

The results of 50 trials are shown in the following display. Asterisks mark the trials favorable to the event "two girls."

HT	HT	HH*	TH	TH
HH*	HH*	TH	HH*	HH*
HT	HH*	HH*	HT	HT
HT	TH	HH*	TH	HH*
HH*	TH	TH	HT	HH*
TH	HH*	HT	TH	TH
HH*	TH	HH*	TH	HT
TH	HH*	HH*	HH*	TH
TH	HH*	TH	TH	HT
HT	HT	HH*	TH	HT

Step 8   Summarize the information and draw conclusions.

It is seen that 19 of the 50 trials are favorable to the event of interest. Therefore, our estimate of the probability that there are two girls in the family, when we know that there is at least one girl, is $\frac{19}{50} = 0.38$.

Now apply the eight-step procedure to the following problems.

Application 1

The Passing Game

A quarterback on a football team completes 50 percent of his passes. Suppose he makes 10 passes in a game. Use a simulation model to find the following estimates.

1.   Estimate the probability that he completes all passes.

2.   Estimate the probability that he completes exactly five passes.

3.   Estimate the probability that he completes at least five passes.

4.   What number of completions, per 10 passes in a game, is most likely?

5.   Guess his average number of completions per game without using simulation.

6.   Calculate the average number of completions per game from your simulation. Is this average close to your answer to question 5?

$$\text{average number of completions} = \frac{\text{sum of number of completions}}{\text{number of trials}}$$

(*Hint:* In this simulation, the probability of the quarterback completing any one pass is one half. This probability is assumed to remain the same for each pass, and the outcome of any one pass is assumed to be independent of those that preceded it. A total of at least 50 trials should be run in the simulation, but these could be combined from more than one student.)

Application 2

All That Jazz

John decides to set up a jazz group with his seven best friends. The group will work only if at least five of his friends can join. Using simulation, answer the following questions.

1. If John thinks that there is a 50 percent chance that each of his friends will join the group, can you estimate the probability of getting at least five friends to join the group?

2. Do you think John is being too ambitious in planning a group of at least five?

3. What is the most likely size of his group? (That is, what number that will join, out of the seven, has the highest estimated probability?)

(*Hint:* You could use the simulation results from the series of true-false questions in Tables 1 and 2 to answer these questions.)

Application 3

Aardvarks Versus Bears

Two evenly matched baseball teams, team A and team B, are to play a five-game series. All five games are played, no matter who wins. For simplicity, we assume that the outcome of any one game is independent of the outcomes of any games that might have preceded it. Use simulation to answer the following questions.

1. Find the probability that team A wins three or more games and thereby wins the series.

2. Find the probability that either team A or team B wins four or more games.

3. Find the probability that no team wins two or more games in a row.

4. Estimate the number of games you would expect team A to win in such a five-game series.

5. What number of wins for team A has the highest probability of occurring?

(*Hint:* In this simulation, team A has a probability of one half of winning any one game since the teams are evenly matched. The outcome of one game can be simulated by a coin toss, with heads denoting "team A wins the game." You can use Table 3 to get the outcome of a coin toss.)

Application 4

The Water System

The diagram below describes the five aging pumping stations and the water-main system for a city. At any particular time, the probability of pump failure at each pumping station is 0.5. For water to flow from A to B, both pumps in at least one path must be working. For example, if pumps 1 and 2 are working, water will flow. If pumps 2 and 3 are working, water will flow. If pumps 2 and 4 are *not* working, water will not flow. Simulate the pumping operation and answer the following questions.

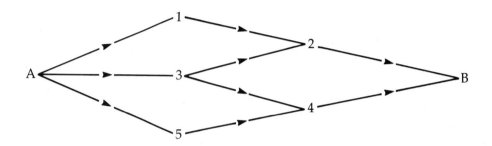

1. Estimate the probability that water will flow from A to B at any particular time.

2. On the average, how many stations were working at any time, according to your simulation?

3. Estimate the probability that the 1–2 path is working at any time.

(*Hint:* It is now important to keep track of which pumps are working. You might let five different students represent the five pumps. Each tosses one coin, with heads representing "the pump works." Then, observe whether or not there is at least one working path from A to B. Water will flow if you get two or more heads in sequence in five coin tosses. Note also that each trial must be counted only once, even if more than one path is open. Repeat the tosses for more trials. Combine the data with other groups of students until at least 50 trials are conducted.)

III. SIMULATION WHEN PROBABILITIES DIFFER FROM ONE HALF

In the examples that we have discussed so far, we have generated the outcomes of our experiments and trials by tossing a coin. We did this because each of the outcomes had an equal chance of happening. Suppose we had a key component that could result in three outcomes, all of them equally likely to take place. The coin would not be the appropriate device in this case. We need some device that will generate one of three numbers without favoring any one of them. There are several devices one can use to accomplish this. We will describe three such devices in this section. You may be able to think of some others yourself.

Spinner

You have all played games that have used spinners. You can make one yourself by following these steps:

A. Draw a circle on a piece of cardboard. Divide the circle into as many equal parts as the number of outcomes. Number each part. If we have three outcomes, then we would divide the circle into three equal parts. (*Hint:* You will need a compass for this.)

B. Take a large paper clip and a sharp pencil. Hold one end of the clip in place at the center of the circle using the tip of the pencil. Spin the other end of the clip and note where it stops. You have now obtained a random number.

Die

Another device you can use is a die. A die has six faces, each with a different number on it, and every time you toss a die, any one of the six faces can be on the top. That means that each of the six numbers has an equal chance of being the number on the top face of the die. See if you can figure out how to use a die to simulate a trial with either two, three, or six outcomes. You may refer to Table 4 (page 16) instead of actually tossing a die.

The dodecahedral die is a die with 12 faces. A dodecahedral die is a useful device to use when 12 outcomes are equally likely. Think about how you might use a dodecahedral die when two, three, four, or six outcomes are equally likely. You may refer to Table 5 (page 17) instead of actually tossing a dodecahedral die. In Table 5, we use the number 0 to represent an outcome of 10, the letter *a* to represent an outcome of 11, and the letter *b* to represent an outcome of 12.

Regular Die

Dodecahedral Die

Table 4
Table of Random Numbers from 1 to 6 Simulating 2,000 Throws of a Regular Die

22212	26352	56651	34314	56215	14453	14662	23224	65354	16664
12415	15552	23426	21231	32432	42526	12562	44664	65436	35464
36551	44222	33121	36121	41615	42115	65445	23222	25241	13333
31552	32655	23655	41311	62642	53314	54514	24355	42555	56351
23514	53141	12444	66246	15634	13151	54541	54341	51321	66144
43265	63546	15164	45546	42162	54232	43143	16663	46253	55665
25363	23343	31462	26134	35333	44632	24634	54561	51565	63526
32311	22213	63121	35255	35336	13531	32461	22346	32235	26353
15416	54541	22632	55614	26543	63255	44662	65632	31433	36423
14255	21451	23564	42463	21244	65222	14565	46532	45313	35451
43623	31264	45635	14121	63252	36453	43454	53114	12254	35151
36425	51555	65426	34525	22425	34641	56162	42444	31232	65331
12356	42164	33251	34512	51412	34326	15213	11315	56351	24662
52444	25262	51452	55254	24233	52254	21223	36616	44224	52313
14532	62522	62532	64445	21426	63116	16365	15261	26352	44512
46216	55534	54264	41432	35565	43111	42524	44656	52261	62464
33646	52544	15662	32424	21323	52354	56545	24156	31132	12353
26461	44564	23643	16325	34563	23442	21422	26513	35113	24633
42131	41436	24443	63453	46656	12541	32614	54513	51352	34164
63533	22111	35511	33344	63656	55213	24626	14156	25456	24143
36261	52416	62663	16412	44525	11561	26146	51136	66531	42421
35244	55231	24525	56466	13433	14534	42145	43443	56624	34561
21614	26362	33265	65245	56663	63631	44342	64655	41322	32111
13621	35363	15536	61566	33425	64541	51156	34316	34556	15115
42141	26564	54215	45424	24655	55565	46114	16565	15352	56314
42524	64442	15624	54224	63426	61366	16122	52225	51111	15521
56113	12124	33111	13554	55553	65135	64562	15363	23456	53311
15555	35611	11314	63631	12522	32541	14524	43363	34322	25224
34364	62151	41423	52545	66522	51433	42563	62153	22163	16166
53215	36451	34221	24556	62133	14352	55416	52333	54243	12521
25446	64511	12443	11543	61163	65552	42134	16245	31452	64341
54245	41443	15125	41463	14534	16641	35356	43114	53335	52323
34663	26566	32565	53334	61523	15622	61141	43655	55246	31551
66162	13421	46652	65453	31363	33536	44414	21466	12213	11143
45633	63221	31542	44224	12345	64342	64542	46635	35613	22135
23566	65522	25122	26255	22442	15613	54225	33113	25312	25541
36314	13244	31254	62551	53223	24264	13446	66416	23412	65534
16536	12363	46616	62326	46521	41655	45422	24236	11441	15516
33632	66322	53121	31645	45211	15443	25351	13644	63641	43656
42465	66126	44535	11223	21631	12326	26213	43265	11132	13442

Table 5
Table of Random Numbers from 1 to 12 Simulating 2,000 Tosses of a Dodecahedral Die (0 = 10, a = 11, b = 12)

64b73	b1ba1	b7730	61528	7b948	4913b	5a941	77a67	25250	00167
64867	89428	b4275	21b31	98b19	8a15b	51246	07b32	56589	85a58
53577	28907	82709	44ab6	1b1a3	a8746	29a30	a7779	154a3	381b6
86311	66b65	8ba32	2500b	91024	4856a	079aa	16014	3749a	85527
97434	48916	8ab79	19b4b	18984	68b00	46424	46900	3b998	b1218
586a9	831b6	b7b34	72468	17a22	747a8	3a0a2	47617	1635a	b3b58
65824	40342	b04a5	aa938	357b0	32661	05966	68484	37b39	98341
a9325	81415	88b05	69359	330b3	516a0	83a82	98965	42219	b0a5b
07818	80447	485a8	603a3	a99a0	509b1	55696	98319	47930	94821
a7171	59170	98aaa	32a78	1ba60	760b9	292a8	89458	71b81	aa299
46018	38558	a9155	67931	b1570	13985	87092	6a431	8987a	466b1
89a58	55493	27030	44b54	87325	9086a	8a647	8372b	27688	4b341
43b69	60415	b7908	32228	5b543	13387	23801	978b9	00892	03098
08597	74421	4458a	17542	97909	36b28	7b304	670a6	694b6	7b20b
025ab	a3792	5948a	281bb	86293	46940	3a656	4012a	44120	9a4a1
32bb3	90845	89b7a	104b2	55a48	b0283	b04a6	98685	74bb6	972a8
88652	31740	57a8a	40b63	8029b	bb927	64a66	a4658	22642	43845
23758	b5922	8b75b	2b758	11995	b4460	64924	36136	40111	4aa28
b87a9	23a42	87272	00636	58a7a	7a873	32370	62608	4b217	90801
4b023	25075	91375	aa7b2	1b761	60a89	b041b	667b4	859a8	a0600
63103	64383	38849	33324	96158	5b566	6a78b	64405	46864	15855
9007b	96b05	ab50b	67491	0b986	24777	6b168	08589	09089	68896
795a1	82331	69b45	65396	26b61	a55a3	87988	14192	15b53	17806
25712	87a09	4867a	798b5	80818	56814	90035	132b3	5b303	b3442
57089	89978	6a452	61596	10850	2420b	87978	97290	6799a	99711
89824	47943	3bb46	63850	71aa5	62b96	09b52	2b212	22391	67925
62a70	508b6	14480	5614a	06a62	6101b	0219b	b7549	75360	00994
14930	36165	b622b	9b264	8118a	70956	a6335	9ba81	92253	29193
a7abb	496ba	8736a	1b39a	90b99	88bb9	03024	72574	24917	59996
68885	33a67	54171	3919a	47a29	6a813	697a0	4a87a	284a1	a7106
32b8b	b295a	92247	b241b	43971	2b5a4	8324a	7a6b4	aa308	95532
37572	53a25	109bb	a8510	04298	87113	2b91b	90195	49201	56957
9a695	00249	35507	63982	8b301	ab401	b8a65	50881	b4271	6b308
31592	15117	49b89	287b2	2bb90	62464	7b2b7	b4779	731a9	50791
30874	19a71	7b116	71605	29099	35885	350a5	713a1	53b95	82800
08173	82603	92281	b109a	a2782	07797	9a435	ab679	02795	4602a
93818	7483a	85b61	376b1	43a65	964a4	16174	51512	80015	12786
48b86	27168	1246a	358b5	37108	2462a	25215	0137a	b5830	b0459
1b6a9	5911a	6b584	a3203	65277	47969	39198	6b92a	37358	3a663
a7453	0b805	57070	6804b	07924	99330	28736	93586	45291	94714

Random Number Tables

Suppose the digits from 0 through 9 are written on ten chips, one number per chip, and placed in a box. The chips are mixed, and one is drawn out without the number being seen. The number selected is called a *random number*, or *random digit*, because it is equally likely to have any value from 0 to 9. By replacing that chip and repeating the selection process, a second random number can be drawn. If this process is repeated many times, a table of random numbers like Table 6 can be formed.

Most random number tables are generated by a computer, but they have the same result as drawing numbers out of a box. Each number drawn is equally likely to take on any of the ten possible values, and the draws are independent of each other.

Consider a key component with ten possible outcomes (like selecting one of ten students to serve on a committee). We can simulate this component by using a random number table. First, number the students from 0 to 9. Second, enter the random number table at any random point. (You may just drop your pencil onto the table and take the number closest to its point.) Third, select the student whose number matches the number selected from the table. We have, by this method, *randomly* selected one student from the ten.

A trial may consist of more than one such key component. For example, three different classes of size ten may each be selecting one person for the committee. We can find three random numbers by locating a random starting point and then reading a series of three numbers going up, down, right, or left on the table. (We do not need to have three different random starting points.)

Random number tables can be used to generate the results of a trial with almost any probability structure. For example, suppose a salesman makes a sale to 35 percent of the customers. We could simulate the result of a contact with a customer by using these tables. Since the salesman makes a sale to 35 out of 100 customers, we can let the first 35 two-digit numbers (00, 01, . . ., 34) represent a sale. This means that, if we read a two-digit number from the table and it is *less than* 35, then it is a sale. (Note that 00 must be included as a possible number.) Table 6 gives 2,000 random digits grouped for convenience into groups of five digits. Suppose we start at the eleventh row of Table 6 and on the eleventh and twelfth columns, reading down. The first five two-digit numbers are 76, 37, 05, 10, 95. So, we now have results of five key components: no sale, no sale, sale, sale, no sale—or two sales in five contacts.

These are only some of the ways you can generate random numbers of any size. If you have a microcomputer available to you, you can probably generate these numbers yourself using a random number generator function that is built into the computer.

Table 6
2,000 Random Digits from 0 to 9

78086	27605	80783	72059	05060	21366	84811	80730	77042	25406
36673	74153	37788	35736	83780	11566	25916	85274	27965	27549
09752	89231	06739	64351	80303	47999	15059	00677	46402	98961
58358	21124	08164	56928	95491	80511	23897	96281	19001	42952
89928	22964	26249	90286	41979	64737	99888	81369	22711	40318
49390	91663	94701	66328	08696	43795	13916	65570	73393	43882
22219	93199	21573	13645	72126	38799	89648	26301	80918	55096
28034	42119	88853	07211	56700	59113	84358	86127	94675	99511
58449	34746	64619	19171	63533	97899	84381	65023	80908	18694
10920	69975	82955	27251	43127	99059	25076	48299	71133	60036
36422	93239	76046	81114	77412	86557	19549	98473	15221	87856
78496	47197	37961	67568	14861	61077	85210	51264	49975	71785
95384	59596	05081	39968	80495	00192	94679	18307	16265	48888
37957	89199	10816	24260	52302	69592	55019	94127	71721	70673
31422	27529	95051	83157	96377	33723	52902	51302	86370	50452
07443	15346	40653	84238	24430	88834	77318	07486	33950	61598
41349	86255	92715	96656	49693	99286	83447	20215	16040	41085
12398	95111	45663	55020	57159	58010	43162	98878	73337	35571
77229	92095	44305	09285	73256	02968	31129	66588	48126	52700
61175	53014	60304	13976	96312	42442	96713	43940	92516	81421
16825	27482	97858	05642	88047	68960	52991	67703	29805	42701
84656	03089	05166	67571	25545	26603	40243	55482	38341	97781
03872	31767	23729	89523	73654	24625	78393	77172	41328	95633
40488	70426	04034	46618	55102	93408	10965	69744	80766	14889
98322	25528	438087	05935	78338	77881	90139	72375	50624	91385
13366	52764	02407	14202	74172	58770	65348	24115	44277	96735
86711	27764	86789	43800	87582	09298	17880	75507	35217	08352
53886	50358	62738	91783	71944	90221	79403	75139	09102	77826
99348	21186	42266	01531	44325	61942	13453	61917	90426	12437
49985	08787	59448	82680	52929	19077	98518	06251	58451	91140
49807	32863	69984	20102	09523	47827	08374	79849	19352	62726
46569	00365	23591	44317	55054	94835	20633	66215	46668	53587
09988	44203	43532	54538	16619	45444	11957	69184	98398	96508
32916	00567	82881	59753	54761	39404	90756	91760	18698	42852
93285	32297	27254	27198	99093	97821	46277	10439	30389	45372
03222	39951	12738	50303	25017	84207	52123	88637	19369	58289
87002	61789	96250	99337	14144	00027	53542	87030	14773	73087
68840	94259	01961	52552	91843	33855	00824	48733	81297	80411
88323	28828	64765	08244	53077	50897	91937	08871	91517	19668
55170	71962	64159	79364	53088	21536	39451	95649	65256	23950

Example

Step 1   State the problem clearly.

Jo drives a minibus in her town. The bus has eight seats. People buy tickets in advance, but, on the average, 10 percent of those who buy tickets do not show up. So Jo sells 10 tickets for each trip. Sometimes more than eight people show up with tickets. Estimate the probability that this will happen.

Step 2   Define the key components.

The key components here are whether or not each person holding a ticket shows up for the trip.

Step 3   State the underlying assumptions.

The probability that any one person with a ticket fails to show up for the trip is 0.1. A ticketholder showing up or not showing up is independent of what other ticketholders do.

Step 4   Select a model for a key component.

We will draw a number from a random number table. The number 0 will represent a ticketholder who did *not* show up for the trip.

Step 5   Define and conduct a trial.

Since 10 tickets are sold for each trip, one trial will consist of drawing 10 random numbers. These numbers represent the ticketholders for one trip.

Our first trial resulted in the numbers 0, 6, 4, 9, 3, 1, 8, 6, 6, 9, which means that 9 of the 10 ticketholders showed up for the trip.

Step 6   Record the observation of interest.

Since nine ticketholders showed up, one did not get a seat. We can easily keep track of the number of ticketholders who did not get seats for each trip.

Step 7   Repeat steps 5 and 6 until 100 trials are completed.

The results of 100 such trials are summarized as follows:

Number Not Getting Seats	Number of Trials
0	26
1	31
2	43

Step 8   Summarize the information and draw conclusions.

The data from step 7 show that more than eight people showed up 74 times out of 100. Therefore, the probability that more than eight ticketholders show up for any one trip is estimated to be $\frac{74}{100} = 0.74$.

Also, the average number of people not getting seats per trip is

$$\frac{0(26) + 1(31) + 2(43)}{100} = \frac{117}{100} = 1.17$$

On the average, Jo can expect between one and two unhappy customers for each trip she makes!

Application 5

Traffic Lights

Coming to school each day, Anne rides through three traffic lights, A, B, and C. The probability that any one light is green is 0.3, and the probability that it is *not* green is 0.7. Use a simulation to answer questions 1 and 2 below.

1. Estimate the probability that Anne will find all traffic lights to be green.

2. Estimate the probability that Anne will find at least one light to be not green.

3. Calculate the theoretical probability that Anne will find all three lights to be green, assuming that the lights operate independently. Compare this answer with your answer to question 1.

(*Hint:* We assume that the lights operate independently. For any one light, the probability that it is green when Anne arrives can be simulated by drawing a random digit from Table 6 and letting "green" be represented by the numbers 0, 1, 2. Drawing a number from 3 through 9 will represent the light not being green.)

Application 6

Working Women

Assume that the percentage of women in the labor force of a certain country is 30 percent. A company employs ten workers, two of whom are women.

1. What is the probability that this would occur by chance? (Estimate the probability by a simulation.)

2. Estimate the probability that a company of ten workers would employ two or *fewer* women, by chance.

3. Estimate the expected number of women that a company of ten workers would employ, making use of your simulation results.

4. In simulating the number of women among the ten workers, what number occurs most frequently?

5. On the basis of your simulation, do you think that women are underrepresented in the company? Why or why not?

(*Hint:* Selecting a female worker by chance means that any one worker employed has a 0.3 probability of being a woman. Assume that the pool of workers is large, so that this probability of 0.3 does not change when a few workers are removed from the pool.)

Random Ties

A man has 10 ties and chooses a tie at random to wear to work each day. Set up a simulation to answer the following questions.

1. Estimate the probability that he wears the same tie more than once in a five-day week.

2. Estimate the probability that he wears the same tie more than twice in a five-day week.

3. Estimate the probability that he wears two different ties more than once each in a five-day week.

(*Hint:* You might simulate this situation by numbering the ties from 0 through 9. Then, select 5 random digits to represent the 5 ties randomly selected through the week. Repeat the simulation for 50 trials, preferably by working in groups.)

Application 8

What's Your Sign?

1. Estimate the probability that, in a group of five people, at least two of them have the same zodiacal sign. (There are 12 zodiacal signs; assume that each sign is equally likely for any person.)

2. Estimate the probability that at least one of the five people has the same zodiacal sign as yours.

(*Hint:* For a trial of this simulation, you must randomly choose 5 numbers from 12 possibilities. Two-digit numbers between 00 and 11 could be selected from a random number table, with each number—00, 01, 02, ..., 11—representing one of the zodiacal signs.)

Multiple Choice

A multiple-choice test consists of ten questions, and each question has four possible answers, only one of which is correct. Using simulation, find answers to the questions below.

1. What is the probability of answering at least three questions correctly, if I guess all the answers?

2. Suppose it is always possible to eliminate one answer as being incorrect. If I guess from the remaining three answers, what is the probability of getting at least three answers correct on the test?

3. On the average, how many questions will a student answer correctly by guessing? (Assume that the student is always guessing from among the four choices.)

Application 10

Waiting in Line

A local bank has two teller windows open to serve customers. The number of customers arriving at the bank varies between one and six customers per minute. Customers form a line, and the person at the head of the line goes to the first available teller. Each teller services one customer per minute. Design a simulation for one 20-minute period, and record the number of people in the waiting line at the end of each minute. Use a table like the following:

Minute	Number Arriving	Number Waiting in Line	Waiting Time for Last Person
1	3	1	1 minute
2	4	3	2 minutes

1. What is the length of the waiting line after the first five minutes?

2. What is the time a person has to wait if he or she arrives on the tenth minute?

3. How many times was the waiting time reduced to zero?

4. What is the average number of people waiting in line over the 20-minute period?

5. If you were the manager of the bank, would you increase or decrease the number of tellers? Repeat the simulation with one teller and with three tellers, and give your recommendation on the number of tellers that will make the average waiting time not more than 3 minutes.

27

Application 11

Shooting Free Throws

Time has run out in the big basketball game, and the score is tied. However, the high school's best free-throw shooter, who has made a basket in 75 percent of her throws, was fouled and gets two shots after a short time-out. What is the probability that she will make at least one shot out of the two and win the game?

1. Hold a paper clip in place with the tip of your pencil and spin the spinner. What does the spin represent? Did she make the first shot?

2. The foul shooter gets another try. Spin again. This completes one trial. Did she break the tie?

3. Record the results of 30 such trials, and estimate the probability that the game is won on these shots.

Application 12

To Walk or Not to Walk?

You have a choice between walking to school and taking a bus. If you walk, the amount of time you take depends on the traffic and the weather conditions. Suppose the time needed to walk to school can be shown by the following diagram:

Time to walk ——— 60 percent of the days it is 5 minutes.
——— 40 percent of the days it is 8 minutes.

How about the time when you take the bus? You find that the time taken by the bus is as follows:

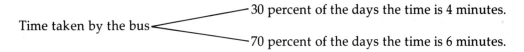

Time taken by the bus ——— 30 percent of the days the time is 4 minutes.
——— 70 percent of the days the time is 6 minutes.

What is your decision in this case? To get the answer, you can go through the following steps:

1. Find the total time taken if you walk for the five days of the week. Our key component is the time taken to walk on a single day. We will simulate an event by using a random number table. Since our probabilities are 0.6 and 0.4 for the two times, we can look for numbers between 0 and 9. We can then say that, for any day, if the number generated is between 0 and 5, which are 6 out of 10 possible digits, then the time will be 5 minutes, whereas if the number generated is between 6 and 9, then the time will be 8 minutes. We have started the table for you and have given the results for the first five trials using the random number table and starting with the first digit from column 6 and row 6. Complete the simulation and then calculate the average total time taken to walk for a week.

Numbers Generated	Time Taken	Total Time
9, 9, 4, 3, 6	8, 8, 5, 5, 8	34
9, 4, 5, 8, 2	8, 5, 5, 8, 5	31
1, 8, 9, 9, 5	5, 8, 8, 8, 5	34
2, 0, 3, 7, 2	5, 5, 5, 8, 5	28
5, 2, 5, 2, 0	5, 5, 5, 5, 5	25

2. Repeat the simulation for the bus. What is the average total time taken by the bus?

3. What have you decided? Is it worth taking the bus?

IV. SIMULATION WITH AN UNKNOWN NUMBER OF KEY COMPONENTS

All the examples and Applications that we have investigated up to this point have had trials with a fixed number of key components. But sometimes the length of a trial changes from trial to trial. We illustrate this case with one example, followed by more Applications of this type of problem.

Example

Step 1   State the problem clearly.

A cereal manufacturer includes a gift coupon in each box of a certain brand. These coupons can be exchanged for a gift when a complete set of six coupons has been collected. What is the expected number of boxes of cereal you will have to buy before you obtain a complete set of six coupons?

Step 2   Define the key components.

A key component consists of buying a box of cereal and observing which coupon it contains.

Step 3   State the underlying assumptions.

Since no other information on the distribution of coupons is given, we will assume that the six coupons occur with equal frequency. The coupon obtained in one box of cereal is independent of the outcomes for other boxes.

Step 4   Select a model for a key component.

We will number the six different coupons from 1 to 6. Since each is equally likely to be present in any one box, we model the outcome of one purchased box by rolling a die and observing the number that comes up. The number on the die corresponds to the coupon number.

Step 5   Define and conduct a trial.

A trial consists of rolling a die until a complete set of numbers (1, 2, 3, 4, 5, 6) is obtained. Our first trial was 4, 5, 1, 3, 1, 1, 1, 1, 6, 5, 3, 6, 6, 1, 3, 6, 3, 5, 3, 6, 4, 5, 4, 1, 1, 4, 1, 5, 4, 1, 6, 3, 6, 2, which took 34 tosses of the die.

Step 6   Record the observation of interest.

The observation of interest is the number of die tosses necessary to obtain a complete set of six numbers. For our first trial, this number was 34.

Step 7   Repeat steps 5 and 6 until at least 50 trials are completed.

We actually completed 200 trials. The second trial gave 4, 2, 4, 3, 4, 1, 6, 5, for a total of only eight tosses of the die. Other trials ranged from 6 to 39 tosses.

Step 8 Summarize the information and draw conclusions.

We performed 200 trials with an average of approximately 15 die tosses per trial. This average forms an estimate of the expected number of boxes of cereal you will have to buy in order to get a complete set of coupons.

Application 13

Mouse Maze

Have you heard of psychologists doing experiments to find out how animals learn? Some of these experiments involve mice who are put in a maze, with food at an exit point of this maze. Suppose an experiment is run with the following maze. A mouse is dropped into the maze at point A, with an exit at the center of the maze at B. The mouse will reach the exit only if it makes a right turn. Suppose our mouse were to take the first right turn every time. Does that mean that we have a "smart" mouse? Or could it be that the mouse was making the turns at random and was just lucky?

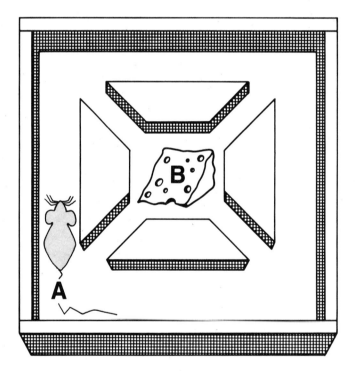

You can answer these questions by using simulation to find the probabilities that the mouse will reach the exit after passing 0, 1, 2, . . . turns. Toss a coin to simulate whether a mouse will make a right turn or keep going. Then record the number of tosses until the mouse reaches the exit. You should assume that the mouse cannot turn around in the maze.

Answer the following questions using simulation. Make sure that you carefully list your assumptions.

1. What is your estimate of the probability of the mouse making a right turn at the first chance?

2. What is your estimate of the probability that the mouse goes around the maze once (that is, passes four intersections) and then makes the very first right turn possible?

3. What is the maximum number of times the mouse will miss the right turn?

4. Do you think that a maze like this one would be very useful for finding out if animals learn from experience? Why or why not?

Donating Blood

In the United States, 45 percent of the people have type O blood. These people are called universal donors since their blood can be used in transfusions to people of any blood type. Assuming that donors arrive independently and randomly at a local blood bank, use simulation to answer the following questions.

1. If 10 donors came to a particular station in one day, what is the probability of at least four having type O blood?

2. On a certain day, a blood center needs four donors with O blood. How many donors, on the average, should they have to see in order to obtain exactly four with type O blood?

3. For your simulation of question 2, what was the maximum number of donors seen in order to find the first four type O donors? What was the minimum number? What number occurred most frequently?

(*Hint:* There are two kinds of simulations required in this activity. The simulation for question 1 is the kind discussed in Section III. The simulation for question 2 is the type considered in this section.)

Drilling for Oil

Suppose the probability that an exploratory oil well will strike oil is about 0.2 and that each exploratory well costs $5,000 to drill. Conduct a simulation to find solutions to the following problems. Assume that the outcome (oil or no oil) for any one exploratory well is independent of outcomes for other wells that may have been drilled previously.

1. Estimate the average number of wells drilled *before* finding oil.

2. In your simulation, what was the maximum number of wells drilled, including the first successful one?

3. What is the average cost of exploration up to and including the first successful well drilled?

(*Hint:* In figuring the cost of exploration, keep in mind that the first successful well costs $5,000 to drill as well as each of the unsuccessful ones. You can find the answer to question 3 by using the solution for question 1.)

Application 16

Family Planning

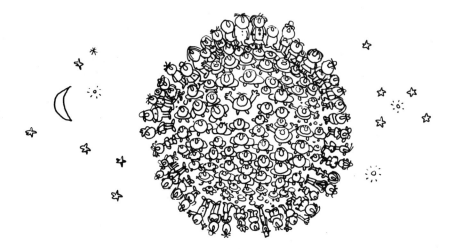

In many countries around the world, couples look to a son to take care of them in their old age. They therefore are inclined to keep having children until they have a son. Governments in overpopulated countries, such as China and India, would like to discourage this practice. However, suppose a government permits people to continue having children until they have exactly one son. Use simulation to answer the questions below.

1.   What is the average number of children per family?

2.   What is the average number of girls per family?

3.   If the government wishes to keep its population from growing, should the government change its policy?

Application 17

Breaking the Bank

You have been playing well at a casino and have $10,000; the bank has $2,000 left. You are playing a game in which your probability of a win is 0.4, and you are making $1,000 bets. Design a simulation and run it until either you or the bank goes broke. Obtain the following data.

1. How often does the bank go broke?

2. How often do you go broke?

3. What is the average number of games you play before you go broke?

4. Are any of your answers surprising? What do you think affects the answers to questions 1, 2, and 3 more, the amount you start with or the probability of winning?

Waiting for the Bus

You are waiting for a bus in a very busy bus terminal. Fifty buses will come by within the next half hour, and any one of four of them can take you to your destination. Assume that the buses arrive in random order. Construct a simulation for bus arrivals, and use the simulation to answer the following questions.

1. How many buses do you expect to see arrive *before* the first one that will take you to your destination?

2. What did you observe to be the maximum number of buses that arrived before you saw a bus that will take you to your destination?

3. What is the probability that you can find a bus to take you to your destination among the first five arrivals?

(*Hint:* For this simulation, you know that there are four specified objects—your buses—among the 50. This could be modeled by using a deck of 50 cards with the four aces representing your buses. Mix the cards and count down from the top until the first ace is reached. This completes one trial of a simulation.)

V. SIMULATING MORE COMPLEX EVENTS

In many cases, a situation under study may have more than one characteristic of interest. For example, a Democratic candidate in an election may be interested not only in the number of registered Democrats but also in how many of the Democrats vote for him or her. Assume for the moment that all voters can be classified as Democrats or Republicans and that there are equal numbers of voters registered as Democrats and Republicans. Each voter now has two characteristics, the party he or she belongs to and the candidate he or she prefers. Suppose, historically in this district, 75 percent of the Democrats vote along party lines, whereas 80 percent of the Republicans vote along party lines. We now have the following information:

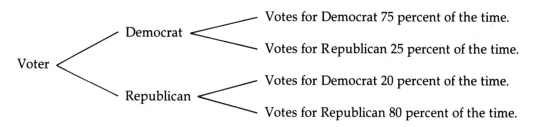

Our objective here is to find the number of voters voting for each of the two candidates. Let us go through the steps.

Step 1   The objective in this simulation is to determine the number of votes that the Democratic candidate gets.

Step 2   The situation is a combination of two key components, the party that a voter belongs to and the candidate that he or she votes for.

Step 3   The assumptions are: (a) there is an equal number of Democrats and Republicans; (b) 75 percent of Democrats vote for the candidate of their party, and 80 percent of Republicans vote for the candidate of their party.

Step 4   We will model the simulation using a random number table and selecting *two* numbers. The first number (a one-digit number) will indicate the voter's choice. We will let D denote that the voter or the vote is Democratic, and R denote that the voter or the vote is Republican.

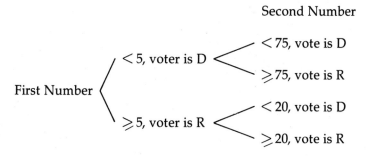

Step 5   Our trial consists of selecting the two random numbers. Our first trial resulted in RR, namely, a Republican voting Republican.

Step 6   The observation of interest is the outcome of the trial, namely:

DD: Democrat voting for a Democrat
DR: Democrat voting for a Republican
RD: Republican voting for a Democrat
RR: Republican voting for a Republican

Step 7   Repeat the trial. The outcomes of 100 trials are shown below.

RR   RR   DR   RR   DD   RD   RR   DD   DD   RD   DR   RR   RD
RR   RD   DD   DD   RD   DD   RR   RR   DD   DD   RR   DD   RR
RR   DD   DD   DR   DD   DD   DD   DD   DD   RR   RR   RR   DD
RR   RD   DD   RR   RR   RR   RR   DR   RR   DD   DD   DR   DD

RR   DD   RR   RR   RR   DD   DD   RD   DD   DD   DD   RR   DD
DR   DD   RR   RR   DR   DD   DD   DD   DD   RD   RR   DD   DR
DD   RR   DD   DD   RR   RR   DD   RR   RR   DD   RD   DD   DD
DD   DD   DD   RR   RR   DR   DD   RR   RD

Step 8   Summarize the information. In this example, we can first count the number of trials with the different outcomes and then set up a table giving the counts for each outcome.

	Voting for Democrat	Voting for Republican
Democrat	45	9
Republican	10	36

This table can help us answer several questions. For example, what is the chance of a randomly selected voter being a Republican who would vote for a Democrat? The answer, based on the table, is $\frac{10}{100}$ or 0.1. Candidates running for office often use simulations like this one to help them in planning their campaign.

Application 19

Inherited Traits

The inheritance of physical traits is determined by the interaction of the parents' genes during reproduction. For example, the reason why you have blue or brown eyes is because of the genes you inherited from each of your parents. The same is true about the color of your skin or hair. One of the first scientists to discover the laws of heredity was Mendel. In his experiment, Mendel crossed two varieties of peas and found that the offspring of the crossed varieties showed the characteristics of the two original peas according to certain rules. We are going to find out the rule in this simulation.

Suppose you have a plant with red flowers and a plant with blue flowers, and you cross the two plants. The genes that determine the color for the flowers consist of two chromosomes, each of which carries either red (R) or blue (B) code. For the red flower, both chromosomes will be R, so the gene for the red flower can be shown as RR. Similarly, the gene for the blue flower will be BB. The plant we get by crossing red and blue flowering plants will inherit one chromosome from each plant. So we get a plant with purple flowers from crossing a red flowering plant and a blue flowering plant.

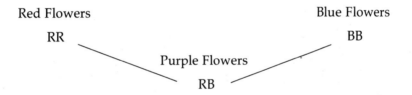

Red Flowers
RR

Blue Flowers
BB

Purple Flowers
RB

What would happen if we crossed two plants with purple flowers? This second-generation cross would also have genes represented by two letters, R and B, in different combinations.

The crossing of two purple flowering plants can be simulated by using two coins. Coin 1 represents one purple plant and coin 2 the second. For each coin, let heads denote the R chromosome and tails the B. Each coin is tossed once to simulate the generation of a particular offspring. If coin 1 comes up heads and coin 2 tails, then the offspring is RB, or another purple flower. Use this simulation model to answer the following questions.

1. What would be the possible colors of the flowers of the second generation of plants when the first-generation plants both have purple flowers?

2. Which color would occur most often? How frequently should it occur?

3. Can you suggest how you could simulate possible colors of flowers of the third generation? Remember, the colors for the offspring depend on the genes of the parents.

Application 20

Turning Left

I can make a left turn onto a highway immediately after stopping if there is no car coming in either direction. The probability that a car is coming from the left is two thirds, and the probability that one is coming from the right is one half.

1. Estimate the probability that I can make a left turn without delay.

2. Find the theoretical probability that a car is *not* coming from the left and a car is *not* coming from the right. Compare your answer with the estimate obtained in question 1. What assumption did you make in this calculation?

3. How would you simulate the probability of making a left turn without delay two times in succession when traveling through this intersection?

Application 21

Power Systems

A primary power system, S_1, on a space shuttle has a backup system, S_2. If S_1 fails during a mission, S_2 automatically takes over. Suppose the probability that S_1 fails during a mission is 0.2, and the probability that S_2 fails is 0.3. Simulate the operation of these systems to answer the following questions.

1. What is the probability that at least one of the two power systems is operating at the end of the mission?

2. What is the probability that S_2 must be used on a mission?

3. What assumptions were made for your simulation? Do they seem reasonable?

(*Hint:* The operation of S_1 can be simulated by selecting a random digit from Table 6 (page 19) and letting 0 and 1 represent failure of the system. If the first number selected is a 0 or 1, S_1 fails, and a second number is selected to represent the operation of S_2; 0, 1, and 2 could represent failure of S_2. Thus, a first digit of 1 and a second digit of 5 would simulate the situation in which S_1 fails and S_2 does not fail.)

Shooting Foul Shots

A basketball player shoots foul shots with a two-thirds accuracy record. That is, she has scored a basket on two out of every three attempts. She is given a free throw from the foul line and is given a second shot only if she has scored a basket on the first shot. In this one-and-one situation, she can score 0, 1, or 2 points. Design a simulation for this player's score on a trip to the free-throw line and use the simulation for 50 trials to answer the following questions.

1. What is the average number of points per trip to the free-throw line?

2. What number of points occurs most frequently?

3. For what fraction of the trips to the free-throw line did the player shoot twice?

VI. SUPPLEMENTARY APPLICATIONS

Application 23

_____

Chances of Meeting

Jon and Andrea want to meet at the library. Each agrees to arrive there between 1:00 and 1:30 P.M. They also agree to wait five minutes after arriving (but not after 1:30). If the other does not arrive during that five minutes, the first person will leave. What is the probability that Jon and Andrea will meet?

(*Hint:* Random times between 0 and 30 minutes can be selected from a random number table. Select two-digit numbers and eliminate those larger than 30.)

_____

Making a Sale

The manager of a store that sells only TV sets has carefully observed her customers and sales for a long period of time. For a certain hour of the day, the probability is 0.3 that the store will have no customers, 0.6 that it will have one customer, and 0.1 that it will have two customers. Each customer has a probability of 0.2 of buying a TV set while in the store.

1. Estimate the probability that the manager will make at least one sale during this hour tomorrow.

2. Estimate the probability that the manager will make two sales during this hour.

3. What is this manager's average number of sales for this hour?

(*Hint:* Two random devices are needed, one to generate the number of customers and one to generate sales per customer. If the first device shows "no customers," then the second need not be used. If the first shows "one customer," the second must be used once to determine "sale" or "no sale." If the first shows "two customers," the second must be used twice.)

Application 25

Back and Forth

Let an x axis represent the path between a child's playground ($x = 0$) and her home ($x = 10$). Suppose we meet the child at $x = 5$. The child moves forward (from x to $x + 1$) and back (x to $x - 1$) with equal probability each minute. Design a simulation, and run it to estimate the mean number of minutes that it takes the child to reach either the playground or her home.

1. What is the average number of minutes it takes the child to reach either the playground or home?

2. For what fraction of the trials did the child reach home?

A Change in the Weather

Observations over a period of years gave the following information for July.

If today is sunny, then *P(tomorrow is sunny)* = 0.7
and *P(tomorrow is dull)* = 0.3

If today is dull, then *P(tomorrow is sunny)* = 0.5
and *P(tomorrow is dull)* = 0.5

Assuming that the first day of the month is sunny, design a simulation to find the mean number of consecutive sunny days in the first week in July.

1. What is the mean number of consecutive sunny days for that week?

2. What is the longest period of sunny days in your simulation?

3. If we assume instead that the first day is dull, do you think that the answers for questions 1 and 2 would change? Verify your answer with a simulation.

Application 27

Selling the News

The operator of a newsstand buys daily newspapers for 15 cents each and sells them for 25 cents each. His daily records show that the probability of selling exactly 20 newspapers is 0.2, and the probability of selling exactly 40 newspapers is 0.3. A newspaper left over at the end of the day represents a total loss, and a newspaper sold yields a profit of 10 cents. Design a simulation to study the number of customers per day—20, 30, or 40—with the given probabilities (use 50 trials).

1. Estimate the average number of customers per day.

2. Using the answer from question 1, estimate the operator's average profit if he buys 20, 30, or 40 newspapers. How many newspapers should the operator buy each day to maximize his profit, given that he can buy newspapers only in multiples of 10?

Unloading Trucks

A pea cannery is to be built in your town. Trucks will arrive randomly, with one arrival every four minutes on the average. Each truck can be unloaded in four minutes, once the cannery crew gets to the truck. Follow the steps below to determine whether this is a good arrangement for the cannery.

A. Use a shuffled deck of 52 cards.

B. Set a 20-minute work period. Each card turned represents one minute.

C. A diamond represents a truck arriving.

D. Keep track of:
   1. What time each truck arrives.
   2. What time each truck is unloaded.
   3. The delay time for each truck driver.

E. Make a summary showing:
   1. The number of trucks arriving per 20-minute period.
   2. The amount of overtime (time worked by cannery workers beyond the 20-minute period).
   3. The total delay time for each truck driver.

Following is an actual experiment, as an example.

Time (minute) Truck Arrived	Time (minute) Truck Unloaded	Delay (minutes)
1	5	0
5	9	0
11	15	0
16	20	0
17	24	3

Number of trucks arriving: 5
Overtime: 4 minutes
Delay time: 3 minutes

Perform the experiment 50 times. Does the situation appear to be good? If not, what changes would you make in the proposed cannery?

Application 29

The Soft-Drink Machine

A soft-drink machine that fills paper cups is set to dispense eight ounces of liquid each time it is operated. However, the actual amount of liquid dispensed will vary, sometimes being slightly over eight ounces and sometimes slightly under. If the machine is operating correctly, the *median* amount of liquid dispensed should be eight ounces.

One way to keep track of the operating characteristics of the machine is to record whether the amount dispensed is above or below the median for a series of fills. For example, a series of ten observations could result in LHLLLHHHHL or LLLHHHHHLL, with L denoting a low observation (below the median) and H denoting a high observation (above the median).

One way to look for a pattern in such data is to observe the number of *runs*, or sequences of like symbols. Series (a) results in 5 runs (3 L runs and 2 H runs), whereas series (b) results in 3 runs (2 L runs and 1 H run). For each series of ten observations, the number of runs could be any integer from 1 to 10. (All the runs could be H or L, or the runs of H's and L's could alternate.)

How can these data lead to decisions about how well the machine is functioning? If the number of runs is small (say, 1 or 2), we might think that something is causing the machine to give too many overfills or underfills. If the number of runs is fairly large, the machine is varying more often from high to low, which might be expected under normal operations. Thus, we might decide to adjust the machine if a *low* number of runs is observed.

We can simulate the behavior of ten observations from this machine by tossing a coin ten times. Let heads denote high (H) and tails denote low (L). If the machine is operating correctly, H and L are equally likely for any one observation. For the ten tosses, the number of runs should be recorded. This corresponds to one trial of ten observations. The simulation should then be repeated for at least 50 trials.

From your simulation results (which can be done by pooling information from groups of students), estimate the probabilities for the various numbers of runs as indicated below:

Number of Runs (in 10 measurements)	Estimated Probability
0	
1	
2	
3	
4	
5	
6	
7	
8	
9	
10	

1. What number of runs has the highest estimated probability?

2. What is the probability that the number of runs is three or fewer?

3. For what numbers of runs would you begin to suspect that the machine may not be functioning properly? Why?

Application 30

An Epidemic

The speed of an infectious disease can be modeled as follows. Suppose that an infectious disease has a one-day infection period, and after that a person is immune. Six people live on an otherwise deserted island. One person catches the disease and randomly visits one other person for help during the infection period. The second person is infected and visits another person at random during the next day (his infection period). The process continues, with one visit per day, until an infectious person visits an immune person and the disease dies out.

This simplified epidemic can be simulated by tossing a die. Suppose that the people, numbered 1 through 6, correspond to the die faces. Person 1 has the disease today. Roll the die to see whom he visits. (If you roll a 1, ignore it and roll again. A person cannot visit himself.) Then, roll again to see whom the second person visits. The die roll is repeated until an infectious person visits an immune person (one who has already had the disease). Construct at least 20 trials of the simulated epidemic. Use the simulation results to answer the following questions.

1. What is the average number of people who get the disease in your simulated epidemic?

2. What is the probability that more than three people get the disease?

3. What is the probability that all six people get the disease?

Exploring Surveys and Information from Samples

Exploring Surveys and Information from Samples was prepared under the auspices of the American Statistical Association—National Council of Teachers of Mathematics Joint Committee on the Curriculum in Statistics and Probability.

This book is part of the Quantitative Literacy Project, which was funded in part by the National Science Foundation.

Exploring Surveys and Information from Samples

James M. Landwehr
AT&T Bell Laboratories
Murray Hill, New Jersey

Jim Swift
Nanaimo School District
Nanaimo, British Columbia

Ann E. Watkins
Los Angeles Pierce College
Woodland Hills, California

DALE SEYMOUR PUBLICATIONS

Acknowledgments

Grateful acknowledgment is made to the following:

The Gallup Organization, Inc. for the article on pages 59–60, "Design of the Gallup Sample." Reprinted by permission.

The New York Times for the article on page 58, "How the Poll Was Conducted," from the June 5, 1985 edition. Copyright © 1985 by the New York Times Company. Reprinted by permission.

Cover: John Edeen and Francesca Angelesco
Editing: Adrienne Harris
Technical Art: Pat Rogondino
Illustrations: John Johnson

This publication was prepared as part of the American Statistical Association Project—Quantitative Literacy—with partial support of the National Science Foundation Grant No. DPE-8317656. Any opinions, findings, conclusions, or recommendations expressed in this publication are those of the authors and do not necessarily represent the views of the National Science Foundation. These materials shall be subject to a royalty-free, irrevocable, worldwide, nonexclusive license in the United States Government to reproduce, perform, translate, and otherwise use and to authorize others to use such materials for Government purposes.

ISBN 0-86651-339-6

Order number DS01707

DALE
SEYMOUR
PUBLICATIONS
P.O. BOX 10888
PALO ALTO, CA 94303

cdefghi-MA-8932109

CONTENTS

PREFACE

Sample surveys provide useful and current information about our people, businesses, and governments. The growth in the use of sample surveys in the last 30 years has been unprecedented. Data from the Consumer Expenditure Survey, reflected in the Consumer Price Index, are used in collective bargaining agreements. Data collected in the Health Interview Survey measure the success of anti-smoking campaigns. The unemployment rate from the Current Population Survey is an important economic indicator making the news every month. In addition, survey data are now used to establish campaign issues for political candidates, to determine the survival of television programs, to set wage rates in certain industries, to locate new stores, and to determine the effectiveness of advertising.

Surveys are carried out by federal, state, and local governments, as well as by universities, businesses, private companies, political candidates, and non-profit groups. The results of these surveys appear in magazines and newspapers and are discussed extensively on television and radio. Because of the growth in the survey industry, there are many different kinds of people doing surveys. Some of these groups have people well-trained in statistical methods guiding their effort; other groups do not realize that there is a statistical basis to sample surveys.

All survey organizations depend on the public for two important reasons. The public provides survey data. Well-designed surveys suffer when people refuse to be interviewed. Some people refuse because surveys seem unimportant or because they don't understand how the views of a sample can represent the views of an entire population. If you, as students, gain a greater understanding of how surveys work and what makes them useful, the value of surveys that you may be asked to participate in will improve.

The public also contains data users. Many people use statistics generated from sample surveys—to see where their candidates stand in polls, to evaluate how well government programs are working, to find out where a new store should be located. Users must question the accuracy of survey results and ask the right questions. Was the sample size large enough so that you can have any confidence in the statistics produced? What were the questions asked? Were there any problems in carrying out the survey that you should know about? To the extent that this book helps you understand the strengths and weaknesses of survey results, you will be able to recognize and use good survey data more effectively.

As an Associate Director of the Bureau of the Census, I applaud the arrival of this book in the classroom. Teaching young people to understand and use sample surveys today will surely result in better surveys and better uses of survey data in the future.

Barbara A. Bailar
Associate Director for Statistical Standards
 and Methodology, United States Bureau
 of the Census
President, American Statistical Association, 1987

I. INTRODUCTION

The United States Constitution requires "enumeration" of the population in order to determine how many seats each state should have in the 435-member House of Representatives. Thus, every 10 years, the Bureau of the Census attempts to count the entire population of the United States. Taking a *census* of the United States is incredibly expensive and difficult. The 1980 census of 86 million households required seven years of planning and about 280,000 workers. The questionnaires filled so many boxes that, if stacked up, they would have been 30 miles high.

The government also needs information about its citizens in the years between censuses. For example, to plan government programs, elected representatives must know how many people are unemployed, poor, and sick. Since the early 1940s, the government has used *sample surveys* to gather this information. Of the approximately 250 surveys taken by the Bureau of the Census each year, the best known is the Current Population Survey (CPS). This monthly survey estimates unemployment, income, schooling, and other measures by questioning about 100,000 people. Based on these people's responses, the bureau estimates the level of unemployment, for example, in the entire U.S. population. The unemployment figures you see on television or in the newspaper come from the CPS.

Another U.S. survey is the National Crime Survey, which the government began in the early 1970s to determine the extent of crime in the United States. Government workers cannot gather this information from police reports because the survey has revealed that people report only about 35% of all crimes to the police. For this survey, interviewers talk to people in about 60,000 households twice a year. (You can see a page from the National Crime Survey questionnaire used by interviewers on page 49.)

The type of survey reported most often in newspapers and on television is the *opinion poll*. The names of the leading polling organizations—Gallup, Roper, Harris, New York Times/CBS—are familiar to most adults. These organizations ask people about their political opinions, the consumer products they prefer, and their views on religion and education. People use the information for everything from planning a presidential candidate's campaign strategy to deciding the flavor of a new toothpaste.

This book will help you understand how statisticians can make statements about an entire group of people, or *population*, after they have questioned only a *sample* from that population. We will study only surveys (or polls) that ask questions people can answer with "yes" or "no." Here is an example of this type of survey.

The March 1985 Gallup survey asked 1,571 American adults this question:

"Do you approve or disapprove of the way Ronald Reagan is handling his job as president?"

Fifty-six percent said that they approved. For results based on samples of this size, one can say with 95% confidence that the error attributable to sampling and other random effects could be 3 percentage points in either direction.

In addition to sampling error, the reader should bear in mind that question wording and practical difficulties encountered in conducting surveys can introduce error or bias into the findings of opinion polls.

Source: Santa Barbara, California, *News-Press*, April 7, 1985.

Gallup surveyed (or polled) a sample of 1,571 adults from a total population of about 170 million adults. Pollsters asked each adult a *yes-no* question. ("Do you approve or disapprove . . . ?") The proportion of *yes* (or approve) responses from this sample was 0.56. The responses of the 1,571 adults might not exactly match those of the entire population. However, based on his calculations, Gallup feels confident that if he polled the entire American adult population, between 53% and 59% of the people would approve (a range of 3 percentage points in either direction from the 56%).

Gallup's statement that between 53% and 59% of the population would approve is a *statistical inference* he made about the population from the sample. In this book, you will learn the basic mathematics and statistics behind such an inference, and you will learn how to interpret the inference.

We will obtain samples from objects in containers, from coins, and from random number tables. During a one-hour class, you will find it much easier to take samples from a container than to take samples of the U.S. population!

Application 1

Guessing the Percentage of Yeses

Your teacher has a container of objects. Some of them are different from the rest; we will call them *yeses*. The ***population percentage*** is the percentage of objects in the container that are *yeses*. This percentage can be found exactly only by examining all the objects in the container. However, if we take a sample of objects from the container, we can estimate the population percentage by the ***sample proportion***. You can find the sample proportion by dividing the number of *yeses* in the sample by the sample size.

1. Mix up the objects and, without looking, take a sample of 10 objects from the container. What is the number of *yeses*?

2. Using the result from question 1, estimate the percentage of objects in the container that are *yeses*.

3. Give an interval around your estimate that is as small as possible but that you believe contains the population percentage. For example, if you get a sample proportion of 0.60, you may believe that the container has from 55% to 65% *yeses*.

4. What is the actual percentage of *yeses* in the container? (Your teacher will tell you.) Does your interval contain this percentage?

In this book, you will learn a method of constructing an interval, called a ***confidence interval***, that will contain the true percentage of *yeses* for most samples. We could, of course, let the interval be 0% to 100%, so that we are sure that the true percentage of *yeses* will be in the interval. But if Gallup, for example, reports that he is confident that between 0% and 100% of the population approve of the way the president is handling his job, we would not be very enlightened! We will construct shorter intervals, with the consequence that the true population percentage won't always be in the interval.

II. SAMPLING DISTRIBUTIONS

Two different samples from a population most likely will not have exactly the same sample proportion. The activities in this section teach you about the *sampling distribution*, which describes the variability among repeated samples from the same population. You will learn how to approximate a sampling distribution through simulation. All the work in this section deals with populations for which we know the true percentage of *yeses*.

Application 2

Tossing Four Coins

We know that about 50% of the student population are girls. Suppose that by random sampling we obtain a sample of 4 students and observe whether there are 0, 1, 2, 3, or 4 girls. Toss four coins to simulate the results we are likely to get from this survey. Let heads correspond to *girl* and tails to *boy*. (If you prefer, you can use a different random device, such as rolling four dice, with 1, 2, or 3 corresponding to *girl*.)

1. Toss four coins all at once (or one coin four times).

    a. How many heads did you get?

    b. What is the sample proportion of *girls* (heads)?

    c. Will you get this same sample proportion each time you toss four coins?

2. Now toss the four coins all at once a total of 40 times (giving 40 *trials*). Tally your results on a table like this one. (Several students may want to form a group and combine results to produce a total of 40 trials.)

Number of Heads	Sample Proportion	Tally	Frequency	Proportion of All Trials
0	$\frac{0}{4} = 0.00$	III	3	$\frac{3}{40} = 0.075$
1	$\frac{1}{4} = 0.25$	HHT III	8	$\frac{8}{40} = 0.20$
2	$\frac{2}{4} = 0.50$	HHT HHT HHT I	16	$\frac{16}{40} = 0.40$
3	$\frac{3}{4} = 0.75$	HHT HHT	10	$\frac{10}{40} = 0.25$
4	$\frac{4}{4} = 1.00$	III	3	$\frac{3}{40} = 0.075$
TOTAL			40	$\frac{40}{40} = 1.00$

3. Combine the frequencies from every group in the class and complete a table like the one for question 2.

4. What is the most likely number of heads?

5. What percentage of the time did your class get 1, 2, or 3 *girls* (heads)?

6. List the 16 ways that four coins can land when tossed. We have listed 3 ways to get you started.

1st Coin	2nd Coin	3rd Coin	4th Coin
H	H	H	H
H	H	H	T
H	H	T	H

7. Look at the chart you completed in question 6. In how many ways can we throw

   a. 0 heads?

   b. 1 head?

   c. 2 heads?

   d. 3 heads?

   e. 4 heads?

8. Use your answers to question 7 to calculate the probability of getting

   a. 0 heads.

   b. 1 head.

   c. 2 heads.

   d. 3 heads.

   e. 4 heads.

9. Complete this sentence using answers from question 8: If we observe four randomly chosen students, the probability of this group containing 1, 2, or 3 girls is ___.

10. Compare your answers to questions 5 and 9. Did the simulation give a reasonably accurate answer?

Tossing Eight Coins

1. In this application we will toss a sample of eight coins. Make a table like the one below for tallying the results. Fill in the sample proportion column.

Number of Heads	Sample Proportion	Tally	Frequency	Proportion of All Trials
0				
1				
2				
3				
4				
5				
6				
7				
8				
TOTAL		10	10	$\frac{10}{10} = 1.00$

2. Each student (or group of students) should toss eight coins (or one coin 8 times) a total of 10 times. Fill in the last three columns of your table.

3. Combine the frequencies from every group in the class and fill in a table like the one for question 1.

Answer questions 4 to 7 using the simulation from question 3.

4. What is the most likely number of heads?

5. Estimate the probability of getting 2, 3, 4, 5, or 6 heads.

6. Complete this sentence: If we observe 8 randomly chosen students, about _____ of the time we will have 2, 3, 4, 5, or 6 girls.

7. Compare the table from question 3 of Application 2 with the one from question 3 here.

   a. Are you more likely to get a sample proportion of exactly 0.50 heads if you toss four coins or if you toss eight coins?

   b. Are you more likely to get a sample proportion of heads between 0.25 and 0.75 if you toss four coins or if you toss eight coins?

8. Are you more likely to get exactly 10 heads from tossing 20 coins, or exactly 50 heads from tossing 100 coins?

9. Are you more likely to get a sample proportion from 0.25 to 0.75 from tossing 20 coins (between 5 and 15 heads), or a sample proportion from 0.25 to 0.75 from tossing 100 coins (between 25 and 75 heads)?

Eight coins can land in 2^8 or 256 ways when tossed. How would you like to spend the next few hours listing all 256 ways in order to calculate exact probabilities? Let's rely on simulation from now on to estimate probabilities!

Using Random Number Tables to Make a Sampling Distribution

About 40% of the American public believe schoolchildren have "too many rights and privileges" (Laramie Sunday *Boomerang*, August 11, 1985). Suppose we plan to choose a sample of 20 Americans. Can you guess how many will say they agree with this statement?

To simulate this example, you could use a physical random device, such as a spinner, that would give a probability of 0.40. Instead, we will use the random number table on pages 90 and 91.

A random number table displays digits 0 through 9 in random order. For a population with 40% *yeses*, we assign four of the digits to *yes* and the other six to *no*. For example, digits 0, 1, 2, and 3 could be *yes*, and digits 4, 5, 6, 7, 8, and 9 could be *no*. (Alternatively, digits 6, 7, 8, and 9 could be *yes*, and digits 0, 1, 2, 3, 4, and 5 could be *no*.) The important thing is to decide, before looking at the random number table, which digits correspond to *yes*. Then we pick an arbitrary point on the random number table to start. One way to pick the starting point is to close your eyes and haphazardly put your finger down on the page.

To obtain a sample of size 20, we look at a sequence of 20 digits, going either left or right or up or down from the starting point. It doesn't matter which direction we go to get the 20 digits, as long as we decide on the direction before looking at the table. We determine how many *yeses* are in our sample by counting the number of digits that are 0, 1, 2, or 3. For example, suppose that our first sample of 20 digits is 84310 76343 64238 59419. Then there are 8 *yeses* in the sample. To draw a second sample of size 20, we continue using the next 20 digits. When we get to the edge of the page of random digits, we continue backward in an adjacent row or column.

1. Construct a table like the one on page 9. You will use this table to tally the results for random samples of size 20. Fill in the sample proportion column.

2. Use the random number table to draw a sample of size 20 from a population with 40% *yeses*. Enter a tally mark in your table.

3. Draw 9 more samples and tally them, giving you a total of 10 trials. Then fill in the two right columns in the table.

4. Combine your results with those of other class members in a similar table. (Now the number of trials will be 10 times the number of students.)

Use the table from question 4 to answer questions 5 through 8.

5. What was the smallest number of *yeses* in any one sample?

6. What was the largest number of *yeses* in any one sample?

7. What is the most likely sample proportion of *yeses*?

Number of Yeses	Sample Proportion	Tally	Frequency	Proportion of All Trials
0				
1				
2				
3				
4				
5				
6				
7				
8				
9				
10				
11				
12				
13				
14				
15				
16				
17				
18				
19				
20				
TOTAL		10	10	1.00

8. Suppose that the newspaper report is correct: 40% of the American public believe schoolchildren have too many rights and privileges. If you have a random sample of 20 Americans, then make the following estimates.

   a. Estimate the probability that exactly 8 people will believe schoolchildren have too many rights and privileges.

   b. Estimate the probability that 6 or fewer people will believe it.

   c. Estimate the probability that the sample proportion believing the statement will be from 0.30 to 0.50, inclusive (that is, the probability that from 6 to 10 people will believe it).

   d. Estimate the probability that all 20 Americans will believe the statement.

You just approximated a *sampling distribution* through simulation—specifically, the sampling distribution of the number of *yeses* in a sample of size 20 drawn from a population with 40% *yeses*. In Applications 2 and 3, you constructed sampling distributions for the number of heads in samples of size 4 and 8 from a population with 50% heads.

The sampling distribution shows the amount of variability from one random sample to another from a specific population. To construct a sampling distribution, we must know both the population percentage and the sample size. A sampling distribution can be used in either of two equivalent forms: the number of *yes*es in a sample, or the sample proportion. For example, using the sampling distribution for a sample of size 20 from a population with 40% *yes*es, we can use the "proportion of all trials" column to estimate the probability of 3 *yes*es, or equivalently the probability of a sample proportion of 0.15.

It is often possible to construct an exact sampling distribution using probability formulas. Using simulation you may obtain a sampling distribution slightly off from the exact one. However, the more trials you run in the simulation, the closer your approximated sampling distribution should be to the exact one. In this book, we will not discuss the probability formulas for deriving the exact sampling distribution; we will always use simulation to approximate the sampling distribution.

9. Describe how the sampling distribution from 10 trials (question 3) differs from the sampling distribution from many more trials (question 4). Which sampling distribution do you think is closer to the one calculated from probability formulas?

III. BOX PLOTS FROM SAMPLING DISTRIBUTIONS

You have used simulation to construct sampling distributions, and you have used tables like the one below to describe these distributions. This table was constructed using samples of size 20 from a population containing 40% *yes*es. We did 40 trials. Next you will learn how to use a 90% box plot to summarize this sampling distribution.

Number of Yeses	Sample Proportion	Frequency	Proportion of All Trials
0	0.00	0	0
1	0.05	0	0
2	0.10	0	0
3	0.15	0	0
4	0.20	1	0.025
5	0.25	3	0.075
6	0.30	4	0.10
7	0.35	8	0.20
8	0.40	9	0.225
9	0.45	1	0.025
10	0.50	5	0.125
11	0.55	8	0.20
12	0.60	1	0.025
13	0.65	0	0
14	0.70	0	0
15	0.75	0	0
16	0.80	0	0
17	0.85	0	0
18	0.90	0	0
19	0.95	0	0
20	1.00	0	0
TOTAL		40	1.00

On page 2, you read a statement by the Gallup poll that "one can say with 95% confidence . . . ." Gallup uses 95% box plots. We will use 90% instead of 95% because the computations necessary to make a box plot are easier with 90%.

Displaying sampling distributions in a plot makes it easier to analyze and compare them. Thus, we will use box plots to focus attention on the most important features of the sampling distributions.

The following figure is a 90% box plot of the sample proportions in this example. The number line at the top is for sample proportions and goes from 0.0 to 1.0, as in the second column of the preceding table. The number line at the bottom of the plot is the corresponding number of *yeses* in the sample, from the first column of the table. We have positioned the box along the number line to represent the frequencies of these sample proportions in the 40 trials (the third and fourth columns of the table). Next we will learn how to construct this 90% box plot.

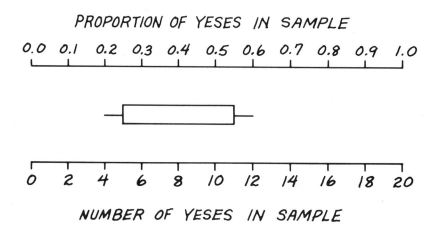

PROPORTION OF YESES IN SAMPLE

NUMBER OF YESES IN SAMPLE

We want to have the sample proportions from the middle 90% of the 40 trials lie inside the box, including the edges. We also want to have the sample proportions from 5% of the 40 trials lie in the lines on either side of the box, the *whiskers*. Ninety percent of 40 is 36. Thus, we want 36 of the observed sample proportions in the box and the remaining 4 in the whiskers (2 in each). Look at the frequency column in our table. Because the whiskers must contain the two smallest sample proportions and the two largest ones, we draw our box starting with the *third* smallest sample proportion (0.25) and extend it to the *third* largest sample proportion (0.55). We then draw the whiskers to represent the remaining 10% of sample proportions: One extends to the left to the smallest recorded sample proportion, 0.20, and the other extends to the right to the largest recorded sample proportion, 0.60.

Because of ties in these sample proportions, we cannot get exactly 36 values in the box. This box actually contains 38 values (including the edges). When ties occur, we will always construct the box so that no more than 5% of the values are in either whisker. One whisker might contain fewer than 5% but never more. Similarly, with ties we might have to put more than 90% of the sample proportions in the box, but we will never put in fewer than 90%.

Constructing a 90% Box Plot

We took 100 random samples, each of size 20, from a population with 50% *yes*es and got these results:

Number of Yeses	Sample Proportion	Frequency
0	0.00	0
1	0.05	0
2	0.10	0
3	0.15	0
4	0.20	1
5	0.25	2
6	0.30	5
7	0.35	12
8	0.40	11
9	0.45	10
10	0.50	16
11	0.55	21
12	0.60	8
13	0.65	8
14	0.70	4
15	0.75	1
16	0.80	1
17	0.85	0
18	0.90	0
19	0.95	0
20	1.00	0
TOTAL		**100**

1. a. When you make a 90% box plot from 100 trials, how many sample proportions should the box ideally contain?

    b. How many sample proportions should each whisker ideally contain?

    c. What is the sixth smallest sample proportion from the 100 trials?

    d. What is the sixth largest sample proportion from the 100 trials?

    e. Make the 90% box plot of the sample proportions from the 100 trials.

    f. How many sample proportions actually ended up in the box?

2. We took 200 random samples, each of size 10, from a population with 50% *yes*es and got these results:

Number of Yeses	Sample Proportion	Frequency
0	0.00	0
1	0.10	5
2	0.20	10
3	0.30	21
4	0.40	42
5	0.50	47
6	0.60	39
7	0.70	26
8	0.80	9
9	0.90	1
10	1.00	0
TOTAL		200

Make a 90% box plot of these sample proportions. The box will start at the 11th sample proportion from each end.

3. Review your work for Application 4 (page 8). For question 4, you constructed a sampling distribution for samples of size 20 from a population with 40% *yes*es and with the number of trials equal to 10 times the number of students in your class.

   a. To construct a 90% box plot, how many sample proportions must you count in from either end to determine the edges of the box?

   b. Construct the 90% box plot for your sampling distribution.

Application 6

Deciding If the Sample Proportion Is Likely or Unlikely

We have constructed the 90% box plot so that it contains the sample proportions from the middle 90% of the trials. We will call the sample proportions inside the box (including its edges) the *likely sample proportions*, because most of the trials (specifically, 90% of them) gave one of these sample proportions. The lines on either side of the box, the whiskers, represent sample proportions from the remaining 10% of the trials, with 5% in each whisker. We call the sample proportions falling in the whiskers the *unlikely sample proportions*.

If you take further samples, you might even get a sample proportion that is outside the whiskers. We also call such sample proportions unlikely. Thus, unlikely sample proportions can fall either in the whiskers or outside the whiskers. You are very unlikely to get a sample proportion outside the whiskers, however.

For example, using the 90% box plot of the sampling distribution for a sample of size 20 from a population with 40% *yes*es, we see that a sample proportion of 0.50 (10 *yes*es out of 20) is a likely sample proportion. However, a sample proportion of 0.60 (12 *yes*es out of 20) is an unlikely sample proportion. Use this 90% box plot to answer the following questions.

PROPORTION OF YESES IN SAMPLE

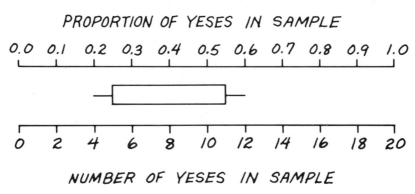

NUMBER OF YESES IN SAMPLE

1. Forty percent of Irish voters voted to lift a constitutional ban on divorce in cases of long-term separation (Newark *Star-Ledger*, June 28, 1986). If you take a random sample of 20 Irish voters, is getting 9 (sample proportion of 0.45) who voted this way a likely or unlikely sample proportion?

2. If you take a random sample of size 20 from a population with 40% *yes*es, will each sample proportion below be a likely or unlikely sample proportion?

   a. 0.40

   b. 0.65

   c. 0.20

   d. 0.90

   e. 0.35

3. For a random sample of size 20 from a population with 40% *yes*es, tell whether each result below gives a likely or unlikely sample proportion.

    a. 20 *yes*, 0 *no*   d. 8 *yes*, 12 *no*

    b. 12 *yes*, 8 *no*   e. 4 *yes*, 16 *no*

    c. 10 *yes*, 10 *no*   f. 0 *yes*, 20 *no*

4. Forty percent of all plain M&M's are brown. If you take a random sample of 20 M&M's, tell whether each number of brown M&M's below is likely or unlikely.

    a. 9 brown

    b. 2 brown

    c. 15 brown

    d. 7 brown

5. The U.S. Bureau of Labor Statistics reports that about 40% of all women with children under the age of 18 do not work. Suppose that you select a random sample of 20 women with children under the age of 18 and ask each woman whether she works. List the likely sample proportions.

6. Complete this sentence:
If we take a random sample of size 20 from a population with 40% *yes*es, 90% of the time we will get a sample proportion of *yes*es between _____ and _____ .

7. According to *On Campus*, the official publication of the American Federation of Teachers, a 1983 Gallup survey found that 40% of the American public favors a longer school year (10 months). Suppose that you select a random sample of 20 Americans and learn that 4 favor a longer school year. If Gallup is right, is 4 out of 20 a likely or unlikely sample proportion? Given this sample proportion, would you think Gallup is right?

8. According to the 1980 U.S. census, about 40% of the population of the city of Chicago is black (*World Almanac*, 1984). In a random sample of 20 Chicagoans, will each result below give a likely or unlikely sample proportion?

    a. all are black

    b. half are black

    c. 12 are black

    d. 30% are black

9. (*Optional*) Ask 20 adults this question: "Do you favor a longer school year?" Do you think your sample is representative of the American public? Why or why not? Is your sample proportion likely or unlikely if Gallup is right (question 7)? On the basis of your survey, do you think Gallup is wrong? Why or why not?

Application 7

Making and Interpreting the 90% Box Plot for a Population with 80% Yeses

About 80% of U.S. adults favor graduation exams even if failure to pass the test could deprive their children of a regular high school diploma (*USA Today*, April 1, 1985).

1. Construct a table like the following one. Fill in the sample proportion column. Then, using a random number table, your class should draw samples of size 20 from a population with 80% *yeses*. Continue until you have 40 trials, and enter the results in the two right columns of the table.

Number of Yeses	Sample Proportion	Tally	Frequency
0			
1			
2			
3			
4			
5			
6			
7			
8			
9			
10			
11			
12			
13			
14			
15			
16			
17			
18			
19			
20			
TOTAL		**40**	**40**

2. Make a 90% box plot of the sample proportions.

3. What percentage of your trials actually ended up inside your box, including the edges? (Your answer must be 90% or larger.)

Use the 90% box plot from question 2 to answer questions 4 through 10.

4. If we ask a random sample of 20 U.S. adults if they favor graduation exams, are the following results likely or unlikely?

   a. 20 *yes*, 0 *no*   d. 10 *yes*, 10 *no*

   b. 18 *yes*, 2 *no*   e. 5 *yes*, 15 *no*

   c. 14 *yes*, 6 *no*

5. About 80% of U.S. adults support the right of school authorities to open school lockers or examine personal property for drugs, liquor, or other contraband (Laramie Sunday *Boomerang*, August 11, 1985). Is it likely or unlikely that a poll of 20 randomly selected adults would show

   a. just 2 favoring this practice?

   b. all 20 favoring it?

   c. 17 favoring it?

   d. 16 favoring it?

6. According to a 1979 census of inmates of juvenile detention and correctional facilities, 80% of those under correctional supervision were male (U.S. Department of Justice, *Report to the Nation on Crime and Justice*, 1983). If we take a random sample of 20 such inmates, is it likely or unlikely that 15 will be male?

7. Complete this sentence:
   If we draw a random sample of size 20 from a population with 80% *yes*es, we estimate that the proportion of *yes*es in our sample will be from _____ to _____ at least 90% of the time.

8. In a random sample of 20 adults, 10 favor graduation exams. Is this a likely sample proportion if 80% of all adults favor graduation exams?

9. About 80% of Americans are against paying higher taxes for defense (*New York Times*, April 4, 1984). If we obtain a random sample of 20 Americans and ask each person if he or she is against paying higher taxes for defense, what are the likely sample proportions?

10. A teacher thought that 80% of the students in his school had seen *E.T.*, but when he asked 20 students at random, he learned that 14 had seen this movie. Do you think he was wrong? Why or why not?

IV. CHARTS OF 90% BOX PLOTS

You have made 90% box plots of sampling distributions for random samples of size 20, including one for populations with 40% *yeses* and one for populations with 80% *yeses*. Here are these box plots placed next to each other:

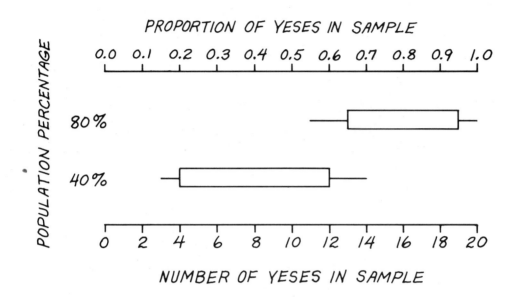

To make these 90% box plots as accurate as possible, we constructed them (using a computer) with many more trials than you did. Thus, your 90% box plots might differ a bit from ours. (They shouldn't differ too much, however.)

We have also made 90% box plots for random samples of size 20 from populations with 5%, 10%, 15%, on up to 100% *yeses*. These box plots, all placed in order next to each other, are on page 92. We constructed these 90% box plots using many trials as well. Note that for a population with 0% *yeses* every sample will, of course, have 0 *yeses*; the sample proportion is always 0.0. Thus, we drew this box as a simple vertical bar at the sample proportion of 0.0. Similarly, for a population with 100% *yeses*, every sample will contain all *yeses*, so we drew the box for the sampling distribution as a vertical bar at sample proportion 1.0.

Remember, each row on the chart of 90% box plots represents a different population, with the indicated percentage of *yeses*. You will find two kinds of questions in the following applications. Given information about the population, you must first find that population in the left column of the chart, then use the information from its box plot to answer the question. Alternatively, if you have information about the sample, you must first find that sample proportion along the scale at the top, then read down to find out the population or populations that answer the question.

Reading Charts of 90% Box Plots

Use the chart of 90% box plots on page 92 to answer the questions below. For questions 1 through 6, first find the appropriate population percentage to the left or right of the chart. Then see if the given sample proportion is in the box for that population percentage. If so, this sample proportion is likely. If this sample proportion is in the whisker or outside the box plot, it is unlikely.

1. A sample of size 20 is selected randomly from a population with 45% *yes*es. Is each of the following results likely or unlikely? Remember that sample proportions falling on the edge of the box are considered inside it and so are likely.

    a. a sample proportion of 0.10 *yes*es

    b. a sample proportion of 0.20 *yes*es

    c. a sample proportion of 0.50 *yes*es

    d. a sample proportion of 0.75 *yes*es

2. A sample of size 20 is selected randomly from a population with 10% *yes*es. Is each of the following results likely or unlikely?

    a. a sample proportion of 0.00 *yes*es

    b. a sample proportion of 0.20 *yes*es

    c. a sample proportion of 0.50 *yes*es

3. About 45% of all mathematicians in the United States are women (*Los Angeles Times*, March 7, 1984). If we take a random sample of 20 mathematicians, are the following results likely or unlikely?

    a. 10 women and 10 men

    b. 15 women and 5 men

    c. 8 women and 12 men

4. Imagine you are taking a true–false test about the Byzantine civil service system. For each of the 20 questions, you discreetly flip a coin and answer *true* if the coin lands heads and *false* if it lands tails. Are each of the following results likely or unlikely?

    a. a 100% score on the test

    b. a 90% score on the test

    c. a 80% score on the test

    d. a 70% score on the test

    e. What scores are you likely to get?

5. According to the National Center for Education Statistics, 30% of male high school seniors have taken trigonometry, compared with 22% of the female students (*Los Angeles Times*, March 7, 1984). If you take a random sample of 20 male high school seniors and ask each if he has taken trig, what are the likely sample proportions?

6. Sixty-five percent of men are fully or partially bald by the time they reach age 55 (*Los Angeles Times*, December 9, 1983). If you check 20 randomly selected 55-year-old men for baldness, what are the likely sample proportions?

To answer the remaining questions, you must first find the appropriate sample proportion across the top of the chart, or the corresponding number of *yes*es at the bottom. Then read down or up to see the population percentages for which this sample proportion is likely.

7. A random sample of size 20 contains a sample proportion of 0.20 *yes*es. For which of the following population percentages is this a likely sample proportion?

   a. one with 5% *yes*es
   b. one with 10% *yes*es
   c. one with 15% *yes*es
   d. one with 20% *yes*es
   e. one with 25% *yes*es

   f. one with 30% *yes*es
   g. one with 35% *yes*es
   h. one with 40% *yes*es
   i. one with 45% *yes*es
   j. one with 50% *yes*es

8. A random sample of size 20 contains a sample proportion of 0.50 *yes*es. For which population percentages is this a likely sample proportion?

9. A random sample of size 20 contains 14 *yes*es. For which population percentages is this a likely sample proportion?

10. A random sample of size 20 contains 20 *yes*es. For which population percentages is this a likely sample proportion?

Application 9

Reading Charts of 90% Box Plots for Samples of Size 100

In this application, the samples will be of size 100. Consequently, you can no longer use the chart on page 92, which was constructed from samples of size 20. Our computer has made a similar chart from samples of size 100. You will find it on page 95. Use it to answer the following questions.

For questions 1 through 5, first find the appropriate population percentage to the left or right of the chart. Then see if the given sample proportion is in the box for that population percentage.

1. For a random sample of size 100 from a population with 55% *yes*es, state whether the following are likely or unlikely results.

    a. a sample proportion of 0.90 *yes*es

    b. a sample proportion of 0.70 *yes*es

    c. a sample proportion of 0.50 *yes*es

    d. a sample proportion of 0.20 *yes*es

2. Ninety percent of U.S. adults agree with the recommendation that high school students take three years of math (*USA Today*, April 1, 1985). Assuming that this suggestion is no April Fool's joke, is it likely or unlikely that a poll of 100 randomly selected adults would show

    a. 100 *yes*es and 0 *no*s?

    b. 92 *yes*es and 8 *no*s?

    c. 84 *yes*es and 16 *no*s?

    d. 62 *yes*es and 38 *no*s?

    e. 40 *yes*es and 60 *no*s?

3. About 25% of Americans bite their fingernails (*Los Angeles Times*, December 9, 1983). If you select a random sample of 100 Americans and check each one for nail biting, what are the likely sample proportions?

4. About 5% of Americans find life dull (*Los Angeles Times*, April 13, 1986). If you ask a random sample of 100 Americans if they find life dull, what are the likely sample proportions?

5. The Census Bureau reports that about 15% of the adults living in the U.S. are illiterate in English (*Cincinnati Enquirer*, April 21, 1986). What are the likely sample proportions if we check a random sample of 100 adults living in the U.S. for illiteracy in English?

To answer questions 6 through 11, first find the appropriate sample proportion across the top of the chart, or the corresponding number of *yes*es at the bottom. Then read down or up to see for which population percentages this sample proportion is likely.

6. A random sample of size 100 contains a sample proportion of 0.20 *yes*es. For which of the following population percentages is this a likely sample proportion?

    a. one with 5% *yes*es

    b. one with 10% *yes*es

    c. one with 15% *yes*es

    d. one with 20% *yes*es

    e. one with 25% *yes*es

    f. one with 30% *yes*es

    g. one with 35% *yes*es

    h. one with 40% *yes*es

    i. one with 45% *yes*es

    j. one with 50% *yes*es

7. A random sample of size 100 contains 50 *yes*es. For which population percentages is this a likely sample proportion?

8. A random sample of size 100 contains 89 *yes*es. For which population percentages is this a likely sample proportion?

9. A study of about 100 divorced couples with children found that 24 were "fiery foes" who rarely communicated (*USA Today*, April 23, 1986). For which population percentages is this a likely sample proportion?

10. A sample (selected at random, we hope) of 100 lower- and middle-class boys found that 8 had conduct disorders, such as stealing, fighting, and running away from home (*Los Angeles Times*, November 25, 1982). For which population percentages is this a likely sample proportion?

11. The same study also investigated about 100 lower- and middle-class boys with symptoms of hyperactivity. Of the boys in this sample, a proportion of 0.27 had conduct disorders. For which population percentages is this a likely sample proportion?

12. Considering your answers to questions 10 and 11, do you think hyperactive boys are more likely than typical boys to have conduct disorders? Explain.

13. Compare the 90% box plots for random samples of size 100 with those for samples of size 20.

    a. Which chart has shorter box plots?

    b. Why do you think this chart has shorter box plots?

Application 10

Reviewing Charts of 90% Box Plots

Use the box plots on page 93, which were constructed from samples of size 40, to answer the following questions.

1. Suppose you reach in a jar of marbles, pull out 40, and find that 18 are blue.

   a. Is this sample proportion likely if 60% of the marbles in the jar are blue?

   b. For which population percentages is a sample proportion of 18 out of 40 likely?

2. Ninety-five percent of U.S. adults believe that students should pass math and reading tests before they graduate from high school (*USA Today*, April 1, 1985). If we take a random sample of 40 U.S. adults,

   a. is it likely or unlikely that a sample proportion of 0.875 will approve of this requirement?

   b. is it likely or unlikely that all 40 will approve?

3. What are the likely sample proportions if we draw a random sample of size 40 from a population with 25% *yes*es?

4. For which population percentages is a sample proportion of 0.25 from a random sample of size 40 a likely result?

5. Alcohol was found in 70% of the blood samples taken from male drivers, age 15 to 34, who died in motor vehicle crashes in four California counties in 1982–83 (*Public Health Reports*, 1985). If we were to take a random sample of 40 such drivers, would we be likely to find

   a. a sample proportion of 0.575 with alcohol in their blood?

   b. 33 drivers with alcohol in their blood?

6. According to General Mills, about 90% of Americans eat breakfast at least some of the time (*Los Angeles Times*, December 9, 1983). If we select a random sample of 40 Americans and ask each person whether he or she eats breakfast at least some of the time, what are the likely sample proportions?

V. CONFIDENCE INTERVALS

This section contains the central idea of this book. We will put together everything we have learned so far and will be able to make statements like this one:

> I took a random sample of 20 students at my school and asked them if they love math. Because 6 of them said *yes*, I am fairly sure that if I ask all students at my school this question, between 15% and 50% will say *yes*. However, for every 100 times that I give such an interval, I expect to be right 90 times and wrong 10 times.

Let's see how to construct the interval we've just described.

Suppose we get 6 *yes*es in a random sample of size 20, for a sample proportion of 0.30. From the chart of 90% box plots on page 92 for samples of size 20, we see that this result is likely from populations with 15%, 20%, 25%, 30%, 35%, 40%, 45%, and 50% *yes*es. We say that 15% to 50% is a **90% confidence interval**. We think that the population has between 15% and 50% *yes*es.

To find the 90% confidence interval for the percentage of *yes*es in a population, lay a ruler down the column giving the sample proportion, as in the diagram below. The line will intersect some but not all of the boxes. If the line falls exactly on the edge of the box, we say that the line intersects this box. The boxes intersected by the line represent the populations for which the sample proportion is likely. Thus, these populations make up the 90% confidence interval.

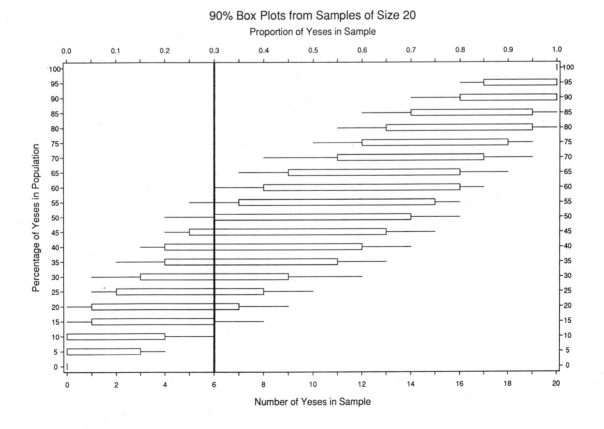

90% Box Plots from Samples of Size 20

Proportion of Yeses in Sample

Let's do another example. Suppose we get 14 *yes*es in a random sample of size 20, for a sample proportion of 0.70. Laying a ruler down the 0.70 column, we find that the ruler intersects the boxes from the 50% to the 85% populations. Our sample is a likely result from populations with 50% to 85% *yes*es. So our 90% confidence interval for the percentage of *yes*es in the population is 50% to 85%.

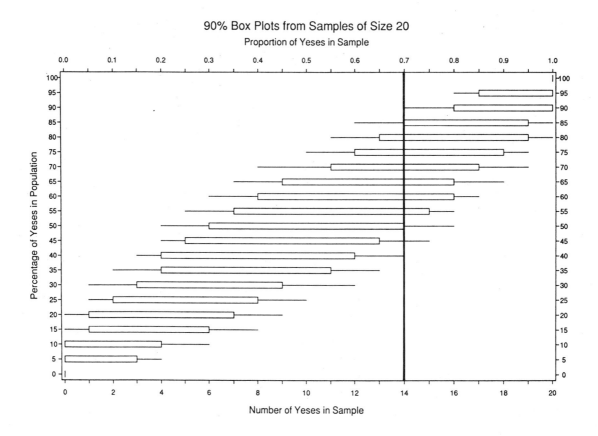

90% Box Plots from Samples of Size 20
Proportion of Yeses in Sample

Further, when we make statements like "The percentage of *yes*es in the population is between 50% and 85%," we will be right 90% of the time and wrong 10% of the time. This last statement is not as obvious as it might seem. You will learn more about this statement through the simulations in Applications 12 and 13, and Application 14 gives the mathematical argument underlying this statement.

Application 11

Finding Confidence Intervals

1. Your teacher has the container of objects you used at the beginning of this book. Draw a random sample of size 20 and find the 90% confidence interval for the percentage of *yes*es in the container. Does your confidence interval contain the true percentage of *yes*es?

2. *Penny Power* magazine gave each of 20 eighth graders three erasable pens and a nonerasable Bic Stic ballpoint pen. Each pen had a medium point and blue ink. The students used the pens for one week while doing their usual schoolwork and homework. At the end of the week, 14 students preferred the Bic Stic to any of the erasables (*Penny Power*, August/September 1984). Assuming that the magazine selected the students and pens randomly, find the 90% confidence interval for the percentage of all eighth graders who prefer the Bic Stic to these erasables.

3. Of the 20 students in question 2, 11 chose the Scripto Erasable as the best of the erasable pens.

   a. What is the 90% confidence interval for the percentage of all eighth graders who prefer the Scripto Erasable to the other erasables?

   b. Can you be fairly confident that at least half of all eighth graders prefer this erasable pen? Why or why not?

4. In a study of advanced chronic multiple sclerosis (MS), 20 patients spent 30 hours in a high-pressure oxygen chamber with 10% oxygen and 90% nitrogen. Only one patient improved (*Los Angeles Times*, January 27, 1983). Find the 90% confidence interval for the percentage of MS patients who will improve with this treatment.

5. In another study of MS patients, 16 of 20 stabilized or improved after treatment with anticancer and steroid drugs to suppress their immune systems (*Los Angeles Times*, January 27, 1983). Find the 90% confidence interval for the percentage of MS patients who will improve or stabilize with this treatment.

6. To improve health care for premature babies, physicians wanted to learn which of three types of milk would give the best results. A Duke University pediatrician studied 60 premature babies who weighed 3 pounds or less. In this sample, 20 babies were fed milk from mothers who had had premature babies, 20 were fed milk from mothers who had had full-term babies, and the remaining 20 were fed formula. By the sixth week of feeding, 18 of the babies on the formula, 17 on the preterm milk, and 12 on full-term milk had gained normal weights. However, several babies in the study unexpectedly became sick. Six babies on formula became sick and 2 of them died. One baby on the full-term milk died. None on the preterm milk died (*Los Angeles Times*, February 3, 1983).

   a. Suppose you were a pediatrician associated with this study. What is the single most important feature of the data you would investigate first?

   b. What is the 90% confidence interval for the percentage of babies on full-term milk who will regain normal weight?

   c. What is the 90% confidence interval for the percentage of babies on formula who will regain normal weight?

   d. What is the 90% confidence interval for the percentage of babies on preterm milk who will regain normal weight?

   e. What overall conclusions would you make if you were a pediatrician?

Application 12

Estimating the Percentage of Digits That Are Even

1. Use the random number table on pages 90 and 91 to get a random sample of 20 digits. (Each student should obtain a different random sample.)

2. What is the number of even digits in your sample? Remember that 0 is an even digit!

3. Using the proportion of even digits in your sample and the chart of 90% box plots on page 92, find the 90% confidence interval for the percentage of even digits in a random number table.

4. What is the true percentage of even digits in a huge list of random numbers?

5. Does your 90% confidence interval contain the true percentage?

6. What percentage of the students in your class do you think will answer *yes* to question 5?

7. Determine the percentage of students in your class who did answer *yes* in question 5. Is this percentage about what you expected?

8. Complete this sentence:
   If 100 students do the experiment described in questions 1 through 5, about _____ of them will answer *yes* to question 5.

9. Complete this sentence:
   If 200 students do the experiment described in questions 1 through 5, about _____ of them will answer *yes* to question 5.

**Determining How Often the Population Percentage
Is in the Confidence Interval**

The data sheet on page 89 shows 12 arrays of X's and O's. Each array contains 10 samples of size 20 drawn from some population. An X is a *yes* and an O is a *no*. Select two or three students to work with each array.

1. The first row of your array is your first sample of size 20.

   a. Count the number of X's in this row.

   b. Find the sample proportion of *yes*es in this row.

   c. Use the sample proportion of *yes*es and the chart of 90% box plots on page 92 to find the 90% confidence interval for the percentage of *yes*es in your population.

2. The second row of your array is your second sample of size 20. Repeat question 1 for the second row and then for each of the eight remaining rows. Complete all but the last column of a chart like the one below.

Row	Number of X's	Sample Proportion of X's	90% Confidence Interval for the Population Percentage of X's	Is the True Population Percentage in the Confidence Interval?
1				
2				
3				
4				
5				
6				
7				
8				
9				
10				

3. You now have 10 confidence intervals. How many of them do you expect to contain the true population percentage?

4. Your class constructed 120 confidence intervals altogether. How many of these confidence intervals do you expect to contain the true population percentage?

5. Ask your teacher for the true population percentages.

   a. Fill in the last column of your chart. How many of your 10 confidence intervals contain the true percentage for your population?

   b. What percentage of the 120 intervals constructed in your class contain their true population percentages?

Now let's see how to answer the question suggested by the title of this application. How often will our confidence interval contain the true population percentage? Your answer to question 5 gives an estimate based on the simulations in your class. Similarly, your answer to question 7 of Application 12 also gives an answer based on different simulations done by your class. Both answers should be about the same. You might expect them to be about 90%, because we are using 90% box plots. Most classes will find, however, that the confidence intervals they have constructed contain the true population percentage a little more than 90% of the time because the boxes actually contain slightly more than 90% of the possible samples (see page 12).

In these two applications, you have been able to check whether each confidence interval included the true population percentage because we know what the true population percentages are. However, in a real survey, we do not know the true population percentage. (If we did know, we'd have no reason to take a random sample to get an estimate!) For real surveys, the true population percentage will either be in the confidence interval or it will not; we never know which. All we can say is that we expect that 90% of the confidence intervals constructed using our method will contain the true population percentage.

Thus, simulations give one way to answer our question. Using mathematical reasoning is a different way to learn that about 90% of our confidence intervals will contain the true population percentage. Application 14 explains this mathematical argument, which does not use simulation.

Analyzing Why 90% of Confidence Intervals Contain the Population Percentage

In this activity, you will see why you can expect 90% of all confidence intervals you construct to contain the true population percentage. As we said on the first page of this section, this conclusion is not obvious. We know that the sample proportion will be in the box 90% of the time. Why does this fact imply that 90% of all confidence intervals will contain the population percentage?

The following discussion and questions 1 through 7 assume that we obtain the sample proportion for a random sample from a population with 20% *yes*es. The figure below is a simplified chart of 90% box plots that we will use to analyze confidence intervals. The population labeled ✳ has an unknown percentages of *yes*es; we will use it in question 9 of this application.

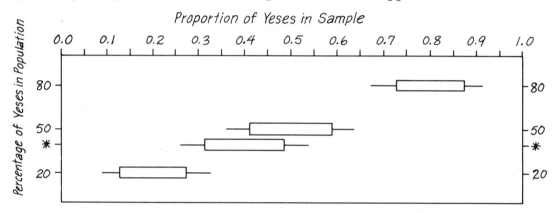

Let's use the above picture to consider what the confidence interval would look like. First, suppose that the sample proportion falls to the *right* of the box for the population with 20% *yes*es, say at X on the picture as shown below.

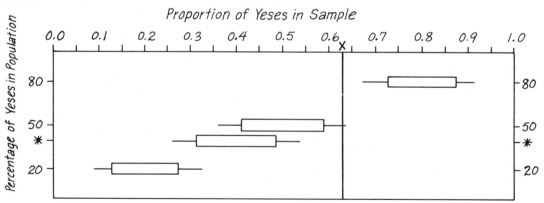

To construct the confidence interval from this sample proportion, we look at a vertical line down from X and see which boxes it intersects. In the above picture, the line clearly does not intersect the box for the population with 20% *yes*es.

32

1. If the sample proportion X falls to the right of the box for the population with 20% *yes*es, will the resulting confidence interval contain 20%? In other words, will the confidence interval contain the true population percentage?

2. Suppose the sample proportion X falls to the left of the box for the population with 20% *yes*es. Will the confidence interval contain 20%? In other words, will the confidence interval contain the true population percentage?

3. Now suppose that the sample proportion falls inside this box. Draw a schematic figure, similar to the preceding ones, to represent this situation.

4. When the sample proportion falls inside this box, will the confidence interval contain 20%?

5. What is the probability that the sample proportion will fall inside the box for the population with 20% *yes*es?

6. Now put together your answers to questions 4 and 5. With random sampling from a population with 20% *yes*es, what is the probability of getting a sample proportion whose confidence interval contains 20%? In other words, what is the probability of getting a confidence interval that contains 20%?

7. What is the probability of getting a confidence interval that does not contain 20%? In what situation will the confidence interval not contain 20%?

8. Now suppose that we obtain the sample proportion for a random sample from a population with 50% *yes*es. What is the probability of getting a sample proportion whose confidence interval contains 50%? (Note that this question is like question 6, but with 50% *yes*es rather than 20%. To answer question 8, you might find it helpful to think through questions 1 through 7, replacing every 20% with 50%.)

9. Now suppose that we obtain the sample proportion for a random sample from a population with some unknown percentage of *yes*es. Call this unknown percentage *, as indicated in the figure on page 32. What is the probability of getting a sample proportion whose confidence interval contains the percentage *?

This analysis applies to every population, whether its percentage of *yes*es equals 20%, 50%, 80%, or *%. In brief, no matter which population a random sample comes from, the sample proportion will be in the box for that population 90% of the time. The sample proportions in the box in turn produce confidence intervals that include this population percentage. Thus, when the sample proportion is in the box, the confidence interval includes the true population percentage. But we know that the sample proportions will be in the box about 90% of the time, so the confidence intervals will also include the true (but unknown) population percentage about 90% of the time.

Working with Different Sample Sizes

So far we have mainly used sample sizes of 20 and 100. This application will show you the effect of different sample sizes on the length of the confidence interval. To answer the questions below, use the charts of 90% box plots for samples of sizes 20, 40, and 80 on pages 92, 93, and 94.

1. Are you likely or unlikely to get a sample proportion of 0.50 *yes*es from a population with 35% *yes*es if the sample size is

   a. 20?

   b. 40?

   c. 80?

2. Are you likely or unlikely to get a sample proportion of 0.70 *yes*es from a population with 80% *yes*es if the sample size is

   a. 20?

   b. 40?

   c. 80?

3. Which sample size has the longest box plots?

4. Which sample size has the shortest box plots?

5. Do larger sample sizes have longer or shorter box plots? Why?

6. A random sample of size 20 contains 10 *yes*es. Find the 90% confidence interval for the percentage of *yes*es in the population.

7. A random sample of size 40 contains 20 *yes*es. Find the 90% confidence interval for the percentage of *yes*es in the population.

8. A random sample of size 80 contains 40 *yes*es. Find the 90% confidence interval for the percentage of *yes*es in the population.

9. Look at your answers to questions 6, 7, and 8, and complete this sentence:
   As the sample size increases, the length of the confidence interval
   _____ .

10. If we were to compare the lengths of confidence intervals for random samples of size 300, 600, and 1200, which one would be shortest?

11. *True or False*: With larger sample sizes, the sample proportion is more likely to be close to the population percentage.

12. To decrease the length of the confidence interval, must a pollster increase or decrease the sample size? Why might he or she choose not to do this?

Application 16

Reviewing Confidence Intervals

1. Assume we select a random sample of size 20 and obtain 13 *yes*es. Is this sample proportion likely or unlikely if the entire population contains 70% *yes*es?

2. According to the 1980 U.S. census, 30% of males 15 years and over have never been married. If we take a random sample of 20 males 15 years and older and ask if they are single (never married), what are the likely sample proportions?

3. If we get 13 *yes*es in a random sample of size 20, what is the 90% confidence interval for the percentage of *yes*es in the population?

4. Assume we take a random sample of size 20 from a population with 10% *yes*es. Are we likely or unlikely to get

   a. 5 *yes*es and 15 *no*s?

   b. all *no*s?

   c. a sample proportion of 0.30?

5. Assume we select a random sample of size 20 and get a sample proportion of 0.90 *yes*es. Is this sample proportion likely from a population with 75% *yes*es?

6. If we take a random sample of size 20 from a population with 25% *yes*es, is 0.40 a likely sample proportion?

7. Find the 90% confidence interval for the percentage of *yes*es in the population if a random sample of size 20 contains 11 *yes*es.

8. About how many of every 300 90% confidence intervals will contain the true population percentage?

9. To decrease the length of the confidence interval, should you increase or decrease the sample size?

10. *(For those who did Application 14)* Explain why 90% confidence intervals contain the population percentage 90% of the time.

VI. METHODS OF SAMPLING

We have used the term *random sample* often in our discussions so far because our method of constructing confidence intervals is legitimate only for samples selected randomly from the population. This section discusses what random sampling (sometimes called *simple random sampling*) is and why it is important.

Definition of Random Sample

A sample is random if it is selected so that:
1. each member of the population is equally likely to be chosen;
2. the members of the sample are chosen independently of one another.

Note that obtaining a randomly chosen sample depends on *the way in which the sample is drawn*, not on the specific members of the population that happen to end up in the sample.

For example, suppose we want to select a random sample of 20 seniors from a class of 300 at a certain school. We could put the name of each senior on a card, put the cards in a box, mix them up, and draw 20. To see if this method gives random sampling, we must check the two parts of the above definition. For this method,

1. every senior had the same chance of being chosen, and

2. we drew the names independently of each other. (In other words, we didn't let best friends staple their cards together or do anything else that would interfere with drawing cards individually.)

Thus, this selection process is random sampling. A sample selected in this way is a random sample, no matter which specific seniors end up in the sample.

A second way to select a random sample of 20 students from a class of 300 is to use a random number table. We could assign each student a different number from 1 to 300, enter a random number table at some arbitrary location, and take three digits at a time as a random number. The 1000 possible values are 000, 001, 002, . . . , 999, and each is equally likely. If a value from 001 to 300 arises, we put the corresponding student in the sample. If 000 or one of the values from 301 to 999 arises, or if a number repeats, we disregard it and go on to the next random number. We continue until we have 20 students in the sample.

Suppose the 20 names we draw all happen to be members of the girls' softball team. Is this group a random sample? Yes, it is, because we selected it randomly from the population of all seniors. Is this group *representative* of the population? No, it is not, because members of the girls' softball team are likely to have characteristics and opinions different from those of seniors in general. Generally, large random samples are representative of the population. Occasionally, random sampling might give a sample that is not very representative, but it is still a random sample if it was selected using the two criteria.

We obtained random samples using different random mechanisms in the sampling experiments in Sections II and III. Sometimes we used a physical device, such as tossing coins, and sometimes we used a random number table. In each case, the sampling process satisfied the definition for selecting a random sample. Random sampling allows us to construct confidence intervals for the population percentage. If we had not obtained samples randomly, we could not have made the statistical inferences we did.

Application 17

Deciding If a Sampling Method Gives Random Samples

1. Use a random number table to draw a random sample of five students from your class. Does your sample appear to be representative?

2. For question 1, what proportion of the two-digit random numbers did you use? What proportion did you disregard? Can you think of a more efficient way to assign the two-digit random numbers to students?

3. Which of the following sampling methods produce a random sample from a class of 36 students?

   a. Select the first six students to enter the room.

   b. Select those students whose phone numbers end with the digit 4.

   c. Suppose that the class has 18 boys and 18 girls. Select a sample of 6 students by using a random number table to choose 1 of the 18 boys, then 1 of the 18 girls, then a boy, then a girl, and so on until you have chosen 6 students.

   d. Suppose that the classroom has six rows of chairs with six chairs in each row. Assign the rows the digits 1 through 6. Throw a die and place all the students in the row corresponding to the number on the die in the sample.

   e. Assign each student a number from 1 to 36. The girls get the numbers 1 to 18 and the boys the numbers from 19 to 36. Use a random number table to select six two-digit numbers between 1 and 36, and place the corresponding students in the sample.

4. For each sampling method below, tell which groups in the population are likely to be underrepresented.

   a. To obtain a sample of households, a television rating service dials numbers taken at random from telephone directories.

   b. In 1984, Ann Landers conducted a poll on the marital happiness of women by asking women to write to her.

   c. To determine the percentage of teenage girls with long hair, *Teen* magazine published a mail-in questionnaire. Of the 500 respondents, 85% had hair shoulder length or longer (*USA Today*, July 1, 1985).

d. To evaluate the reliability of cars owned by its subscribers, *Consumer Reports* magazine publishes a yearly list of automobiles and their frequency-of-repair records. The magazine collects the information by mailing a questionnaire to subscribers and tabulating the results from those who return it.

e. A college psychology professor needs subjects for a research project to determine which colors average American adults find restful. From the list of all 743 students taking introductory psychology at her school, she selects 25 students using a random number table.

f. For a survey of student opinions about school athletic programs, a member of the school board obtains a sample of students by listing all students in the school and using a random number table to select 30 of them. Six of the students say that they don't have time to participate, and they are eliminated from the sample.

5. If a sample of 20 adults ends up containing only men, two explanations are possible. The first is that the sampling procedure wasn't random; the second is that the sampling procedure was random but that a nonrepresentative sample resulted. Which explanation would you be more inclined to believe? Explain. (*Hint*: Look at the charts of 90% box plots.)

6. Repeat question 5 but assume that the sample of size 20 had 13 men.

7. Describe how you could actually obtain a random sample of 30 students from the population of students in your school. You may want to consult with someone in the records office.

Other Ways to Obtain a Sample

Obtaining a random sample can be very difficult. For example, there may be no easy way to list all members of a population so that we can assign a number to each member. Even if we could make such a list, it might be very difficult to contact some members in order to include them in the sample.

Suppose we want to conduct a survey to determine which of two candidates will win the next election for dogcatcher in our town. We would like to sample the population of all those who will vote in the election. But who knows who will vote? Nobody. Suppose, then, we define the population as all those who voted in the last election and are still registered. Such information is publicly available, and we could conceivably make a list of all these people, and choose a random sample using the list. But constructing this list would be a lot of work, probably more than we want to do. Alternatively, we could take as the population all voting-age residents of the town and try to take a random sample of them. But who has a complete list of residents of the town? We might find a list of all household addresses, but we would have to know how many people live at each address to produce a complete list for sampling.

Another possibility is to use telephone numbers; more than 90% of households have a telephone. But if we use the telephone book as our list of residents in the population (or at least as a list of households), we will miss all those people with unlisted numbers. Around 20% of all residential phone numbers are not listed in current telephone directories, and this percentage varies depending on the demographic characteristics of the region. Moreover, people with unlisted numbers might have different views about the candidates for dogcatcher than those with listed numbers. If everyone in our town has telephone numbers with the same first three digits (a big if), then we could obtain a sample by dialing these three digits followed by four digits selected at random using a random number table. It will be difficult to reach people who are not home very often, so these people will be less likely to be in the sample. On the other hand, those households with two telephone numbers will be more likely to be in the sample. As you can see, devising a procedure to obtain a random sample for a real question and a real population of interest can be very difficult, if not impossible.

If a method of selecting a sample tends to overrepresent or underrepresent some part of the population, then the method is *biased* (and the resulting samples tend not to be representative of the population). Ideally, pollsters prefer random sampling, but as we saw with the dogcatcher example, random samples are difficult to obtain. In practice, some bias is almost inevitable in the method of sampling.

The rest of this section and Applications 18, 19, and 20 explore the advantages and disadvantages of different sampling methods. You will learn how to evaluate the ways in which a method of selecting a sample might be biased, thereby giving samples that tend not to be representative of the population.

Convenience Sampling

The easiest way to obtain a sample is simply to choose it, without any random mechanism. For example, if we want a sample of 5 from a class of 30 students, we could choose the first 5 students who raise their hands, or choose the 5 in the front row, or choose the 5 tallest, or choose 5 close friends, or choose 5 enemies, or simply name 5 people haphazardly without using any special criteria. Obtaining a sample by such methods is called *convenience sampling*. Convenience sampling uses no explicit random mechanism. It is easy, but is it useful? Can we make confidence interval statements relating the sample to the population, as in Section V, using convenience sampling? Unfortunately, we can't.

Why can't we use convenience sampling to construct confidence intervals? First, our method of constructing a confidence interval (laid out in Sections II through V) depends fundamentally on using a sample selected by random sampling. We made our 90% box plots by observing the variability in different random samples from the same population. Convenience sampling gives us no straightforward way to model the variability from one sample to the next, so we cannot construct box plots or a confidence interval.

Second, convenience sampling is often biased, as you will see in the examples in Applications 18 and 19. With random sampling, we expect no bias. A specific sample may happen not to be representative. However, we know that on average random samples are representative: about 90% of the time the confidence interval will contain the population percentage.

Self-Selected Samples. When people participate in a survey by voluntarily returning a form printed in a newspaper or magazine, they make up a *self-selected sample*, which is one type of convenience sample. People who care enough to respond may not be representative of the whole population. For example, in a mail-in survey of 5,400 *USA Today* readers, an amazing 43% of the respondents in Delaware, Indiana, Kentucky, Michigan, New York, Ohio, and Pennsylvania reported symptoms that pointed to a serious risk for clinical depression. The newspaper notes, however, that "Mail-in surveys always attract the most concerned and motivated. It's not a random sample . . . ." (*USA Today*, July 12, 1985). Such a study cannot reliably tell us the percentage of the overall population at risk for depression.

Judgment Sampling. In another form of convenience sampling, an expert selects a sample that he or she considers representative. For example, a produce buyer might select and taste several grapes from a shipment in order to determine the quality of the grapes as a whole. A judgment sample may give a better estimate than most random samples would, if the expert is really good at selecting the sample. However, there is no easy objective way to quantify such a claim.

In summary, random sampling is useful because we can calculate confidence intervals from samples drawn in this way. However, random sampling is difficult to do in practice. Alternatively, convenience sampling can be easy to do, but it is not always useful for learning about the population as the method may be biased.

Probability Sampling

In the face of all these difficulties in obtaining a sample, what methods do organizations performing large sample surveys actually use? They use procedures called *probability sampling*. Random sampling is one special type of probability sampling.

Probability sampling always includes a random mechanism to choose the members of the sample. Each member of the population is chosen using known probabilities, but the probabilities do not have to be equal; thus, each member of the population is not necessarily equally likely to be chosen. Further, the members of the sample are not necessarily chosen independently.

Three other common types of probability sampling methods are described next. Statisticians have developed formulas for obtaining confidence intervals from probability samples, but the formulas are complicated and we will not discuss them in this book.

Cluster Sampling. Suppose an organization wants to poll voters in a town. It might first select some streets at random in the town, then select some households at random on these streets, and then poll everyone in these households. This sample is not a convenience sample, because at no time does the interviewer decide who to include in the sample. However, it is also not a (simple) random sample, even though each voter in the town has an equal chance of being part of the sample. The reason it is not a random sample is that the people are not chosen independently of one another. If one person is in the sample, every voter in his or her household will be, too; moreover, neighbors on that person's street are more likely to be included than are residents on other streets. This type of sampling is called *cluster sampling*, because the items enter the sample in clusters, not individually.

Stratified Random Sampling. A common type of probability sampling is ***stratified random sampling***. In this method, polling organizations divide the population into separate strata, or subgroups, so that each population member is in one, and only one, stratum. Then they take a random sample in each of the strata. For example, to obtain a sample of 40 students from a high school, we could divide the students into the two strata of boys and girls and take a random sample of 20 from each. Alternatively, we could define the four strata as freshmen, sophomores, juniors, and seniors and take 10 students at random from each.

One reason for using stratified random sampling is that the separate strata may be of interest, not just the whole population. In the high school example, we may want to know how the student body as a whole answers the survey question, and we may also want to know how the views of boys and girls compare. Thus, we must make sure we have enough boys and enough girls in the sample, so we define them as the strata.

Another important reason for using stratified random sampling is to insure that the sample is more representative of the population than a (simple) random sample might be. This increased representativeness causes the confidence interval from a stratified random sample generally to be shorter than the confidence interval from a random sample (of the same total size). That is, stratified random sampling usually gives more precise estimates than random sampling.

Systematic Sampling. Another popular type of probability sampling is ***systematic sampling***. If you were to select a sample of students from your class by choosing every fifth student who walks into the classroom, you would be using systematic sampling. To use systematic sampling, we first order the members of the population in some way. Next we decide to sample, say, 1 out of every 20. For a 1-in-20 systematic sample, we randomly choose one of the first 20 members of the population and then every 20th member from then on. We might get, for example, members 8, 28, 48, 68, and so on; alternatively, we might get members 17, 37, 57, 77, and so on.

Systematic sampling has several advantages. It is often easier to do than random sampling. It also guarantees that the sample is taken from throughout the ordered population; thus, the sample may be more representative than one from random sampling. A danger, however, is that the way we order the population may be connected to the problem we are studying. For example, suppose we study freeway traffic by taking a systematic 1-in-7 sample of days. We could get Sunday, Sunday, Sunday, which would not allow us to learn much about overall congestion! Systematic sampling is most useful when random sampling is too difficult, and we see no reason for the ordering of the population to create a nonrepresentative sample.

Using Different Sampling Methods

1. Describe how you would select a sample of 30 juniors from your school using the following methods.

    a. random sampling

    b. convenience sampling

    c. sampling by self-selection

    d. stratified random sampling

    e. systematic sampling

    f. cluster sampling

2. Retailers at the local shopping mall want to survey their Saturday customers about their satisfaction with the eating facilities within the mall. One merchant went to business school and learned about the importance of statistics, so he wants to obtain a random sample. He proposes the following method: Interviewers should stand at the center of the mall and select the first 100 people who walk by after 11:00 a.m. He believes this approach will provide a random sample because the interviewers will not exercise any decision over whether or not to include specific individuals in the sample.

    a. What kind of sample would the merchant really get?

    b. In what way might this sampling method be biased?

    c. Describe how the merchant could modify this approach to use a version of systematic sampling.

    d. If the retailer were to use stratified random sampling, what strata would you recommend that he choose?

    e. How would you improve the merchant's sampling procedure?

3. The Educational Testing Service (ETS) needed a representative sample of college students. ETS first divided all colleges into groups of similar ones (such as public colleges with more than 25,000 students, small private schools, and so on). Then they used their judgment to choose one representative school from each group, thus obtaining the sample of schools. Each school in turn picked a sample of students (Freedman, Pisani, and Purves, *Statistics*).

    a. ETS divided the colleges into strata but did not perform stratified random sampling. Explain.

    b. Suggest ways to improve this sampling scheme.

4. Researchers wanted a representative sample of Japanese-Americans living in San Francisco. "The procedure was as follows. After consultation with representative figures in the Japanese community, the four most representative blocks in the Japanese area of the city were chosen; all persons resident in those four blocks were taken for the sample. However, a comparison with Census data shows that the

sample did not include a high-enough proportion of Japanese with college degrees" (Freedman et al.).

   a. What kind of sampling did this study use?

   b. Why do you suppose the sample did not have enough college graduates?

   c. Can you think of a way to improve this sampling scheme? Can you think of a reasonable way to use random sampling to obtain the sample?

5. The headline on page 1 of an Illinois newspaper stated, "More people using drugs at work, survey reports." The article gave the following information: "The survey questioned 227 people who called the national [cocaine] helpline, chosen at random, during a six-week period in February and March . . . Ninety-two percent of the callers said they sometimes worked while under the influence of drugs" (*Rockford Register Star*, March 25, 1985).

   a. What kind of sampling was used?

   b. What population would you say this sample is drawn from?

   c. Describe why this survey does not justify the claim made in the headline.

6. A newspaper article began, "Almost half of the USA's secretaries would rather work for a man than a woman, even though a male boss is more likely to ask them to clean the coffeepot, says a *Working Woman* survey" (*USA Today*, April 23, 1986). This is the result of a "poll of 1,100 readers in the magazine's May issue." Of these readers, 46% prefer to work for a man, 5% for a woman, and 49% say it doesn't matter.

   a. What kind of sampling do you think was used?

   b. What population do the results apply to, according to the newspaper?

   c. In what way might the sampling method be biased? (*Hint*: What kind of secretaries would not read *Working Woman*?)

Analyzing the Largest Sample Survey Ever

In the 1936 presidential election, Franklin D. Roosevelt ran for reelection against Alfred Landon. The *Literary Digest*, a popular magazine that ran preelection polls, had correctly predicted the winner in all presidential races since 1916. In 1936, based on responses from about 2.4 million people, the magazine predicted that Landon would win, 57% to 43%. In fact, Roosevelt won, 62% to 38%. What happened?

To obtain its sample, the magazine compiled a list of about 10 million names from sources such as telephone books, lists of automobile owners, club membership lists, and its own subscription lists. All 10 million people received questionnaires, and about 2.4 million returned them; these people made up the sample.

1. What method of sampling did the magazine use?

2. What percentage of people returned the questionnaire? In what ways do you think people who returned the questionnaire might have differed from those who did not? Do you think that the proportion favoring Roosevelt among those who returned the questionnaire was about the same as the proportion favoring Roosevelt among all those receiving the questionnaire? That is, do you think a **nonresponse bias** existed?

3. Discuss other sources of bias in the magazine's sample selection. In other words, in what ways were the people receiving the *Literary Digest* questionnaire likely to differ from the population of voters in 1936?

4. Why do you think the *Literary Digest* survey successfully predicted the winner from 1916 to 1932 but not in 1936?

It so happened that in 1936 a young man named George Gallup was setting up an organization to do surveys. He predicted the *Literary Digest*'s predictions (with 1% error) well before the magazine published them. Gallup obtained his sample by randomly choosing 3,000 people from the same lists the *Digest* used and mailing them postcards asking how they planned to vote. Gallup also ran a different, larger survey that predicted Roosevelt would win. (For further discussion of this and other election examples, see Freedman, Pisani, and Purves, *Statistics*.)

Good Housekeeping magazine runs an annual "Most Admired Men" poll in which the editors list several columns of prominent men and ask readers to send in their votes. Here is a newspaper comment on this poll. "*Good Housekeeping* magazine has its fifth annual 'Most Admired Men' poll underway, by its very size—circulation in the millions—out-polling all the Nielsens, Trendexes, etc., surveys now cluttering up the nation's opinions. And it's a fascinating project, certainly democratic across the range of G. H. readers, not just the inefficient 1,200 questionees of the noisier nose-countings; some contact 500 persons or less and accept their aggregate word as national opinions, or trends. . . . The *Good Housekeeping* poll strikes us as a far more definitive reflection of opinion" (Newark *Star-Ledger*, August 19, 1985).

5. Discuss why the *Good Housekeeping* survey might not reflect national opinion as accurately as some other, much smaller polls.

Other Sources of Bias

Even if a survey organization uses random sampling or probability sampling to choose a sample, survey results can be biased for other reasons. For example, people may refuse to respond, they may not tell the truth, the survey may occur at a bad time, it may be poorly worded, or interviewers may not be well trained. Unfortunately, it is always difficult and sometimes impossible to estimate the errors caused by such factors.

Nonresponse Bias

Many people neglect or refuse to respond to surveys; the nonresponse rate can vary from a very low percentage for some governmental surveys to over 90% for some long questionnaires delivered by mail. For example, the city of Laramie, Wyoming, sent out 2,000 surveys to a random sample of Laramie households as part of its second annual Citizen's Attitude survey. Only 481 surveys were returned. What was this survey's response rate? A related problem is that some people, such as those who work long hours, are difficult to contact. Unfortunately, people who refuse to respond and people who are difficult to contact tend to give answers different from other people's.

Untruthful Answers

People give untruthful answers for several reasons. If an interviewer asks a sensitive question, people may give an answer they think is socially acceptable, or tell the interviewer what they think he or she wants to hear. For this reason, in Gallup's presidential election polls, interviewers hand interviewees a ballot that they can mark secretly.

Another problem is that people, not wanting to appear ignorant, will try to answer a question even if they know nothing about the subject. "In one study, educators were asked how they would rank Princeton's undergraduate business program. In every case, it was rated among the top 10 departments in the country, even though Princeton does not offer an undergraduate business major" (*Los Angeles Times*, November 21, 1982).

People often do not remember numbers they are asked about. For example, one study (*Sociological Methods and Research*, November 1981) asked students to report their grade point averages (GPAs). Researchers then determined the actual GPAs. Over 17% of the students reported a GPA 0.4 or more above their actual average, but about 2% of the students reported a GPA more than 0.4 below their actual GPA!

Survey Details

Factors such as the timing of a survey, the specific way questions are worded, and the competence of the interviewers can all affect the survey results. For example, in a National Football League poll in January 1971, football emerged as the nation's favorite sport (Moore, *Statistics: Concepts and Controversies*, first ed.). What happens in January that could have biased this result?

Subtle differences in the phrasing of a question can sometimes cause a large difference in the results. For example, Americans are much more willing to "not allow" speeches against democracy than they are to "forbid" them (Schuman and Presser, *Questions and Answers in Attitude Surveys*). In a 1981 survey, fewer than 10% of the respondents said they would cut programs involving "aid to the needy." But rephrasing the question led 39% to say they supported cuts to "public welfare programs" (*Los Angeles Times*, April 20, 1982).

Similarly, interviewers can sometimes phrase questions to make people respond a certain way. For example, try to say "no" to this question: "Do you favor paying hard-working teachers a little more so that our fine young people can have a decent education?"

Interviewers must not misinterpret people's answers. Consequently, the Census Bureau and other large survey organizations require that their interviewers follow very explicit procedures, and they monitor the interviews closely, with random follow-up by supervisors.

Look at the reproduction on page 49 of part of the questionnaire used by National Crime Survey interviewers. This page is designed to determine background information before getting to the questions on crime. These questions help the Department of Justice to study why people may or may not become victims of crime. Notice that the questionnaire spells out everything the interviewer must say and provides a place to record every response. Such uniformity is necessary to insure that all people surveyed answer the same questions. Otherwise it would be impossible to aggregate the answers into a valid national summary.

Notice also that the questionnaire does not ask, "Are you employed?" Instead, the questions focus on specific activities during the last week in order to get more detailed and reliable information about employment.

PERSONAL CHARACTERISTICS

18. NAME (of household respondent)	19. TYPE OF INTERVIEW PGM 4	20. LINE NO. (cc 12)	21. RELATIONSHIP TO REFERENCE PERSON (cc 13b)	22. AGE LAST BIRTH-DAY (cc 17)	23. MARITAL STATUS (cc 18)	24. SEX (cc 19)	25. ARMED FORCES MEMBER (cc 20)	26. Education — highest grade (cc 21)	27. Education — complete that year? (cc 22)	28. RACE (cc 23)	29. ORIGIN (cc 24)
Last / First	**085** 1 ☐ Per. — Self-respondent 2 ☐ Tel. — Self-respondent 3 ☐ Per. — Proxy ⎫ Fill 14 on 4 ☐ Tel. — Proxy ⎭ cover page 5 ☐ NI — Fill 20—29 and 15 on cover page	**086** Line No.	**087** 1 ☐ Ref. person 2 ☐ Husband 3 ☐ Wife 4 ☐ Own child 5 ☐ Parent 6 ☐ Bro./Sis. 7 ☐ Other relative 8 ☐ Non-relative	**088** Age	**089** 1 ☐ M. 2 ☐ Wd. 3 ☐ D. 4 ☐ Sep. 5 ☐ NM	**090** 6 ☐ M 7 ☐ F	**091** 1 ☐ Yes 2 ☐ No	**092** Grade	**093** 6 ☐ Yes 7 ☐ No	**094** 1 ☐ White 2 ☐ Black 3 ☐ American Indian, Aleut, Eskimo 4 ☐ Asian, Pacific Islander 5 ☐ Other — Specify	**095** Origin

▶ **INTERVIEWER:** If respondent 12—15 go to Check Item A. If 16+ read, then go to Check Item A.

Before we get to the crime questions, I have a few (additional) items that are useful in studying why people may or may not become victims of crime.

CHECK ITEM A Look at item 3 on cover page. Is box 1 marked?
☐ No — **Ask 30**
Yes — Is this person a new household member?
100 1 ☐ Yes — **Ask 30** 2 ☐ No — **SKIP to Check Item C**

30. How long have you lived at this address?
101 _____ Months (If more than 11 months, leave blank and enter 1 year below.)
OR
102 _____ Years (Round to nearest whole year)

CHECK ITEM B Is entry in 30 —
☐ 5 years or more? — **SKIP to Check Item C**
☐ Less than 5 years? — **Ask 31**

31. Altogether, how many times have you moved in the last 5 years, that is, since _____, 197__?
(Mo. of Int.) (5 yrs. ago)
103 _____ Number of times

CHECK ITEM C Is this person 16 years old or older?
☐ Yes — **Ask 32a**
☐ No — **SKIP to 37a**

32a. What were you doing most of LAST WEEK — (working, keeping house, going to school) or something else?
104 1 ☐ Working — **SKIP to 32c** 6 ☐ Unable to work — **SKIP to 35**
2 ☐ With a job but not at work 7 ☐ Retired
3 ☐ Looking for work 8 ☐ Armed Forces — **SKIP to 36a**
4 ☐ Keeping house 9 ☐ Other — Specify
5 ☐ Going to school

b. Did you do any work at all LAST WEEK, not counting work around the house? (Note: If farm or business operator in HHLD, ask about unpaid work.)
105 1 ☐ Yes 2 ☐ No — **SKIP to 33a**

c. How many hours did you work LAST WEEK at all jobs?
106 _____ Hours — **SKIP to 36a**

33a. If "with a job but not at work" in 32a, **SKIP to 33b.**
Did you have a job or business from which you were temporarily absent or on layoff LAST WEEK?
107 1 ☐ Yes 2 ☐ No — **SKIP to 34a**

b. Why were you absent from work LAST WEEK?
108 1 ☐ Layoff — **SKIP to 34c**
2 ☐ New job to begin within 30 days — **SKIP to 34c**
3 ☐ Other — Specify ⎱ **SKIP to 36a**

34a. If "looking for work" in 32a, **SKIP to 34b**
Have you been looking for work during the past 4 weeks?
109 1 ☐ Yes 2 ☐ No — **SKIP to 35**

b. What have you been doing in the last 4 weeks to find work? Anything else?
Mark all methods used. Do not read list.
Checked with —
110 1 ☐ Public employment agency
2 ☐ Private employment agency
3 ☐ Employer directly
4 ☐ Friends or relatives
5 ☐ Placed or answered ads
6 ☐ Other — Specify (e.g., CETA, union or professional register, etc.)
7 ☐ Nothing — **SKIP to 35**

c. Is there any reason why you could not take a job LAST WEEK?
111 1 ☐ No
Yes — 2 ☐ Already had a job
3 ☐ Temporary illness
4 ☐ Going to school
5 ☐ Other — Specify

35. If "layoff" in 33b, **SKIP to 36a**
When did you last work at a full-time job or business lasting 2 consecutive weeks or more?
112 1 ☐ 6 months ago or less
2 ☐ More than 6 months but less than 5 years
3 ☐ 5 or more years ago ⎱ **SKIP to 37a**
4 ☐ Never worked full time 2 weeks or more
5 ☐ Never worked at all

36a. For whom did you (last) work? (Name of company, business, organization or other employer)

b. What kind of business or industry is this? (e.g., TV and radio mfg., retail shoe store State Labor Department, farm)
113

c. What kind of work were you doing? (e.g., electrical engineer, stock clerk, typist, farmer, Armed Forces)
114

d. What were your most important activities or duties? (e.g., typing, keeping account books, selling cars, finishing concrete, Armed Forces)

e. Were you —
115 1 ☐ An employee of a PRIVATE company, business, or individual for wages, salary, or commissions?
2 ☐ A GOVERNMENT employee (Federal, State, county, or local)?
SELF-EMPLOYED in OWN business, professional practice, or farm? If yes
Is the business incorporated?
3 ☐ Yes
4 ☐ No (or farm)
5 ☐ Working WITHOUT PAY in family business or farm?

Evaluating Bias in Surveys

Identify any sources of bias in each of the following surveys.

1. The rating service Arbitron estimates the popularity of radio stations in the Los Angeles area. Four times a year, Arbitron takes a random sample of about 10,000 listeners. Every member of the household over age 12 is asked to fill out a diary, showing what he or she listens to every quarter hour from 6:00 a.m. to midnight, for one week. Each diarist receives 50 cents for his or her trouble. At the end of 12 weeks, Arbitron tallies the results from the usable diaries—usually between 33% and 50% of the 10,000 sent out (*Los Angeles Times*, January 31, 1984).

2. One year after the Detroit race riots of 1967, interviewers asked a sample of black residents in Detroit if they felt they could trust most white people, some white people, or none at all. When the interviewer was white, 35% answered "most"; when the interviewer was black, 7% answered "most" (Moore, *Statistics: Concepts and Controversies*).

3. In response to recent proposals for improving the quality of education, a Louis Harris poll was commissioned to find out how teachers feel about certain questions. "We undertook the Metropolitan Life survey of teachers, interviewing a cross-section of elementary and secondary teachers across the United States. In all, we surveyed 1,981 teachers. It can be said theoretically that every public school teacher had an equal chance of being drawn into the final sample." Among the many results: "While they have reservations about merit pay as such, a 71% to 28% majority believe such a system could work if there were an objective standard on which a teacher's individual merit could be judged" (Newark *Star-Ledger*, July 22, 1984).

   The management-oriented Educational Research Service also conducted a survey of teachers at about the same time. Among other results, this study found that 50.8% of a random sample of 1,013 teachers "either agreed or tended to agree that merit or incentive pay should be given to teachers who meet appropriate performance criteria" (Newark *Star-Ledger*, September 22, 1984). Comment on the apparent difference in opinion on merit pay between the surveys.

4. To find out how people reacted to the clothes of vice-presidential candidate Geraldine A. Ferraro, researchers ran a survey shortly after the 1984 Democratic convention in three locations: the Wall Street area of New York City, State Street in Chicago, and Crown Center in downtown Kansas City. The researchers stopped people at random and asked them if they had seen the Democratic convention on television. Those who had were not used. Those who had not "were asked if they would be willing to contribute a minute or two of their time to help a woman candidate choose a suitable picture for a campaign poster. We wanted to enlist only those who had a positive attitude toward women running for office." The 347 respondents were then shown pictures of women wearing three outfits, and the pictures

did not show the women's faces. Then the respondents were asked several questions (*Los Angeles Times*, August 3, 1984).

5. The following quotation is from a report on a survey of high school students' views of nuclear war. "[It] is based on 5,553 responding high school students (10th, 11th, and 12th graders). Thirty-three northern New Jersey public and private high schools, selected solely upon their willingness to have the questionnaire administered to a group of their students, participated in the study. The students came from various economic backgrounds and environments: inner city (297), urban and suburban middle class (2,217), affluent suburbs (2,313), and rural areas (722). They ranged from fewer than 50 in social studies or other classes in some schools, to virtually the entire 10th, 11th, and 12th grades in others." Among other results reported, one question concerned the likelihood of a nuclear blast caused by an act of war somewhere on earth in the next 20 years. Thirty-seven percent said this event is likely, 37% said it is somewhat likely, and 26% said it is unlikely (*Physicians for Social Responsibility*, July 1984).

6. On the recent deregulation of banking, "[the head of California's Security Pacific Bank] reckons the higher interest accounts, and all the other new financial services, are designed for the most affluent 15% to 20% of Security Pacific Bank's customers. By extension—as 2 million customers are surely a sample of the general population—the new world of deregulated finance benefits the top-earning 15% to 20% of U.S. households" (*Los Angeles Times*, December 4, 1983).

7. A Gallup poll found that 81% of U.S. parents say they have spoken with their teenagers about the dangers of drinking and driving. Only 64% of the teens say they remember such a discussion (*USA Today*, December 19, 1984).

8. The U.S. census of 1980 states that 32,194 Americans are 100 years old or older. However, Social Security figures show only 15,258 adults of this advanced age (*Los Angeles Times*, December 16, 1982).

9. In a 1983 survey of fourth graders (nine-year-olds), *Weekly Reader* found that 30% felt peer pressure from other children to drink alcoholic beverages (*Cincinnati Enquirer*, April 22, 1986). The newspaper article did not publish the wording of the question. (*Hint*: Try to write a question that you are sure nine-year-olds will understand that asks if they feel peer pressure to drink.)

10. In a census in Russia, 1.4 million more women than men reported that they were married (*U.S. News & World Report*, August 30, 1976).

VII. LARGE SURVEYS

Large surveys, such as the Gallup poll, differ from the surveys we studied in Sections II through V in four major ways:

1. As we saw on page 2, large survey organizations report an "error attributable to sampling and other random effects," or "sampling error," rather than confidence intervals.

2. Large surveys use a 95% box plot rather than the 90% box plot we have used.

3. The sample size is at least several hundred and is usually about 1,500.

4. As we discussed in Section VI, the samples for large surveys are usually not obtained using random sampling. Instead, pollsters use a form of probability sampling for which they can compute confidence intervals.

You will learn more about these differences in this section.

Reminder

The 90% confidence interval contains all of the population percentages for which the sample proportion is likely.

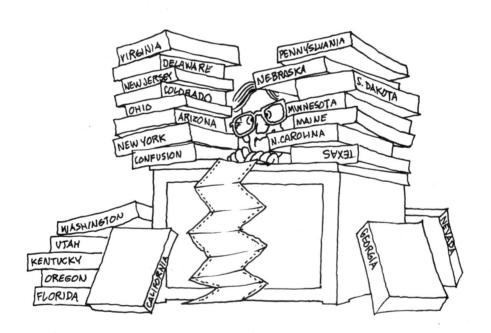

Application 21

Calculating Sampling Error

According to a study reported in *USA Today* (see page 23), about 60 of the 100 divorced couples with children (sample proportion 0.60) are "unfriendly." From the box plots for samples of size 100 (page 95), we find that the 90% confidence interval for the percentage of divorced couples with children who are unfriendly is 55% to 65%. Another way to say the same thing is that we think that about 60% of all divorced couples with children are unfriendly, with a *sampling error* of 5% either way.

The term sampling error refers to the size of error that occurs because the sample proportion from a random sample is not usually the same as the population percentage. (Less frequently used synonyms for sampling error are margin of error, chance error, sampling tolerance, standard margin of error, and error attributable to sampling.) The sampling error *does not* include errors resulting from possible sources of bias, such as nonresponse bias, untruthful replies, or bad wording of questions.

In each of the surveys described below, find

    a. the sample proportion.

    b. the 90% confidence interval.

    c. the sampling error.

1. In a survey of 20 people, 10 people are TV addicts.

2. A survey of 40 women finds 12 who do not work.

3. A survey of 40 students finds 20 who like cafeteria food.

4. A random sample of 100 boys includes 35 with conduct disorders.

5. A random sample of 100 students includes 60 nonsmokers.

Complete these sentences by looking at your answers to the questions above.

6. For a sample of size 20, the sampling error is about _____%.

7. For a sample of size 40, the sampling error is about _____%.

8. For a sample of size 100, the sampling error is about _____%.

9. As the sample size increases, the sampling error _____ .

95% Box Plots

Let's review confidence intervals. If we take random samples from a population and construct a confidence interval from each sample, then the population percentage should be inside 90% of the intervals we construct. In other words, we expect that in 10 out of every 100 surveys, the confidence interval will *not* contain the population percentage.

If large polling organizations used 90% box plots, they would be wrong in about 10 of every 100 surveys. Thus, they use 95% box plots and are wrong in about 5 of every 100 surveys. Using 95% box plots lengthens both the box and the confidence interval.

Large Sample Sizes

Perhaps you suspect that polling organizations do not compute confidence intervals from charts of 95% box plots. If so, you are right! Now that you understand the basic ideas of confidence intervals, we can simplify our procedure.

A simple formula is available to determine the sampling error in a survey that uses random sampling. It is

$$2\sqrt{\frac{p(1-p)}{n}} \, ,$$

where p is the sample proportion and n is the sample size. The formula gives a decimal, which we can convert to the corresponding percentage. To use this formula, you need $np \geqslant 5$ and $n(1-p) \geqslant 5$. The formula can be derived using a complicated statistical theory that we will not go into. This theory says that when we use this formula, the population percentage will be in the confidence interval at least 95% of the time.

For example, suppose we take a sample of size 100 and get 70 *yes*es. Then

$$n = 100 \, ,$$

$$p = \frac{70}{100} = 0.70 \, ,$$

and the sampling error is

$$2\sqrt{\frac{p(1-p)}{n}} = 2\sqrt{\frac{0.70\,(1-0.70)}{100}}$$

$$\cong 0.09 \text{ or } 9\% \, .$$

The 95% confidence interval for the true population percentage is 61% to 79%.

For the remainder of this book, round any sampling error to the nearest whole percent.

Application 22

Finding the Sampling Error

Assume random sampling and find the sampling error as a percentage for each of the surveys below. Use the formula $2\sqrt{p(1-p)/n}$.

1. In a sample of 25 students, 20 said *yes*.

2. In a sample of 100 students, 80 said *yes*.

3. In a sample of 400 students, 320 said *yes*.

4. In a sample of 1600 students, 1280 said *yes*.

5. Look over your answers to questions 1 through 4. When you multiply the sample size by 4, what happens to the sampling error?

6. In a sample of 200 taxpayers, 76 cheated on their income tax (*Los Angeles Times*, April 13, 1986).

   a. Find the sampling error.

   b. Find the 95% confidence interval for the percentage of taxpayers who cheat.

7. In a study of 500 children, ages three to seven, 68% didn't know their home phone number (*USA Today*, August 7, 1985).

   a. Find the sampling error.

   b. Find the 95% confidence interval for the percentage of three- to seven-year-olds who don't know their home phone number.

8. If $p = 0.50$, what sample size gives a sampling error of

   a. 1%?

   b. 2%?

   c. 3%?

   d. 4%?

   e. 5%?

   f. 6%?

   g. 7%?

   h. 8%?

Working with Large Surveys

In each of the surveys described below, assume the sample is obtained by random sampling and

a. identify or compute the sample proportion.

b. find the sampling error to the nearest percent using the $2\sqrt{p(1-p)/n}$ formula.

c. find the 95% confidence interval.

1. The National Assessment of Educational Progress asked 2,000 17-year-olds to estimate the answer to 3.04 × 5.3. The percentage who got the right answer was 36.6 (*The Third National Mathematics Assessment: Results, Trends, and Issues*, 1983).

2. When the Gallup survey interviewed 416 teenagers, ages 13 to 18, on their drinking and drug use, 108 said they used marijuana (*Los Angeles Times*, September 8, 1984).

3. Of 1,557 cars traveling on a residential street, 701 made a full stop at a new stop sign (*Los Angeles Times*, September 6, 1984).

4. A survey by A. C. Nielson Co. of 1,100 owners of videocassette recorders found that 65% of those questioned used the "fast forward" feature to skip commercials on TV programs they had taped (*Los Angeles Times*, September 2, 1984).

5. In Puerto Rico, investigators found that 7 of 61 infants hospitalized with salmonella infections had probably acquired their infection from pet turtles (*Harvard Medical School Health Letter*, September 1984).

6. A survey of 300 mathematically gifted teenagers found that 70% were nearsighted (*Los Angeles Times*, January 6, 1984).

7. In a survey of 506 full-time college students, 48% said they drink at least once a week (*USA Today*, April 1, 1985).

8. Of 2,265 high school seniors surveyed, 73% said they had used crib notes to cheat on a test (*Los Angeles Times*, April 17, 1986).

9. In 200,000 taste tests, the Coca-Cola Company found that 55% of the participants preferred the "New Coke" to the old Coke (*Los Angeles Times*, July 30, 1985).

10. In a *USA Today* survey of 999 college students, 88% said that they want to have children (May 13, 1986).

We have learned that survey organizations use probability sampling, not true random sampling. Therefore, the sampling error reported in a newspaper is not necessarily the same one we would compute using the $2\sqrt{p(1-p)/n}$ formula. Depending on the type of probability sampling, the sampling error could be larger, about the same, or even smaller than the sampling error obtained from random sampling. Generally, it will be a bit larger.

In the surveys described below,

a. compute the sampling error to the nearest percent using the $2\sqrt{p(1-p)/n}$ formula, as if the sample were random.

b. decide if the reported sampling error is the same, larger, or smaller than that for a random sample.

c. find the 95% confidence interval using the reported sampling error.

11. A survey of 1,574 registered voters found that 60% would vote for Ronald Reagan for president. The pollster reported the sampling error as 4 points (*Los Angeles Times*, September 2, 1984).

12. *Los Angeles Times* reporters randomly surveyed 113 businesses to determine why no freeway congestion occurred during the Summer Olympics in Los Angeles. Of those business managers surveyed, 24% said they had continued to work a five-day week but had altered their hours. The article said that the error attributable to sampling for such a survey is 9% (September 2, 1984).

13. When the *Los Angeles Times* surveyed 1,093 regular freeway commuters, 14% reported leaving town during at least part of the Olympic Games. The article says that "such a poll has a margin of error of about 3%" (September 2, 1984).

14. Pollsters questioned 874 men, of whom 33% said working mothers are worse mothers than those who stay at home. The reported margin of error was 3 points (*Los Angeles Times*, September 10, 1984).

15. In a telephone poll of 1,504 adults, 58% reported attending an art exhibition in 1984. A *New York Times* article about the poll says that "the results are within plus or minus three percentage points of what they would have been had the entire population been polled" (December 4, 1984).

16. The following letter appeared in the *Los Angeles Times* on September 7, 1984.

Polls

Polls, polls, polls, that's all you hear every week during presidential campaigns! I say they're hog-wash.

No pollster has ever called me or knocked on my door to get my opinion on any issue whatsoever, and until such time as one ever singles me out for my opinion, I will continue to disbelieve all polls, and denounce them all as nothing but propaganda devices.

Write a response to the letter's author.

National Surveys

Polling organizations conduct most national surveys either by telephone interviews or by personal interviews. Using a mail questionnaire is another possibility, but the nonresponse rate tends to be higher, leading to less reliable results.

Large survey organizations occasionally print explanations of how they do their polling. Here are reports from the *New York Times*/CBS News poll and the Gallup survey. You will now be familiar with many of the technical words and concepts in these articles. You will also find some terms that we have not discussed and that will probably be unfamiliar to you. Note that for sampling error, Gallup uses the term *sampling tolerance*.

How the Poll Was Conducted

The latest *New York Times*/CBS News Poll is based on telephone interviews conducted May 29 through June 2 with 1,509 adults around the United States, excluding Alaska and Hawaii.

The sample of telephone exchanges called was selected by a computer from a complete list of exchanges in the country. The exchanges were chosen to insure that each region of the country was represented in proportion to its population. For each exchange, the telephone numbers were formed by random digits, thus permitting access to both listed and unlisted residential numbers.

The results have been weighted to take account of household size and to adjust for variations in the sample relating to region, race, sex, age and education.

In theory, in 19 cases out of 20 the results based on such samples will differ by no more than 3 percentage points in either direction from what would have been obtained by interviewing all adult Americans. The error for smaller subgroups is larger. For example, the margin of sampling error for Democrats or Republicans is plus or minus 4 percentage points.

In addition to sampling error, the practical difficulties of conducting any survey of public opinion may introduce other sources of error into the poll.

Source: *New York Times*, June 5, 1985.

Design of the Gallup Sample

The Gallup Organization, Inc., maintains a national probability sample of interviewing areas for use in personal interview surveys. The sampling procedures used in the selection of these areas, and in the selection of households and individuals within these areas, are designed to produce sample estimates of the adult population (18 years of age or older) living in the United States (the 50 states and the District of Columbia), *excluding* military personnel living on military bases and persons residing in institutions, such as prisons or hospitals.

The sample follows a replicated, multi-stage area probability design, using stratification by geography, urbanization, and size of community. The areal selection is to the block level in urban areas and to segments of townships (or equivalents) in the case of rural areas. Approximately 300 sampling locations are used in full-scale national surveys.

The sample design first stratified the population by size of community and urbanization, using 1980 census data, into the following categories:

1. Population of central cities of 1,000,000 of more persons.
2. Population of central cities of 250,000 to 999,999 persons.
3. Population of central cities of 50,000 to 249,999 persons.
4. All population not covered in 1, 2, or 3 above, yet located in urbanized areas (as defined by the Bureau of Census).
5. Population of cities and towns (incorporated places and census-designated places) of 2,500 to 49,999 persons.
6. Population of towns and villages (incorporated places and census-designated places) of less than 2,500 persons.
7. All other population.

Population in each of these city size/urbanization categories was further stratified into eight geographic regions: New England, Middle Atlantic, East Central, West Central, Southeast, South Central, Mountain, and Pacific. Within each community size/urbanized area/regional stratum, the population was then arrayed in a serpentine geographic order and zoned into equal-sized units. Replicate sets of localities were selected in each zone, with probability of selection of each locality proportional to its population size.

In the next stage of sample selection, the designated localities were further subdivided and subdivisions were drawn with the probability of selection proportional to the size of population in each subarea. In localities for which subdivision population data are not reported, small definable geographic areas were selected with equal probability.

For each personal interview survey, within each subdivision for which block statistics are available, a separate sample of blocks or block groups is drawn, with probability of selection proportional to the number of dwelling units. In all other subdivisions or areas, blocks or segments are drawn with equal probability.

Within each cluster of blocks and each segment, a randomly selected starting point is designated on a map of the area. Starting at this point, the interviewer is required to follow a predetermined travel path, attempting an interview at each household on this route. The interviewer continues until his or her assignment, which includes a set number of interviews with male and female respondents, has been completed.

(continued)

Interviewing is conducted on weekends or on weekday evenings, when adults are most likely to be at home. Only one interview is conducted in each household.

Allowance for persons not at home is made by a "times-at-home" weighting procedure rather than by call-backs. This method helps reduce the sample bias that would otherwise result from underrepresentation of persons who are seldom at home. . . .

While an estimate of the standard error for any obtained proportion can be computed, it may be helpful to consider the "typical" range of sampling error found in Gallup surveys. Based on numerous estimates, the sampling tolerance for mid-range proportions obtained using a standard 1,500-case national sample is approximately plus or minus 3 percentage points, at the 95% confidence level. For proportions outside the middle range (e.g., reflecting 90%—10% or 80%—20% divisions of behavior or opinion), somewhat smaller sampling tolerances are appropriate. For proportions based on sub-samples (e.g., men only) larger tolerances are appropriate.

It should be noted that these tolerances reflect random variations in the sampling process, design effects due to clustering and weighting, and other random variations introduced in interviewing and data processing. The tolerances *do not* take into account sources of nonrandom error or other possible biases. While every effort is made to avoid such errors, it should be borne in mind that sampling tolerances alone do not reflect all possible sources of inaccuracy in the survey research process.

Source: The Gallup Organization, Inc.

Application 24

Comparing the New York Times/CBS and Gallup Polls

1. Which poll uses the telephone and which uses personal interviews?

2. What is the sample size for each poll?

3. What sampling error does each poll report?

4. When a person is not at home, does Gallup call back later? How does Gallup try to minimize the probability that the person is not at home?

5. Does the article say how the *New York Times*/CBS poll deals with the problem of nonresponse?

6. Does either poll use random sampling? If not, what kind of sampling does each use?

7. What variable(s) does the Gallup poll use for stratification? What variables does the *New York Times*/CBS poll use?

8. Assuming that 170 million adults live in the United States, what is the probability that an adult would be interviewed in a specific Gallup survey?

9. Does either article mention possible sources of error other than sampling error? Does either article give examples of such sources of error? Does either give any number for the potential size of such error?

Planning and Carrying Out Your Own Survey

Work on your own or in a small group on this project.

1. Write a *yes-no* question on a topic that interests you for a survey of 40 students.

2. Decide exactly what population you will sample from. For example, your population could be all girls in your school, all seniors, or all students enrolled in history courses.

3. As a pretest, ask your question to a few members of your class to see if they interpret it exactly as you intend. How can you increase the chances that students will tell the truth? Will you ask for a verbal response? A secret ballot answer? Change your procedures or the wording of your question, if necessary.

4. How will you use random sampling to select 40 students?

5. Obtain 40 students for your sample and ask your question.

6. What is your sample proportion?

7. What is the 95% confidence interval for the percentage of *yes*es in the population? (Use the formula.)

8. Write an article for the school newspaper reporting the results of your survey. Explain the meaning of the confidence interval in your article.

Assessing Opinions About Populations

A Vanderbilt University psychologist had each of 12 pairs of siblings wear one of his or her T-shirts to bed three nights in a row. The T-shirts were then put in individual boxes with small openings in the lids. Each child received two boxes, one of which contained the T-shirt of his or her brother or sister. Of the 24 children, 19 (sample proportion 0.79) identified, by smell alone, the T-shirt worn by a brother or sister (*Science 83*, March 1983).

In the next application, you will answer questions about similar situations. Study these sample questions and answers first.

a. Construct the 95% confidence interval for the percentage of children that choose the correct box.

The sampling error is

$$2\sqrt{\frac{p(1-p)}{n}} = 2\sqrt{\frac{0.79\,(1-0.79)}{24}}$$

$$= 0.17, \quad \text{or} \quad 17\%\,.$$

Thus the 95% confidence interval is 79% ± 17%, or 62% to 96%.

b. Do you think that children have some ability to identify siblings' clothing by smell?

Yes, we do. If children did not have this ability, in the long run they would choose the correct box 50% of the time. However, 50% is not in the confidence interval of 62% to 96% for the true percentage of children that choose the correct box.

As another example, suppose a teacher claims that exactly 10% of people who have recently left teaching say that students' lack of motivation was one of the main reasons they left. A study of 500 recent former teachers found that 8% gave this reason (*American Educator*, Summer 1986).

a. Construct the 95% confidence interval for the percentage of recent former teachers who would give lack of student motivation as one of the main reasons they left teaching.

The sampling error is

$$2\sqrt{\frac{(0.08)(0.92)}{500}} = 2\%\,,$$

so the 95% confidence interval is 6% to 10%.

b. Should you tell the teacher that he or she is wrong?

No, you should not—for statistical as well as political reasons. The 95% confidence interval for the true percentage of recent former teachers giving lack of student motivation as a reason includes the teacher's figure of 10%. Thus, 10% could well be the exact percentage.

Assessing Opinions

For each of the surveys below, assume the samples are random.

1. A study of 300 mathematically gifted children found that 20% were left-handed (*Los Angeles Times*, January 6, 1984).

   a. Construct the 95% interval for the percentage of mathematically gifted children who are left-handed.

   b. About 8% of the whole student population is left-handed. Do you think the proportion of left-handers is greater among mathematically talented students than among students in general? Explain.

2. Out of the same 300 mathematically gifted children, 60% had allergies or asthma.

   a. Construct the 95% confidence interval for the percentage of mathematically gifted children who have allergies or asthma.

   b. Ten percent of the whole student population has allergies or asthma. Do you think a greater percentage of mathematically gifted children have allergies or asthma than do students in general? Explain.

3. A handwriting analyst examined 10 pairs of handwriting samples. One sample in each pair was from a psychotic and the other was from a normal person. The handwriting analyst correctly identified the psychotic in 6 of the 10 pairs (Larsen and Stroup, *Statistics in the Real World*).

   a. Construct the 95% confidence interval for the percentage of pairs of handwriting samples the analyst will get correct in the long run.

   b. Do you think the analyst can identify the handwriting of a psychotic? Explain.

4. Observations of 255 right-handed mothers during the first four days after delivery showed that 212 of the mothers held their babies on the left (Nemenyi, P. et al., *Statistics from Scratch*).

   a. Construct the 95% confidence interval for the percentage of right-handed mothers who hold their babies on the left.

   b. Do you think it is just as likely for a right-handed mother to hold her baby on the left as on the right? Explain.

5. In a survey of 416 teenagers ages 13 to 18, 23% said they do not drink (*Los Angeles Times*, September 8, 1984).

   a. Construct the 95% confidence interval for the percentage of teenagers who say they do not drink.

b. Among people 18 and older, 35% do not drink. Do you think teenagers aged 13 to 18 tend to drink more than those 18 and older? Explain.

6. Ask a friend to estimate the percentage of college undergraduates who say that they are bored in class.

   a. A Carnegie Foundation survey of 5,000 undergraduates found that 36.9% say they are bored in class. Construct a 95% confidence interval for the percentage of undergraduates who say they are bored in class.

   b. Do you think your friend's estimate is the true population percentage? Explain.

VIII. A CAPTURE-RECAPTURE METHOD

Sometimes the people responsible for managing wildlife populations need to count the total number of animals in a population. For example, they might want to know how many deer are in a forest, how many fish are in a lake, or how many seals are on an island. It is impossible to count these animals directly, so naturalists use ingenious *capture-recapture methods*. These methods include several statistical procedures, some quite complicated. In this section, we will discuss the simplest type of capture-recapture method.

In 1970, naturalists wanted to estimate the number of pickerel fish in Dryden Lake in central New York State. They captured 232 pickerel, put a mark on their fins, and returned the fish to the lake. Several weeks later, another sample of 329 pickerel fish were captured. Of this second sample, 16 had marks on their fins (Chatterjee in Mosteller et al., *Statistics by Example: Finding Models*).

Let N be the total number of pickerel fish in the lake. Because the proportion of marked fish in the population should be approximately equal to the proportion of marked fish in the sample, we can write the following equation.

$$\frac{\text{number of marked pickerel fish in the population}}{\text{total number of pickerel fish in the population } (N)} = \frac{\text{number of marked pickerel fish in the sample}}{\text{number of pickerel fish in the sample}}$$

Then we can estimate N by solving this equation. Thus, in Dryden Lake,

$$\frac{232}{N} = \frac{16}{329}$$

$$16N = (232)(329)$$

$$N = \frac{(232)(329)}{16}$$

$$N = 4{,}770.5$$

The *estimate* for the number of pickerel fish in the lake is 4,771.

Application 27

Practicing with the Capture-Recapture Equation

1. Your teacher has a container with a number of cards in it. Draw out 25 of the cards and mark them with a pen or pencil. Return the cards to the box and mix them thoroughly. (It is difficult to mix them well.) Draw a sample of size 20 and count the number marked. What is the estimate for the number of cards in the box?

2. Suppose that naturalists catch, tag, and release 50 deer in a forest. After allowing time for the tagged deer to mix with the others, they catch a sample of 100 deer, 10 of which have tags. What is the estimate for the number of deer in the forest?

3. Suppose that wildlife workers capture 328 penguins on an island, mark them, and allow them to mix with the rest of the population. Later, they capture 200 penguins, 64 of which are marked. What is the estimate for the number of penguins on the island?

4. Suppose that the high school in a town has 500 students. A random survey of 200 people in the town finds 40 high school students. What is the estimate for the number of people in the town?

5. Visitors conducted a capture-recapture experiment to determine the number of taxicabs in Edinburgh, Scotland. On the first day, observers saw 48 taxicabs. The next day they observed 52 cabs, 10 of which they had seen the previous day (The Wildlife Society, October 1978). What is the estimate for the number of taxicabs in Edinburgh?

6. In a study of raccoons in a certain region of northern Florida, 48 animals were captured using cages baited with fish heads. The raccoons were marked and released. In the following week, 71 raccoons were captured, 31 of which had been marked (Pollock in Brook and Arnold, *The Fascination of Statistics*). What is the estimate for the number of raccoons in this region?

Experimenting with the Capture-Recapture Model and Its Assumptions

The capture-recapture equation and its use can, at first, appear deceptively simple. In this application we do several experiments to learn what the assumptions are behind this method and why they matter.

1. Use the container from question 1 of Application 27, which contains 25 marked cards. Mix the cards thoroughly, draw a sample of size 20, and count the number marked. What is the estimate for the number of cards in the box this time?

2. Repeat question 1 four more times. Write the four new estimates.

The capture-recapture method gives only an estimate for the number of cards in the container. Each time you did the experiment, you probably came up with a different estimate. Perhaps you were even surprised at how different the estimates were from one another. Can you guess what we need in addition to the estimate? We need a confidence interval to give us an idea of how precise the estimate is. Later in this section we will learn how to construct a confidence interval for this capture-recapture method.

First, however, we must be aware of some potential problems with this method and the assumptions it is based on. For example, suppose some of the marked animals become afraid of being caught again and avoid traps. How will this behavior affect the estimate of the population size? The following experiments and questions deal with this situation.

3. Ask your teacher how many cards are in the box.

4. Did your estimates from questions 1 and 2 tend to be too large or too small? (They should have been about evenly divided between too large and too small.)

5. Remove 10 of the *marked* cards from the box. These cards represent animals who are "trap shy" and don't want to be captured again. Repeat questions 1 and 2. Write the five estimates.

6. Did the estimates from question 5 tend to be too large or too small? (The population size is still the same as before.)

7. Complete this sentence: When some of the marked animals hide, the estimate of the population size tends to be too _____ .

8. Sometimes some "trap happy" animals are easier to capture and easier to recapture than others. Thus, an animal captured the first time is also likely to be in the second sample. What do you think this behavior will do to the estimate of the population size? Design an experiment with the box of cards to find out if the estimated population size would tend to be too big or too small.

Questions 5 through 8 show that when we use this capture-recapture method, we are assuming that all animals are equally likely to be captured in both trappings. When this assumption is not true, the method can give bad estimates.

In using this capture-recapture method, we have also made two additional assumptions. We assumed that the marks would not be removed, wear off, or become invisible in some way before the recapture. Finally, we assumed that the population was closed during the period of the study—that is, it had no additions due to births or animals entering the area nor deletions due to deaths or animals leaving the area.

9. Complete this sentence. If some animals lose their marks during the study, the estimate of the population size will tend to be too _____ . (If you are unsure of the answer, design and run an experiment to find out.)

10. Suppose the time between the capture and the recapture is too long and some marked animals die. Suppose also that some new animals are born so that the population size remains constant. Will the deaths tend to make the estimate of the population size too large or too small? Explain.

11. Reread question 5 of Application 27. Discuss which assumptions of the capture-recapture model this example may violate.

To use this capture-recapture method, naturalists and statisticians must be convinced that the three basic assumptions are satisfied reasonably well. More complicated capture-recapture methods are available if these assumptions cannot be satisfied.

Confidence Intervals for Capture-Recapture Problems Using Charts of 90% Box Plots

As you have seen, the method of capture-recapture gives an estimate of the population size. We want a confidence interval to accompany the estimate. Now we will see how to adapt our method for the sample survey problem to give a confidence interval for this capture-recapture method.

Suppose we capture and tag 150 birds in a park. We later capture 100 birds and see that 30 have tags. Thus, the sample proportion of tagged birds is

$$\frac{30}{100} = 0.30$$

What percentage of all birds in the park are tagged? Our estimate is 30%, but we don't know the population percentage for sure. Checking the charts of 90% box plots for a sample of size 100 on page 95, we see that a sample proportion of 0.30 is a likely result from populations with from 25% to 35% *yes*es. Therefore, it is likely that from 25% to 35% of the birds in the park have tags. The 90% confidence interval for the *percentage* of birds in the population that have tags is 25% to 35%.

We can now use this confidence interval for the percentage of birds tagged to construct a confidence interval for the total *number, N*, of birds in the park. Suppose the true percentage of tagged birds in the population is at the lower end of the confidence interval, 25%. We estimate the total number of birds using this percentage:

$$\frac{\text{number of tagged birds in the population}}{\text{total number of birds in the population } (N)} = \text{smallest percentage in confidence interval}$$

$$\frac{150}{N} = 0.25$$

Solving this equation, $N = 600$.

Similarly, suppose the true percentage of tagged birds is at the upper end of the confidence interval, 35%. Then we estimate the total number of birds using this percentage:

$$\frac{\text{number of tagged birds in the population}}{\text{total number of birds in the population } (N)} = \text{largest percentage in confidence interval}$$

$$\frac{150}{N} = 0.35$$

$$N \cong 429$$

Thus, a 90% confidence interval for the *number* of birds in the park is 429 to 600. Remember that for every 100 times we construct a confidence interval this way, the true number of animals will be inside the confidence interval about 90 times. Remember also that to use this capture-recapture method, the assumptions discussed in Application 28 need to be satisfied.

Finding Confidence Intervals for Capture-Recapture Problems
Using Charts of 90% Box Plots

1. Suppose you capture, tag, and release 200 fish in a lake. You later capture a sample of size 20 and find that 6 have tags. Use the chart of 90% box plots on page 92 to answer these questions.

    a. Is catching 6 tagged fish out of 20 a likely result if 15% of the fish in the lake are tagged?

    b. Is this result likely if 35% of the fish in the lake are tagged?

    c. List the population percentages that are likely.

    d. What is the 90% confidence interval for the *percentage* of tagged fish in the lake?

    e. What is the 90% confidence interval for the *number* of fish in the lake?

2. Suppose biologists capture, tag, and release 100 snakes in a desert. They then capture a sample of size 100, 40 of which have tags. Use the chart of 90% box plots on page 95 to answer these questions.

    a. Find the 90% confidence interval for the percentage of tagged snakes in the desert.

    b. Find the 90% confidence interval for the number of snakes in the desert.

3. Suppose a biology class captures, marks, and releases 75 mice in a field. Later they capture a sample of 80 mice, 40 of which have marks. Use the chart of 90% box plots on page 94 to answer these questions.

    a. What is the 90% confidence interval for the percentage of marked mice in the field?

    b. What is the 90% confidence interval for the number of mice in the field?

4. Suppose visitors note 100 taxicabs in a city. The next day they observe 100 taxicabs, and 35 are ones they saw the day before.

    a. Find the 90% confidence interval for the percentage of taxicabs the visitors originally noted.

    b. Find the 90% confidence interval for the number of taxicabs in the city.

Using the $2\sqrt{p(1-p)/n}$ Formula to Construct Confidence Intervals for Capture-Recapture

Gorbatch seal rookery, a breeding ground on St. Paul Island in Alaska, wanted to estimate the number of fur seal pups in the rookery. In early August 1961, wildlife workers captured and marked 4,965 pups by shaving some of the black hair from the tops of their heads. They then released the pups and allowed them to mix with the others. In late August, when the workers captured a sample of 900 pups, 218 of them had marks (Chatterjee in Mosteller et al., *Statistics by Example: Exploring Data*).

We want to estimate the number of pups in the rookery and to construct a confidence interval for this number. However, we do not have charts of 90% box plots to use for a sample of size 900. Instead, we can use the $2\sqrt{p(1-p)/n}$ formula to obtain a 95% confidence interval. (Recall that this formula gives a 95% confidence interval, not a 90% one.)

The sample proportion is

$$\frac{218}{900} = 0.24 \,.$$

The true percentage of tagged pups in the population is probably not exactly 24%, so we will construct a confidence interval to get limits of likely population percentages. Because a sample of size 900 with $p = 0.24$ has a sampling error of

$$2\sqrt{\frac{(0.24)(1-0.24)}{900}} = 0.03 \text{ or } 3\% \,,$$

the 95% confidence interval for the percentage of marked pups in the population is 21% to 27%. In other words, if we choose a random sample of size 900 and find a proportion 0.24 marked in our sample, this sample proportion is a likely result from populations with from 21% to 27% marked.

Next we use this confidence interval for the capture-recapture problem exactly as we did when we obtained the confidence interval from the charts of 90% box plots. If the true percentage of marked pups in the population is at the lower end of the confidence interval, 21%, we use

$$\frac{\text{number of marked pups in the rookery}}{\text{total number of pups in the rookery } (N)} = \text{smallest percentage in confidence interval} \,,$$

$$\frac{4,965}{N} = 0.21 \,.$$

Solving gives $N = 23,643$. Similarly, using the largest percentage in the confidence interval gives

$$\frac{4,965}{N} = 0.27 \,,$$

or $N = 18,389$. Thus, the 95% confidence interval for the number of pups is 18,389 to 23,643. These population sizes are likely to have 24% marked in a sample of size 900.

Finding Confidence Intervals for Capture-Recapture Problems Using the Formula

For these questions, use the $2\sqrt{p(1-p)/n}$ formula when you must find sampling errors and confidence intervals.

1. Suppose we capture, tag, and release 100 fish in a lake. We then catch a sample of size 100, 40 of which have tags.

    a. What is the estimate for the percentage of tagged fish in the lake?

    b. What is the sampling error for the percentage of tagged fish in the lake?

    c. What is the 95% confidence interval for the percentage of tagged fish in the lake?

    d. What is the 95% confidence interval for the total number of fish in the lake?

2. Suppose rangers catch, tag, and release 180 deer in a game preserve. They then capture a sample of size 90, 15 of which have tags.

    a. What is the estimate for the percentage of tagged deer in the preserve?

    b. What is the sampling error for this percentage?

    c. What is the 95% confidence interval for the percentage of tagged deer in the preserve?

    d. What is the 95% confidence interval for the number of deer in the preserve?

3. Suppose the number of students in the town high school is 500. A random survey of 200 people in the town finds 40 high school students. What is the 95% confidence interval for the number of people in the town?

4. To find out how many largemouth bass are in Dryden Lake in central New York State, a naturalist captured 213 largemouth bass and made a mark on their fins. The fish were returned to the lake. About a month later, the naturalist caught 104 bass, and 13 of them had marks (Chatterjee in Mosteller et al., *Statistics by Example: Finding Models*). Find the 95% confidence interval for the number of largemouth bass in the lake.

5. In the taxicab experiment in Application 27, observers noted 48 taxicabs. The next day, they saw 52 taxicabs, and 10 were those they had seen the day before.

    a. Find the 95% confidence interval for the number of taxicabs in the city.

    b. The true number of cabs was 420. Is this number in the confidence interval?

IX. THE GERMAN TANK PROBLEM

In the early years of World War II, American and British intelligence information about Germany's war production proved to be inaccurate and contradictory. Thus, in 1943, statisticians at the United States Embassy in London began trying to estimate German war production by analyzing the serial numbers on captured German equipment. On some types of equipment, such as tire molds and tank gearboxes, the Germans numbered the items sequentially 1, 2, 3, 4, and so on.

Suppose the Allies captured four German tanks that bore the serial numbers 41, 23, 43, and 52. What is the best estimate for the total number of tanks?

This problem is different from the one we have been doing throughout most of this book: estimating the population percentage. In that problem, we took a random sample and used the sample proportion to estimate the population percentage. The estimator to use, the sample proportion, was obvious, so we worked on how to find the sampling error. In the capture-recapture problem of Section VIII, we wanted to estimate the total population size, just as we do here. In capture-recapture, the *estimator* we used was

$$N = \frac{\left(\begin{array}{c}\text{number of marked fish} \\ \text{in the population}\end{array}\right)\left(\begin{array}{c}\text{number of fish} \\ \text{in the sample}\end{array}\right)}{\left(\begin{array}{c}\text{number of marked fish} \\ \text{in the sample}\end{array}\right)}.$$

However, the information we have available now is completely different.

In the German tank problem, the challenge is to choose a good estimator for the total number of tanks. It is not obvious how to construct an estimator. We must first think of several ways to estimate the number of tanks and then decide which estimator works best. We will again use simulation to help us solve this new problem.

Solving the German Tank Problem

Let's do some experiments to simulate the German tank problem. Your teacher has a container of objects numbered 1, 2, 3, and so on, up to N. Your job is to estimate the total number of objects, N. Without looking into the container, one student should capture a sample of three "tanks."

1. What are the numbers of the three tanks?

2. Write a *method* or a formula for estimating the total number of tanks in the container. (You may want to work with several other students.) This method or formula is your *estimator*.

3. Using your method, how many tanks do you estimate are in the container?

We are now going to see which group has the best method of estimating the total number of tanks.

4. Your teacher will write a chart like this one on the board. Copy it onto your paper.

Estimators

Trial						
1						
2						
3						
4						
5						

In the boxes at the top of the chart, write the methods suggested by the different groups in your class. Across from "trial 1," write the estimate of the number of tanks given by each method.

5. Replace the three tanks, mix the objects in the container, and have another student capture three tanks. What are the numbers of these three tanks?

6. Estimate the number of tanks in the container using your method. Pretend that you did not see the results from trial 1.

7. Place your estimate and those of the other groups in the row headed by "trial 2."

8. Repeat questions 5, 6, and 7 for trials 3, 4, and 5.

9. Look in the container. How many tanks are in it?

To determine which method is the best estimator, statisticians sometimes use a rule called *least squared error*. For example, suppose the container actually had 40 tanks in it, and your method produced an estimate of 42 on trial 1, 35 on trial 2, 40 on trial 3, 51 on trial 4, and 31 on trial 5. Your estimate was 2 too big on trial 1, 5 too small on trial 2, just right on trial 3, 11 too big on trial 4, and 9 too small on trial 5. Your errors are 2, −5, 0, 11, and −9. The total of your errors is −1. So that negative errors and positive errors don't cancel each other out like this, statisticians add up the squared values of the errors. In this example, the sum of the squared errors is 4 + 25 + 0 + 121 + 81, or 231.

10. Find the sum of the squared errors for each method in your table.

11. Which method has the smallest sum? Congratulate the students who invented this method.

Statisticians also like to use estimators that are *unbiased*—that is, estimators that do not consistently give answers that are too large (or too small).

12. Were any methods your class used biased? Try to determine why these methods were biased.

Now read the note at the end of this application to discover the method statisticians used during the war. This method worked out very well. The records of the Speer Ministry, which was in charge of Germany's war production, were recovered after the war. The table below gives the actual tank production for three different months, the estimate from serial number analysis, and the number obtained by traditional American/British intelligence gathering.

Month	Actual Number of Tanks Produced	Serial Number Estimate	Estimate by Intelligence Agencies
June 1940	122	169	1000
June 1941	271	244	1550
September 1942	342	327	1550

Source: *Journal of the American Statistical Association*, 1947.

13. During World War II, Allied statisticians also conducted a serial number study of tires on several German Mark V tanks to determine the production of one tire manufacturer. Each tire was stamped with the number of the mold in which it was made; captured tires had 20 different mold numbers from this manufacturer. The largest mold number was 77.

    a. What is the best estimate of the total number of molds?

    b. What additional piece of information do you need to estimate this manufacturer's daily tire production?

14. Suppose you are standing on a corner watching taxis go by. You see that the numbers of the first five taxis are 284, 570, 321, 319, and 35. What is the best estimate for the total number of taxis? List the assumptions you are making to get this estimate.

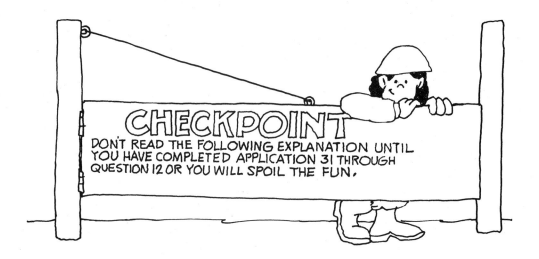

A good method for estimating the number of tanks is to multiply the largest tank serial number by $(n+1)/n$, where n is the number of tanks in the sample. For example, if the Allies captured four tanks with serial numbers 41, 23, 43, and 52, the estimate for the total number of tanks would be

$$\frac{5}{4}(52) = 65 .$$

Among all estimators that are unbiased, this estimator is the best because it tends to minimize the sum of the squared errors.

The explanation of why this estimator is reasonable is simple. Suppose, for example, that we capture four tanks. Imagine each tank on a number line above its serial number:

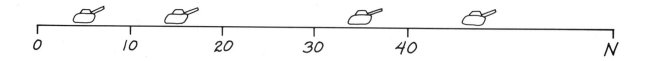

These four tanks divide all of the tanks into five groups. We would expect that the serial number, m, of the largest-numbered tank captured would be 4/5ths of that of the last tank in the population, N. That is,

$$m \cong \frac{4}{5} N$$

so
$$N = \frac{5}{4} m \,,$$

which is our formula

$$N = \left(\frac{n+1}{n}\right) m$$

where N is the total number of tanks,
        n is the number of tanks captured,
        m is the largest serial number of the captured tanks.

Alternatively, we can write the formula

$$N = \left(\frac{n+1}{n}\right) m$$

$$= \frac{nm+m}{n}$$

$$= m + \frac{m}{n}$$

which can be interpreted as adding the average gap between serial numbers to the largest serial number.

Finding the Confidence Interval for the German Tank Problem

So far we have learned to estimate the total number of German tanks by multiplying the maximum of the n observed serial numbers by $(n+1)/n$. It would be useful to construct a confidence interval for the number of tanks, just as we formed confidence intervals for the sample survey and capture-recapture problems. This application shows how we can use the same methods we used for the other two problems to get a confidence interval here.

Let's call the unknown number of tanks (the size of the population) N. We get the maximum of the n observed serial numbers from the sample; call this maximum m. We know both n and m but not N.

The steps that follow are exactly the same as those in the sample survey problem. First we simulate the sampling distribution of the observation m, assuming some population size N and sample size n. Then we summarize the sampling distribution by a 90% box plot. Next we arrange the 90% box plots, for different values of N, in a chart. From these box plots we can read off, for each N, which values of m are likely sample maximums and which are unlikely. Moreover, by reading in the vertical direction, we can learn which values of N make the observed m a likely sample maximum. These values of N give the confidence interval.

We will obtain the confidence interval for question 13 of Application 31, in which a sample of size $n = 20$ gave a maximum value of $m = 77$. Clearly, N must be greater than or equal to 77.

First we estimate the sampling distribution of m for samples of size 20 for several different N. Let's start with $N = 77$. Using the random number table, we obtain a sample of 20 different values from the population 1, 2, 3, . . . , 76, 77. We need 20 different values because we can't catch the same tank twice. Here are the 20 values:

63, 28, 32, 15, 40, 61, 59, 01, 73, 33, 02, 50, 05, 12, 58, 49, 67, 42, 09, 51.

The maximum, m, is 73. We need the maximum in many samples, each of size 20, to get the sampling distribution. We did 40 trials and obtained these maximums:

73, 71, 76, 75, 69, 70, 76, 72, 77, 76, 76, 68, 74, 76, 71, 55, 76, 77, 67, 74, 76,

77, 56, 73, 73, 76, 75, 77, 68, 76, 75, 77, 68, 69, 61, 70, 77, 77, 75, 75.

The next step is to summarize the 40 trials for $N = 77$ by a 90% box plot. Using the 40 values listed above, and constructing the box exactly as we did in Section III, we get the following plot.

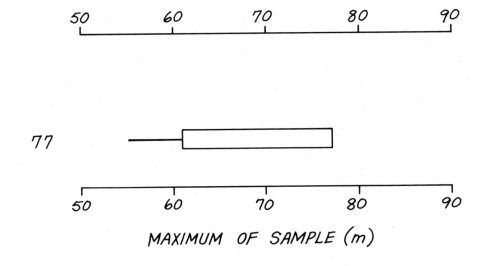

1. We must calculate the sampling distribution for many different population sizes N. We did this for $N = 77$. Now you will do it for $N = 85$. For $N = 85$, use the random number table to generate a sample of 20. What is the maximum, m?

2. Combine results from students in the class until you have generated 40 such samples for $N = 85$, and list the 40 sample maximums.

3. Take your 40 trials for $N = 85$ and construct the 90% box plot. Place this box plot above the one for $N = 77$ on a chart like the one above.

4. Why doesn't your box for $N = 85$ extend to the right of $m = 85$?

5. Is $m = 72$ a likely sample maximum for a population size of $N = 77$? For $N = 85$?

6.   a. Find a value of m that is a likely sample maximum for $N = 77$ but not for $N = 85$.

     b. Find a value of m that is a likely sample maximum for $N = 85$ but not for $N = 77$.

     c. Find a value that is likely for both $N = 77$ and $N = 85$.

Now you see what we must do. We have to fill in the chart from question 3 for many more values of N. But generating all these samples is boring. This is a good job for a computer! We used a computer to produce the following box plots. We could have given more values for N, but this chart will give you the idea.

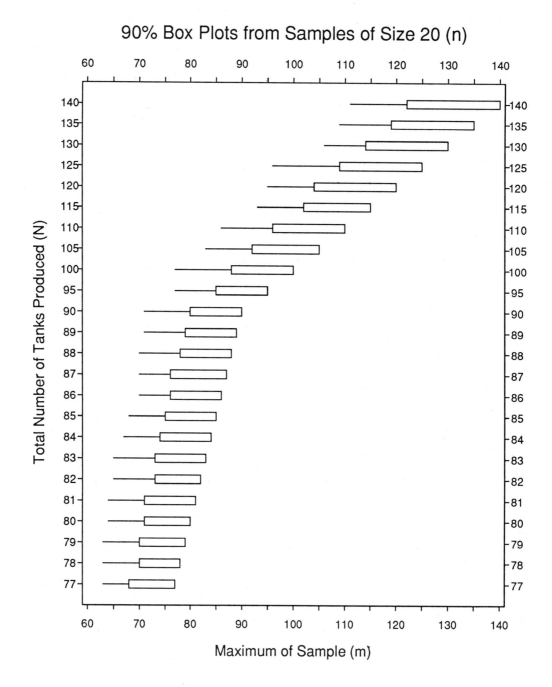

90% Box Plots from Samples of Size 20 (n)

Maximum of Sample (m)

Total Number of Tanks Produced (N)

Use this chart to answer the following questions.

7. a. Is $m = 80$ a likely sample maximum if $N = 90$?

    b. Is $m = 80$ a likely sample maximum if $N = 100$?

    c. List all the population sizes N that have $m = 80$ as a likely sample maximum.

To find the confidence interval for the total population size, we read down the chart as before. The 90% confidence interval includes all those populations that have the sample maximum m as a likely sample maximum.

8. What is the 90% confidence interval for the total population size if $m = 80$?

9. Give the 90% confidence interval for the total population size if $m = 85$.

10. From this chart, you cannot calculate the confidence interval for the total population size if $m = 125$. Explain why not.

11. Give the confidence interval for the total population size if $m = 77$, which applies to question 13 of Application 31. What estimate of N did you give then? Is your estimate inside this interval? Is it at the center of this interval?

12. What is the probability that an interval calculated in this way will contain the true population size N?

X. CONCLUSION

We hope that you have enjoyed working through this book and that you will now be able to understand and evaluate the surveys and polls you read about. For example, consider this article:

> "The Gallup poll, commissioned by the teachers' union, found that 57% of those surveyed believed their local schools were having a hard time attracting good teachers. Most pointed to low pay as the root of the problem . . . . Gallup questioned 1,501 adults by telephone in late April and May. The standard margin of error was plus or minus 3 percentage points" (Newark *Star-Ledger*, July 2, 1985).

Here are the important points to keep in mind when reading this article.

1. In any survey that involves a sample and not the entire population, we do not expect the result to be exact. If Gallup took a census of the whole adult population, the percentage of people who agreed with the statement would probably not be exactly 57%.

2. However, the larger the size of the sample, the closer the sample proportion tends to be to the true percentage.

3. Gallup reports a sampling error of 3%. This statement means that the true population percentage is probably somewhere between 54% and 60%. We say "probably" because the true population percentage is within the given interval in 95 out of every 100 such surveys. However, in 5 out of every 100 surveys, the true population percentage will be outside the given interval. This is what we can expect; it does not necessarily mean that the pollster made some mistake in conducting or analyzing the poll.

4. When we say that the true population percentage is probably between 54% and 60%, we mean that from any of these populations—with percentages either 54%, or 55%, or 56%, or 57%, or 58%, or 59%, or 60%—a sample proportion of 0.57 is likely.

5. The random variability from sample to sample is only one of several sources of error. In addition, bias can result because people may refuse to respond; they may not tell the truth; the survey question may be poorly worded; the timing of the survey may be bad; or the interviewer may make a mistake. When such sources of bias are present, it is always difficult and sometimes impossible to estimate how far the sample proportion is from the population percentage.

We hope that this book has also helped you understand and appreciate some of the basic concepts and methods of *statistical inference*. We used these methods throughout most of the book to solve the sample survey problem, but we also used exactly the same ideas to solve two other problems, capture-recapture and German tank.

All three of these problems involve the same key ideas. We want to learn about a specific *population*. We obtain a *random sample* from the population and use the sample to *estimate* what we want to know about the population. But estimating is not enough. We must also evaluate how good our estimate is. Since we don't know the precise population, we can't just compare the estimate to the population. What we can do, however, is use *simulation* to learn how the value of the estimate varies from one random sample to another. By simulating many samples from a population, we get the *sampling distribution* of the estimate. We sample from many different possible populations in order to get the sampling distribution for each. (More advanced mathematics and statistics courses use mathematical probability formulas instead of simulation to find the sampling distribution, but the overall approach is exactly the same.) Finally, from the sampling distributions, we can calculate a *confidence interval* for the population.

This book has shown you the fundamentals of making a statistical inference about a population from a sample. You can use these methods to solve many other statistical problems as well.

Bibliography

Surveys

Ferber, R., Sheatsley, P., Turner, A., and Waksberg, J. *What Is a Survey?* Washington, D.C.: American Statistical Association (no date). This 25-page booklet is available free from the American Statistical Association, 806 Fifteenth Street, N.W., Washington, D.C. 20005. It contains sections on types of surveys, designing and conducting a survey, and using the results of a survey.

Freedman, D., Pisani, R., and Purves, R. *Statistics.* New York: W. W. Norton, 1978. See Part VI on sampling.

Hollander, M., and Proschan, F. *The Statistical Exorcist: Dispelling Statistics Anxiety.* New York: Marcel Dekker, 1984. This book contains chapters about sampling, the *Literary Digest* poll, using a table of random numbers, the German Tank Problem (called the Racing Car Problem), and capture-recapture.

Moore, D. *Statistics: Concepts and Controversies*, 2nd ed. New York: W. H. Freeman, 1985.

Tanur, J. M. (Ed.). *Statistics: A Guide to the Unknown*, 2nd ed. San Francisco: Holden-Day, 1978. Chapters include "Opinion Polling in a Democracy" by George Gallup, "How Accountants Save Money by Sampling," "How to Count Better: Using Statistics to Improve the Census," and "Information for the Nation from a Sample Survey."

Williams, B. *A Sampler on Sampling.* New York: John Wiley, 1978.

Capture-Recapture

Chatterjee, S. Estimating the Size of Wildlife Populations. In Mosteller, F., Kruskal, W. H., Pieters, R. S., Rising, G. R., Link, R. F. (Eds.). *Statistics by Example: Exploring Data.* Reading, MA: Addison-Wesley, 1973.

Chatterjee, S. Estimating Wildlife Populations by the Capture-Recapture Method. In Mosteller, F., et al. (Eds.). *Statistics by Example: Finding Models.* Reading, MA: Addison-Wesley, 1973.

Swift, J. H. Capture-Recapture Techniques as an Introduction to Statistical Inference. In Sharron, S. (Ed.). *Applications in School Mathematics, 1979 Yearbook.* Reston, VA: National Council of Teachers of Mathematics.

The German Tank Problem

Larsen, R. J., and Marx, M. L. *An Introduction to Mathematical Statistics and Its Applications.* Englewood Cliffs, NJ: Prentice Hall, 1981. This calculus-based college textbook has a good discussion of estimators. See pages 193–194, 201–203, 207–211, 218, 224–227, 247–248.

Noether, G. E. *Introduction to Statistics: A Nonparametric Approach,* 2nd ed. Boston: Houghton-Mifflin, 1976. See pages 2–11 and 30–35.

Ruggles, R., and Brodie, H. An Empirical Approach to Economic Intelligence in World War II. *Journal of the American Statistical Association, 42,* 1947, 72–91. This completely nontechnical article makes fascinating reading.

Vannman, K. How to Convince a Student that an Estimator Is a Random Variable. *Teaching Statistics, 5,* May 1983, 49–54.

Data Sheet for Application 13

Population A
```
XOOOXXXXXOOOXXOXXXXO
OXOOOXOXXOOOOXOOXOOO
OXOOOXOXXOXXOXXXXXOX
OXXOOXOXXOOXOXOOOOOO
OXOOXXXOOOOOOOOOOOXX
OOXXOOOXXOOOOOOOXXXO
XXOOXOOXXXXOOOXXOOOO
XOXOOOOOOOOXOOOOOOO
XXOXXOXOOXOOOOXXOOXO
XXOOOXXXOOXOXOOOOOOO
```

Population B
```
OOOOOOOOOOOOOXOOOOOX
OOOOOOOOOOOOOOOOXOX
OOOOOOOOOOOOXOOOOOOO
OOOOOOOOOOOXOOOOXOOO
OOOOOOOOOOOOOOOOOOOO
OOOOOOOOOOOOOOOOOOOO
OOOOOOOOOOXOOOOOOOOO
OOOOOOOOOOOOOOOOOOOO
OOOOOOOOOOOOOOOOOOOO
OOOOOOOOOOOOOOOOOOOO
```

Population C
```
OOOXOXOXOXXXOXOOXOOX
OOXOXOOOOOOXOOOOXOO
XXXXOOOXOOOOOXOOXXXO
OOOOXXOOXOOOXXOXOXXX
OXOOOOXOOOXXXXXOOXOO
XXOXOOXOOXXOOOOOXOXX
XXOOOOOOOXOOXXXOOXXO
OXOOXOXOOOOXOOOOXOOO
XOOOXOOXXOOOXXOXOXOO
XOOXOOOOXOOXOOXXXOOO
```

Population D
```
XXOOOXXXOXXOXXOXXOXX
OXOXOXXXXOOOXXXXXXOO
XOXXXOXOOOOXOOXXOOOO
OXXXXXXXXXXXXXXXXXX
XXOOXXXOXOXOXXOXXXXO
OOOXOOXOXXXXXXXXOXXX
XXOOXXXOXXOXOXOOXXOX
OXOOOOOOXXOXXXXOXOXO
OOOOOXOXOOOOXOOOXOXO
OOOOOOXOXOOOOOOXXOOX
```

Population E
```
XXOXXXXXXXOXXOXXXXXX
XXOXOXXXOXXXOXXXOOXX
XXXOXXXOXOOXOOXXXOXX
XXOXOXOXXXXXXOXXXXX
XXOOXXOXXOXXXOXXXOX
XOXXXOXOXXXOXXXXXOXX
OXOOXOXXXXXOXOXOOXXX
OXXOXXOOOXOOOXXXXXOX
XXXOXXOXXOXXXXXXXOXX
XOOXXOOXXXXXXOXXXXXX
```

Population F
```
XXXXOXXXXXXXXXXXOOOOX
XXXXXXXXXXXXXXXXXXXX
XXXXOXXXXXXXXXXXOOXX
XOOXXXXXXXXXXOXXXXXOX
XOXXXXOXXXXXXXXXXXXX
XXXXXXXOXXOXXXXXXXXX
OXXXXOXXXXXXXXXOXXXOXX
XXXXXXXOXXXXXXOXXXXXX
XXXXXOXXXXXXOXXXXXXX
XOXOXXXXXOOXXXXXXXXX
```

Population G
```
XXXXXXXXXXXXXXXXXXXX
XXXXXXXXXXXXXXXXXXXX
XXXXXXXXXXXXXXXXXXXX
XXXXXXXXXXXXXXXXXXXX
XXXXXXXXXXXXXXXXXXXX
XXXXXXXXXXXXXXXXXXXX
XXXXXXXXXXXXXXXXXXXX
XXXXXXXXXXXXXXXXXXXX
XXXXXXXXXXXXXXXXXXXX
XXXXXXXXXXXXXXXXXXXX
```

Population H
```
OOOOOXOOOOOOOXOOOOO
OOOXXOXXXOOOOOOXOOOX
OXOOOOOOOOOOOXXOXOOO
OXOXOOXOXOOOOOOOXOOO
OOOXOXOOOOOOOXOOOOOO
OOOOOXOXXOOOOOOOXOOO
OOOOOOOOXOOOOOOOOOX
OOOXOOOOOOXOOOOOOOO
OOOOXOOXOOOOOOOOOOO
OXOOOOOOOXOOOOOOOOOX
```

Population I
```
OOOOOOOOOOOOOOOOOOOO
XXOOOOOOXOOOOOOOOOOX
OOOOOOOOOOOOOOOOOOOX
OOOXOOOOOXOOOOOXOOXO
OOOOOOOOOOOOOOOXOOO
OOOOOOOOOOOXOOOXOOO
OXOOOOOOOOOOOOOOXOO
OXOOOOOOOOOOOOOOXOO
OOOOOOOOOOOOOOOOOOOO
OOOOOOOOOXOOOXOOOOOX
```

Population J
```
OOXOOOOXOXOXXXXOXOXX
OOXXOOXOOXOOOOXXXXX
XXOOXOOXOXOXXXOXXXOO
OOXOXXXXOOXOOOOXXXOX
OXOXOOOXOXOOXOOXXOXO
XXOXOOXXXOOOXOOOXOOX
OXOXOXOXOXXOOXXXXOX
XOOOOXXOXXXXXXOOXOO
XOOOOOXOXXOOXOOOXXXO
XXOXXOXXOXOXOXXXOXOX
```

Population K
```
XXXXXXXXXXXOOXOXXXXO
XXOXOXOXOOXXXXXXXOXX
XXXOXXXXXOXXXXXXOXXO
XXXXOXXXXXXXOXOOXXX
XXXXOOXOOOOXXXXXXXX
OXOXXXXXOXXXXXXXOOO
XXOXXXXXXOOXOXOXXOX
XOXXOXOXXOXXXXXXOOXX
OXXOOXOXXXXXXXOXXOOX
XXXXXXOOXXOXXOOXXXXX
```

Population L
```
OOOOOXXOOXOOOXOXXOOO
OOOXXOXXOOOOXOXXOXOO
OOOXXOXOOOXOOOOOXOOX
OOOOOOOOOXXOXXOOOOXO
XOOOOOOOOXOOOOXOOXO
OXOOXOOOOOXXOOOOXOXO
OOXXOOXOOOOXOOOOXXOO
XOXOOOXOOXXOXOOOOOOX
OXXOOXXOOOOXOOOOOXO
OOOOOXOXOOOOOOOXOOO
```

Table of Random Numbers

39634	62349	74088	65564	16379	19713	39153	69459	17986	24537
14595	35050	40469	27478	44526	67331	93365	54526	22356	93208
30734	71571	83722	79712	25775	65178	07763	82928	31131	30196
64628	89126	91254	24090	25752	03091	39411	73146	06089	15630
42831	95113	43511	42082	15140	34733	68076	18292	69486	80468
80583	70361	41047	26792	78466	03395	17635	09697	82447	31405
00209	90404	99457	72570	42194	49043	24330	14939	09865	45906
05409	20830	01911	60767	55248	79253	12317	84120	77772	50103
95836	22530	91785	80210	34361	52228	33869	94332	83868	61672
65358	70469	87149	89509	72176	18103	55169	79954	72002	20582
72249	04037	36192	40221	14918	53437	60571	40995	55006	10694
41692	40581	93050	48734	34652	41577	04631	49184	39295	81776
61885	50796	96822	82002	07973	52925	75467	86013	98072	91942
48917	48129	48624	48248	91465	54898	61220	18721	67387	66575
88378	84299	12193	03785	49314	39761	99132	28775	45276	91816
77800	25734	09801	92087	02955	12872	89848	48579	06028	13827
24028	03405	01178	06316	81916	40170	53665	87202	88638	47121
86558	84750	43994	01760	96205	27937	45416	71964	52261	30781
78545	49201	05329	14182	10971	90472	44682	39304	19819	55799
14969	64623	82780	35686	30941	14622	04126	25498	95452	63937
58697	31973	06303	94202	62287	56164	79157	98375	24558	99241
38449	46438	91579	01907	72146	05764	22400	94490	49833	09258
62134	87244	73348	80114	78490	64735	31010	66975	28652	36166
72749	13347	65030	26128	49067	27904	49953	74674	94617	13317
81638	36566	42709	33717	59943	12027	46547	61303	46699	76243
46574	79670	10342	89543	75030	23428	29541	32501	89422	87474
11873	57196	32209	67663	07990	12288	59245	83638	23642	61715
13862	72778	09949	23096	01791	19472	14634	31690	36602	62943
08312	27886	82321	28666	72998	22514	51054	22940	31842	54245
11071	44430	94664	91294	35163	05494	32882	23904	41340	61185
82509	11842	86963	50307	07510	32545	90717	46856	86079	13769
07426	67341	80314	58910	93948	85738	69444	09370	58194	28207
57696	25592	91221	95386	15857	84645	89659	80535	93233	82798
08074	89810	48521	90740	02687	83117	74920	25954	99629	78978
20128	53721	01518	40699	20849	04710	38989	91322	56057	58573
00190	27157	83208	79446	92987	61357	38752	55424	94518	45205
23798	55425	32454	34611	39605	39981	74691	40836	30812	38563
85306	57995	68222	39055	43890	36956	84861	63624	04961	55439
99719	36036	74274	53901	34643	06157	89500	57514	93977	42403
95970	81452	48873	00784	58347	40269	11880	43395	28249	38743
56651	91460	92462	98566	72062	18556	55052	47614	80044	60015
71499	80220	35750	67337	47556	55272	55249	79100	34014	17037
66660	78443	47545	70736	65419	77489	70831	73237	14970	23129
35483	84563	79956	88618	54619	24853	59783	47537	88822	47227
09262	25041	57862	19203	86103	02800	23198	70639	43757	52064

Table of Random Numbers

59718	77768	50032	53440	41359	33021	01938	86092	87426	80010
91977	35682	34043	26290	40447	12411	32837	12151	21227	81491
88224	92826	92683	66928	95518	70106	92397	62132	97206	26324
01288	56565	78378	72344	12566	58325	40257	93212	49208	51320
19483	45024	12857	46267	94007	98674	54199	29738	24084	91964
33652	12588	55326	05702	43815	61284	13606	65461	70415	91440
32207	57357	18841	61415	57755	46846	41422	35285	37870	55929
99945	87321	41676	70537	39314	45154	93823	14053	81888	11464
29773	64388	95180	80750	12815	77661	89578	42194	99329	21247
92329	55414	05162	94197	19267	68846	27895	12005	80292	49745
75834	71767	45378	40316	61259	13140	66115	61564	76757	62599
22755	89933	41019	18996	13005	31853	72795	22193	59897	62049
09056	73260	95209	33157	15608	37565	93590	85486	80932	76059
66250	96883	74585	74550	89984	28356	77938	69704	19034	19744
37052	83115	38995	52825	93308	75276	21274	48777	75400	62004
81653	74197	85789	50614	52742	48213	94759	80701	08234	44686
41417	37426	42282	34323	83341	38345	83018	25015	68282	94820
27862	25188	15227	90981	06296	86815	04322	44750	01554	91302
85083	13672	29208	17587	12217	24032	52318	83860	81936	29114
05649	48381	63320	11822	11590	75112	54027	56579	81397	14691
91654	28637	01627	24482	33119	29924	69390	85040	66927	63521
43540	82299	18928	35588	55113	78385	61536	49596	05202	40993
33276	99974	62800	97999	56683	61505	85617	32656	16834	88980
18139	96834	07488	32049	53532	12159	75508	10924	25298	96474
07403	42795	55422	49346	44612	61632	81241	04660	95163	16285
05374	34289	66087	74636	64247	73598	42730	79472	79834	72702
63121	17926	84377	16927	91950	26475	10086	61879	03475	64750
66148	59081	34743	69023	50306	63739	14717	32374	19119	96284
92153	23320	34180	78025	42391	35908	73996	49173	47360	92856
06629	93991	80847	49133	45105	34818	10122	31369	33312	94856
74784	07080	13104	64110	98440	56468	88959	67988	58764	70414
59043	74797	24791	65130	97918	99820	32673	44512	36847	14028
58572	79127	74870	47218	03752	92434	71791	28040	60536	37429
75069	76687	43795	50161	20794	95015	42376	33178	10265	03394
72258	09820	54814	84454	32761	59316	14974	80017	37524	25760
16186	64983	27652	53966	75826	16790	13767	52267	65505	56954
54047	17961	92967	27968	12463	85270	13763	96297	43279	93087
42301	36874	19357	14982	22806	69213	79929	48973	21969	28172
87940	43389	26009	52702	03148	70789	88539	19084	59200	88168
91551	24267	81423	17461	09300	11928	98793	97748	95430	11644
03166	69589	65596	56997	70092	63418	92825	91586	76847	51167
64280	45356	96248	79274	15733	72317	44107	80124	99672	44523
28464	37825	88800	20180	28989	75914	46882	28736	60408	63180
36861	76806	80789	30886	71013	56044	52405	81063	04283	41256
43125	34876	18177	22382	37920	77067	93319	29881	37050	32533

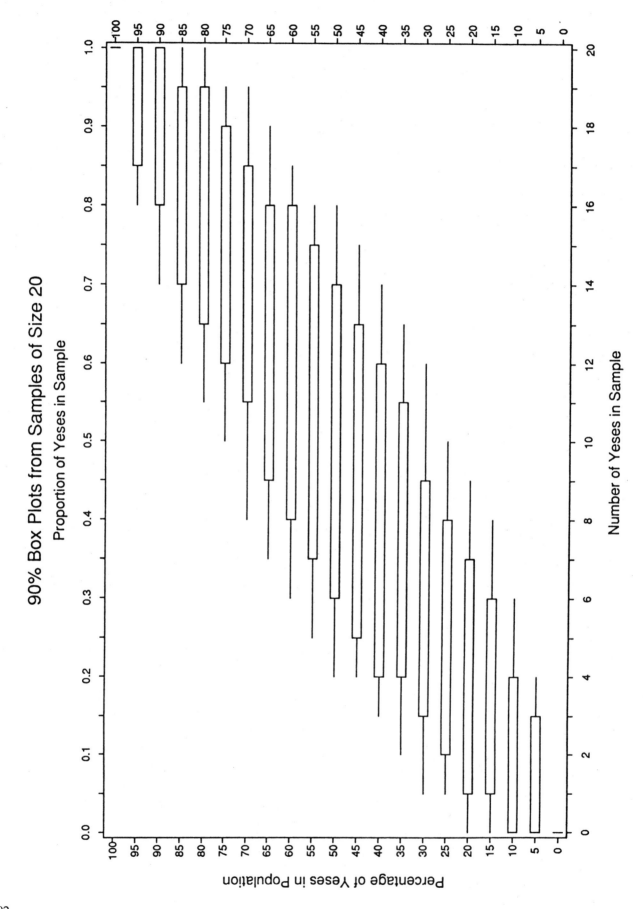

90% Box Plots from Samples of Size 20
Proportion of Yeses in Sample

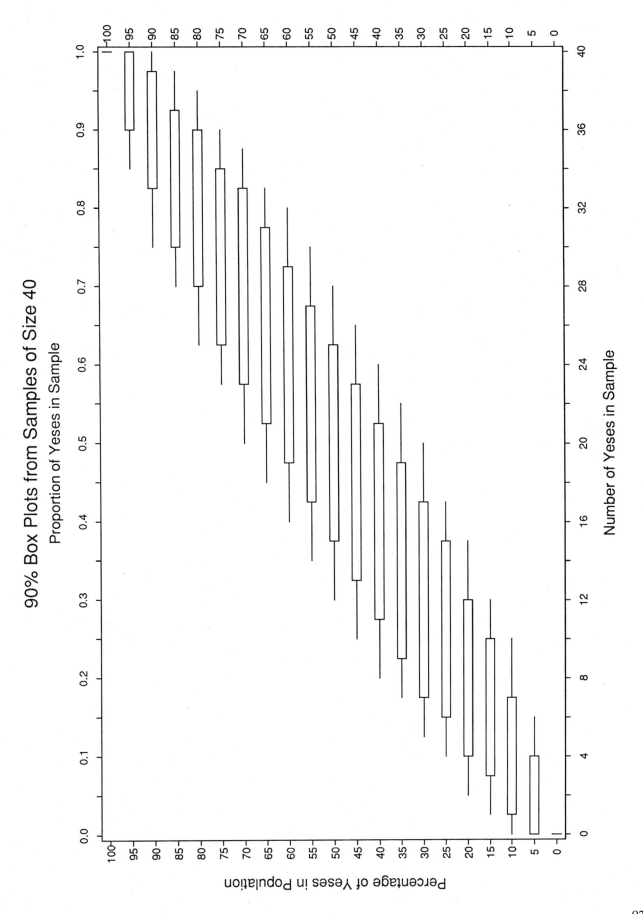

90% Box Plots from Samples of Size 40
Proportion of Yeses in Sample

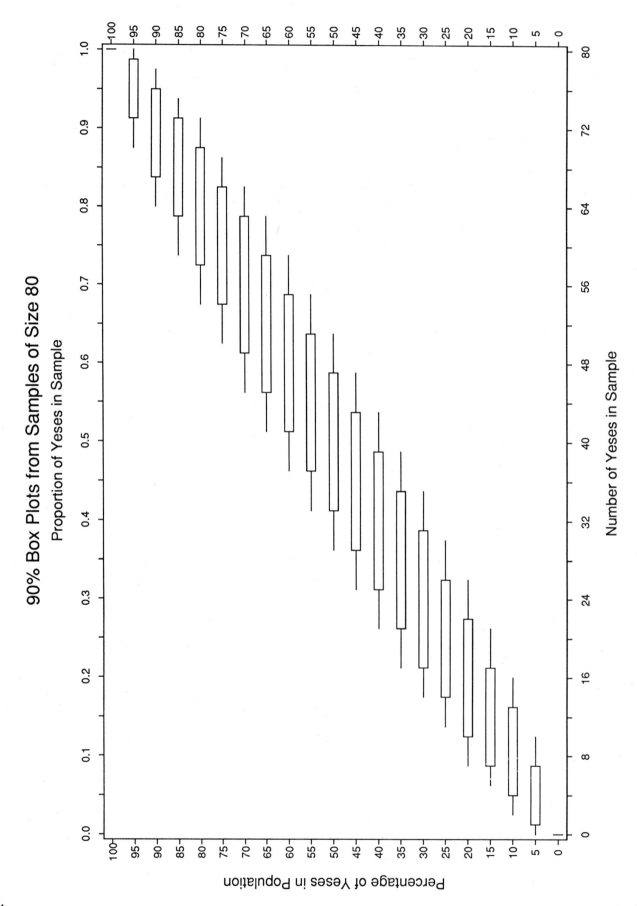

90% Box Plots from Samples of Size 80
Proportion of Yeses in Sample

Percentage of Yeses in Population

Number of Yeses in Sample

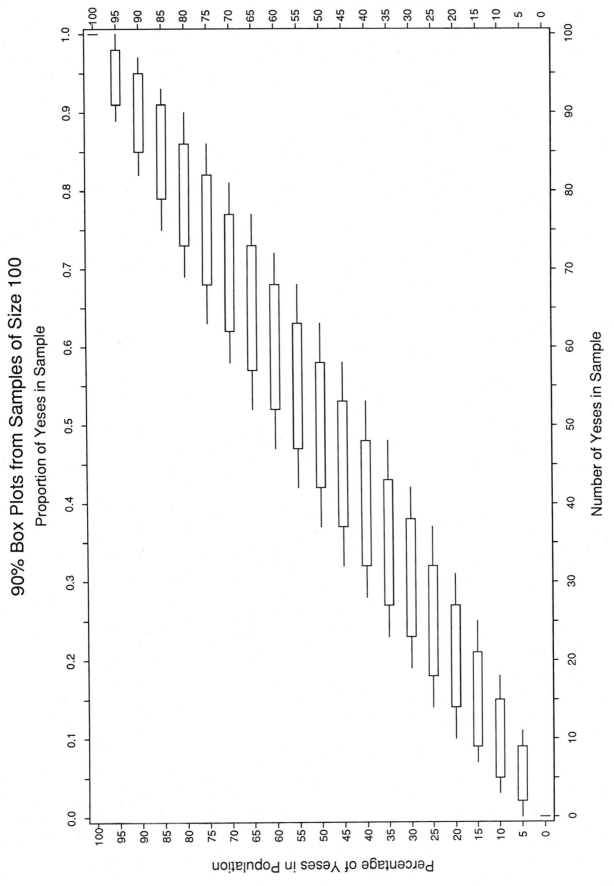

90% Box Plots from Samples of Size 100

Proportion of Yeses in Sample

Percentage of Yeses in Population

Number of Yeses in Sample

INDEX OF STATISTICAL TERMS